WIN AT CHESS!

A Comprehensive Guide to Winning Chess for the Intermediate Player

Ronald H. Curry

Thinkers' Press

Davenport, Iowa

1999

Win at Chess!

First Printing:
July 1995
Second Printing:
May 1997
Third Printing:
August 1999

ISBN: 0-938650-64-5

Requests for permission and republication rights (whether as an article or for a foreign language), or a catalog of our chess publications, should be addressed in writing to:

Thinkers' Press
Senior Editor
P.O. Box 8
Davenport Iowa 52805-0008

DEDICATION

Dedicated to the only critic I love — my wife, Suzanne, who lovingly encourages, and so graciously puts up with my devotion to this noble pastime.

ACKNOWLEDGMENTS

My sincere gratitude is extended to my deserving wife, Suzanne, for patiently typing the manuscript, and to my editor, Bob Long, for transforming a good manuscript into an excellent book. My appreciation is expressed to Paul Arms, Henry Krysiak, Wilfred Marsh, Frank Riley, and Ned Smith for proofreading the text and offering many helpful suggestions. I am also deeply grateful to my many chess students for their inspiration and encouragement.

Win at Chess!

CONTENTS

Part II — The Middlegame

Part IV — Practice & Progress

INTRODUCTION

Chess, like love, like music, has the power to make men happy.
— Tarrasch

Every chessplayer wants to play better chess and win more games. To improve, you will need to STUDY and PLAY chess — especially study. To learn to play better, an intermediate chessplayer needs information and guidance that is reliable, practical, clear, and well-organized. The comprehensive, Master-proven principles and techniques in this book will improve your chess game and help you progress toward chess mastery.

The chessplayer who understands WHY will consistently defeat opponents who only know HOW! So, the focus of this book is on understanding important principles rather than memorizing lengthy sequences of moves. The Masters' key secrets of winning chess play are explained and illustrated with numerous examples throughout this book, and the emphasis is on practical winning principles and methods. Essential principles of winning opening, middlegame, and endgame play are covered, as well as comprehensive tactical and positional themes, maneuvers, and techniques. Numerous exercises are included to test your progress. *Win At Chess!* is a complete chess manual for improving your chess game.

The chess instruction in this manual is theoretically sound and practically reliable. All the principles and techniques have been proven effective by chess Masters in countless games over the centuries (and by the author, a chess Expert, in national and international tournament competition). During the past twenty years, scores of the author's students have successfully used the ideas in this book to improve their chess games significantly. You can apply these winning principles and techniques in your games with confidence!

Study, then *apply* these vital, Master-proven chess ideas, principles, and techniques — and win at chess!

Ronald H. Curry
Wilmington, Delaware
May 1995

CHAPTER 1

CHESS GROWTH

Chess is a game of understanding, not memory.
— Znosko-Borovsky

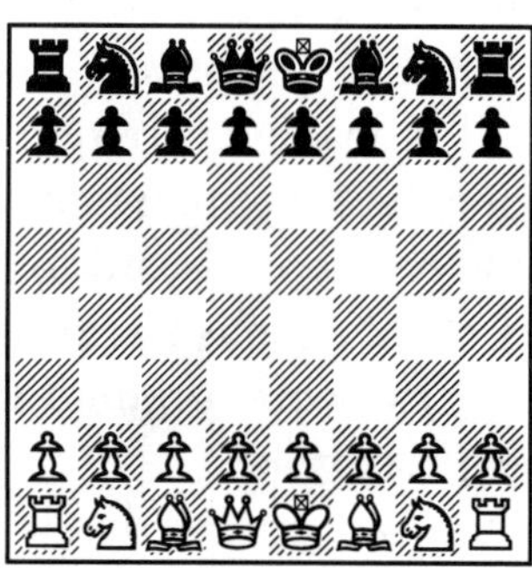

Diagram 1

Chess, the game of kings and king of games, is a game of skill and a fascinating intellectual challenge. Chess is not simple; it is a complex game founded on rules, guided by rational thinking, and often influenced by emotion. There are no axioms or unalterable laws governing every chess position — precepts and guidelines can blaze a safe and promising trail, but you must ultimately select your own path to chess mastery.

Chess requires and rewards logic, imagination, a competitive spirit, patience, and, above all, *understanding*. Learning and applying sound principles, rather than memorizing moves, is the key to success. Winning chess games requires knowledge in the opening, imagination in the middlegame, and technique in the endgame.

In the soul of every chessplayer breathes the spirit of a Bobby Fischer or Gary Kasparov, but the bleak truth is that most chessplayers do not advance beyond a low intermediate strength. The anchor retarding their progress is lack of knowledge — they seldom study.

The secret to improving your chess is to combine STUDY with PLAY. Study alone is sterile; play alone is limiting (you tend to repeat and reinforce your mistakes). **A note of caution:** *many experienced but relatively weak chessplayers are prisoners of their pasts*. Clinging to incorrect or incomplete old chess ideas, and shackled by vestigial notions and inadequate playing habits, they are reluctant to adopt new ideas, change their games for the better, and grow. Change and growth are essential for improvement in chess. No chessplayer improves without taking risks ("Behold the turtle, who makes no progress until he sticks his neck out."). Changing established chessplaying patterns takes courage, patience, and time, but the rewards are worth the effort.

This book is for the chessplayer who seriously wants to improve. In reading this book you will probably encounter some new or different ideas on how to play better chess. For maximum benefit, set up each of the diagrammed positions on a chessboard for study. While the text explains and summarizes, the diagrams clarify and reinforce important principles and techniques. ***If you are unfamiliar with any of the chess terms used, consult the Glossary.***

The chapters in this book are arranged in logical progression; but if you are impatient and anxious to improve your chess game immediately, read Appendix B ("The Condensed Chess Course") for concise, comprehensive instruction. If one area of your chess game particularly needs improvement, read the chapter on that topic.

To become a *complete* chessplayer, however, be certain to read *all* the chapters to increase and balance your chess improvement. Do all the practical exercises included in several chapters — they simulate game conditions and afford you instructive practice in applying the principles you have learned.

You WANT to improve your chess, you CAN improve your chess, and you WILL improve your chess. Let's get started!

CHESS PROGRESSION

First, let us find out where you are on the ladder of chess and what lies ahead for you.

As you improve, you will grow through several distinct stages of development. At each stage, a dominant theme may emerge for your focus and mastery before you can progress to the next level. Naturally, you retain and increase your proficiency with previous themes as you continue your improvement.

In reviewing my own chess career, I find a definite, typical, hierarchical pattern of development. Although many of the themes in chess development overlap strength levels, the pattern of progression is clear. You can assess your present status as an amateur chessplayer and learn what challenges await you by comparing your level of knowledge and skills with mine at various stages of development. My various chess strengths are expressed as United States Chess Federation (USCF) national ratings.

1000 — When my chess strength was approximately 1000 (low intermediate), my play was characterized by careless openings, premature attacks, aimless moves and captures, inferior and passive defense, an impotent, embryonic endgame, and no sound ideas of purposeful pawn play. Worse yet, my major problem was *losing material,* because I frequently overlooked opponents' one-move threats, even obvious ones, and left my pieces *en prise* (attacked and unprotected). Often before I could begin to attack my opponent, he had already attacked me and won several pieces and pawns, or even checkmated me (sound familiar?). In fact, I was losing many chess games before I ever had a chance to win. Before I could win at chess, I had to learn to avoid losing. The major culprit was *overlooking opponents' threats*. The effective remedy, which I did not know at the time, was simple: after *each* of my opponents' moves I should have asked the vital question, "What is the THREAT?" and before *each* of my moves I should have asked the key question, "Is this move SAFE?" To win a chess game, you must first avoid losing it!

1200 — Having learned to sidestep some of my opponents' threats, I could still win material only if my opponents left their pieces and pawns *en prise* or inadequately guarded. My attacks were obvious, and mostly unsuccessful. At this level I discovered the marvelous and intriguing world of TACTICS (pins, skewers, Knight forks, double attacks, discovered attacks, etc.). I learned the critical truth that *chess games are decided by tactics*. Although I missed many (perhaps most) tactical opportunities in my games, I did occasionally manage to play a convincing tactic if the conditions were pre-established. I also learned the useful method of counting the *number* and *value* of attackers and defenders, to determine the safety of captures and occupation of squares by either side. My defense also improved, for I began to recognize more threats and avoid many simple tactics by my opponents. I also learned a few standard opening moves and improved my inept endgame by studying fundamental endgame techniques ("queening square," opposition, triangulation, *zugzwang*). I learned the value — nay, necessity — of *playing each move with a specific purpose*, and I started winning more games. Chess was becoming fun!

1400 — Buoyed up to 1400 by my newly acquired tactical skills, I discovered that peer chessplayers were far less obliging than weaker opponents in succumbing to my new expertise. I learned that against strong chessplayers, *tactics must be forced or induced.* This illuminating realization exposed a fundamental weakness in my game — *relying on opponents' errors* — and led me to understand the essential truism that *every successful chess tactic is based on one or more weaknesses in the position.* Thus I discovered that the secret of playing effective tactics is to recognize — create (force or induce) if necessary — and ATTACK WEAKNESSES. To recognize weaknesses, I had to learn to analyze positions more thoroughly for *both sides*.

This new skill of regularly and, sometimes, accurately analyzing each position for weaknesses enabled me to pinpoint more tactical opportunities, and to defend better against possible tactical threats by my opponents. I also began playing modest combinations and sacrifices, *relying more on sound principles than memory*. I was becoming a chessplayer.

The Seven Basic Factors Which Characterize a Chess Position Are:

1. King Safety
2. Material
3. Possible Tactics
4. Piece PLacement and Mobility
5. Pawn Structure
6. Control of Important Squares
7. Tempi

1600 — Although I was winning more often, my game was still based disproportionately on move-to-move threats and tactics. My chess strategy could best be described as "get my pieces out, castle, and wait for my opponent to make a mistake." Planning, if any, was rudimentary and haphazard. Against 1600-strength peers, this strategy proved inadequate. My opponents were downright disobliging at making tactical errors, and I was frequently stymied. In many middlegame positions, I simply had no idea of what to do. At this plateau I sought counsel from several stronger chessplayers, read a chess book or two, and discovered the miraculous element of PLANNING. Planning, while important and beneficial, was the most difficult theme I had encountered in my chess development. However, after considerable study and practice (I enlisted stronger players to criticize my games, and started a diary of my losses to learn a pertinent lesson from each game), I was finally able to incorporate short- and long-term planning as an integral part of my game and to liberate myself substantially from my former myopic method of move-to-move chess. Soon I began winning more games, even against stronger players, thanks to better planning.

1800 — At this level I began to appreciate seriously the role and value of POSITIONAL PLAY, especially the significance of pawn structure and proper pawn play. I learned that *pawn structure always influences — and sometimes dictates — strategy and tactics* by defining the squares and lines available for pieces. I learned that positional play, essentially the control of important offensive and defensive squares and lines, depends on *active piece placement* and *sound pawn formations*. I developed more skill at handling a variety of positions: open, semi-open, and closed. I reinforced and expanded my skill at avoiding and inflicting weak pawns (isolated, doubled, backward), and developed greater awareness of "holes" in pawn structures (possible outposts) and offside pawn majorities (potential new Queen). Extensive experience against stronger players convinced me that, while tactics always win chess games, proper positional play is a necessary prelude to effective tactics. *A superior position is almost invariably a prerequisite for game-winning tactics*. My games with peers were typically closer and longer, so I studied and improved my endgame knowledge and techniques (King role, distant opposition, pawn structure). To secure consistently promising middlegames against stronger opponents, I also continued to broaden my knowledge of openings. Further, I realized that the attacker wins more often in chess, so I incorporated and emphasized more aggressive play, including active defense. I learned that there is a "thread" — a series of related themes — running through most chess games, and it is important to hew to that thread. As a result, my play became more coordinated, deeper, and longer-range — sounder.

2000 — Improvement at this level has been more mental than technical:

- Being aggressive (always alert for weaknesses)
- More consistently evaluating positions correctly and analyzing variations accurately
- Employing a systematic method of searching for moves
- Uniformly playing according to the offensive opportunities and defensive necessities in each position
- Accurately applying more of my appropriate chess knowledge to each position
- Evaluating plans more critically
- Being more flexible
- Being defensively tenacious and resourceful
- Mentally playing *both* sides of the board at all times
- Carefully pacing myself (being patient) during each game

These characteristics improved my chess. The solid, aggressive style of play I had developed earlier was further enhanced by understanding more fully the importance of the INITIATIVE. With the *initiative* (ability to create threats), you control the game, direct the flow of events, and generally make your opponent "dance to your tune." Painfully I discovered that when my opponents seized and maintained the initiative, I usually lost; when I developed a strong initiative, I often won. The initiative is primarily achieved by gaining tempi and superior development, and it is frequently maintained by threats and hindrance. Like most chessplayers, I prefer to attack rather than defend, so concentrating on seizing and maintaining the *initiative* is a current paramount concern. I am still working at this level, plus reinforcing my knowledge and skills learned at previous stages. Of course, I am looking forward to the next level.

This has been my progression in chess; it may or may not be yours — you may learn and apply some important chess themes and principles before I did. You will encounter various personal stages of development.

Chapter 2

CHESS NOTATION

Language is mankind's greatest invention.

Chess moves and positions are usually recorded in modern Algebraic notation, which comprises a coordinated system to: 1) identify squares on the chessboard, and 2) provide symbols describing moves and captures by the chessmen. The following symbols are used for the chessmen:

King	K	♔	♚
Queen	Q	♕	♛
Rook	R	♖	♜
Bishop	B	♗	♝
Knight	N	♘	♞
pawn	(omitted)	♙	♟

Special Symbols

†	Check
‡	Double-check
#	Checkmate
0–0	Castles Kingside
0–0–0	Castles Queenside
...	Precedes Black move (in text)

Definitions

Files and Ranks

(Note: The chessboard is always positioned so that each player has a *light* square in his lower right-hand corner.) The eight vertical columns of squares on the chessboard are FILES, designated a, b, c, d, e, f, g, and h, from White's *left*. The horizontal rows of squares are RANKS, numbered 1 to 8 from the *White* side (Diagram 2):

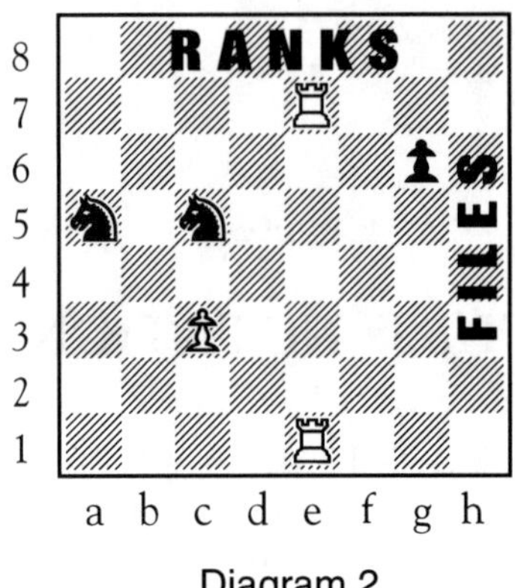

Diagram 2

Squares

Squares are identified by their rank-and-file coordinates. In Diagram 2, the white pawn is on the square c3, and the black pawn is on the square g6; the white Rooks are on e1 and e7, and the black Knights are on a5 and c5. (The square a1 is always in White's lower left corner.)

Diagonals

Diagonals are designated by their terminal squares (e.g., a1-h8, f1-a6).

Moves

Moves are described by specifying the letter for the piece moved (no letter is used for pawns) followed by its arrival square. *Nf3* describes a Knight move to the square f3, while *e5* describes a pawn move to the square e5. Rank-and-file modifiers are used to prevent ambiguity. In Diagram 2, for example, both white Rooks are capable of moving to e5; therefore, *R1e5* specifies the Rook on the *first* rank moving to e5. Similarly, if the black N/a5 moved to b3, this move would be written *...Nab3*.

Game moves are recorded using the move number, White's move, then Black's move (e.g., *1. e4 Nf6*). Individual Black moves in text are preceded by ellipses "..." (e.g., *...Bg4*) to distinguish them from White moves.

Captures

Captures are indicated by the symbol for the capturing piece (file designations are used for pawns) followed by an "x" and the designation of the *square* on which the capture takes place. *Bxc4* indicates a Bishop captured a chessman on the square c4; *exd5* indicates a pawn on the e-file captured a chessman on the square d5. Rank-and-file modifiers are used if necessary to prevent ambiguity (e.g., *Naxb3* or *R1xe5*).

Pawn Promotions

Pawn promotions in this book are indicated by an equal sign "=" (e.g., *f8=Q* indicates that a pawn advanced to the square f8 and "promoted" to a Queen; *exf8=N†* indicates that a pawn on the e-file captured a piece on the square f8 and "underpromoted" to a Knight giving check).

Positions

The position in Diagram 2 can be recorded as: White — R/e7, R/e1, P/c3; Black — N/a5, N/c5, P/g6.

Annotation Symbols

The following supplementary symbols are frequently used by annotators to comment tersely on the quality of chess moves:

!	Strong move
!!	Outstanding move
?	Weak move
??	Blunder
!?	Sharp move, but risky
?!	Trappy move, but unsound

These symbols merely reflect the annotator's opinion.

For experience with Algebraic notation, play through the following game:

1.	e4	e5	4.	c3	dxc3
2.	Nf3	Nc6	5.	Bc4	Bb4
3.	d4	exd4	6.	0–0	cxb2

7.	Bxb2	Nf6
8.	Nc3	d6
9.	Nd5	Bg4
10.	Nxf6†	gxf6

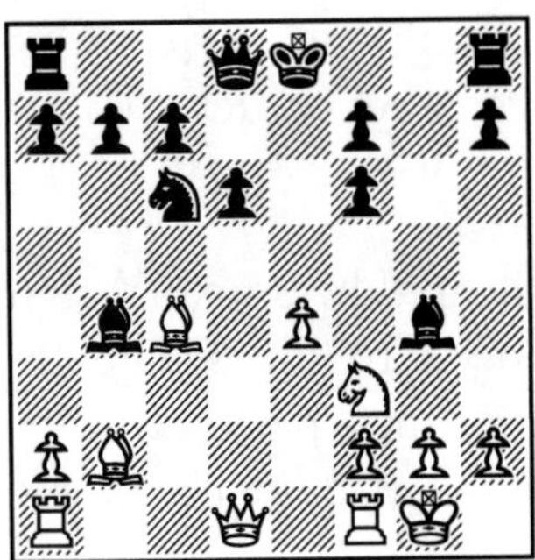

11.	h3	Bh5
12.	Qd5	Bg6
13.	Ng5	Qd7
14.	Bxf6	Rg8
15.	Rad1	Na5
16.	e5	Nxc4
17.	Qxc4	Bc5
18.	Rfe1	Bb6
19.	exd6†	Kf8
20.	Re7	Qc6
21.	Nxh7†	Bxh7
22.	Qxf7#	

Summary

Algebraic notation is simple, accurate, and concise. Easy to read and record, it is recommended for all chessplayers.

Part I

THE OPENING

Chapter 3

THE OPENING

A chess game begins on the first *move!*

Goals in the Opening

In the opening (first 10-15 moves), pieces and pawns are mobilized for attack and defense. Checkmate is not a realistic prospect in the opening, barring suicidal blunders by your opponent, so the four primary opening goals are:

- Control the center
- Develop all pieces
- Safeguard the King
- Hinder your opponent

Each move in the opening should contribute toward one or more of these important goals; otherwise, the move is probably weak or an outright mistake.

The outcome of the opening determines or influences your strategic alternatives and tactical opportunities for many subsequent moves. The major objective in the opening is to build a safe, solid, active, and flexible position which will provide promising tactical and positional opportunities in the middlegame. A well-played opening does not aim for an immediate knockout; rather, the opening builds for the future.

Let us examine these four goals in greater detail.

Control the Center

In the opening, it is very important to occupy and attack the center squares (d4, d5, e4, e5) to gain space for your pieces and restrain enemy pieces and pawns from occupying and controlling the center. Controlling the center allows you to post active, mobile pieces on strong central squares while denying your opponent similar desirable development. Achieving a strong, supported Ideal Pawn Center (two central pawns safely abreast on the fourth rank, protected by pieces — see Diagram 3) gains valuable central space, releases both your Bishops, and restricts your opponent's access to important central squares, hindering his development. A mobile Ideal Pawn Center can later advance to gain more space for your pieces and cramp the opponent.

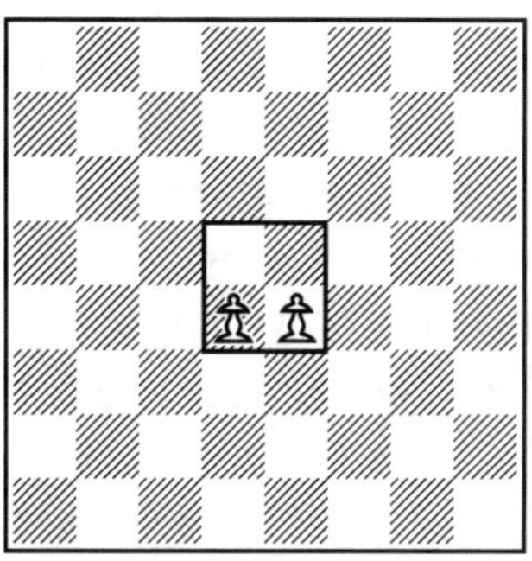

Diagram 3

An advanced pawn wedge in the center (pawns on d4 and e5, or d5 and e4) also divides and restricts opposing pieces and pawns.

Controlling the center squares is also important because Knights and Bishops exert their maximum power in or near the center, and many attacking lines crisscross through the center in the middlegame. The center is the hub of the chessboard, and the side which controls the traffic in the center controls the game. Try to gain and maintain control of the center.

Develop All Pieces

Every piece should be moved to its most effective and safe square in the opening. Develop *all* your pieces in the opening; do not try to wage a chess war with half your forces sitting idly on their original squares. Seek effective, strong squares which allow your pieces the most scope, mobility, and aggressive prospects.

Knights and Bishops belong near the center, attacking it (Bishops can also control the center from the wings, by fianchettoed development (i.e., Bishops on b2, g2, b7, or g7) or by pinning opposing Knights which attack the center). Rooks belong on open files, or files likely to become open, especially central files. The Queen's placement is flexible — develop the Queen, but not too early. The Queen is the most powerful piece, and will strongly influence the game; but premature, aggressive attacks and pawn-grabbing expeditions with the Queen are usually abortive, and lose time and position when the powerful Queen is harassed by opposing minor pieces and pawns. A long-range piece, the Queen can function effectively close to home in the opening.

Develop a new piece in preference to moving an already developed piece twice; ideally, move each piece only once in the opening. (The position of each piece can be improved later, as circumstances change.) Moving the same pieces multiple times in the opening costs valuable moves (*tempi*) which can usually be used to better advantage to develop new pieces. White tempi losses, in effect, reverse the colors in the game and give Black the initiative. Black tempi losses are even more serious, as Black begins the game one move behind and falls even further behind in development. Avoid losing tempi in the opening.

Safeguard the King

King safety is paramount. Left on a central file, a King becomes vulnerable in the early middlegame when central lines begin to open. For that reason, both Kings are normally whisked to safety by castling in the *opening*, before any middlegame activities (especially line-openings and attacks) occur.

Kingside castling is usually safer, since all pawns sheltering the castled King are protected and no open lines lead directly to the King. Queenside castling is typically more aggressive but more risky, since a Rook is developed to a central file immediately but the a-pawn is unprotected, and an open diagonal (c1-h6 or h3-c8) often leads directly toward the castled King. A recent survey of several hundred Grandmaster games revealed that Grandmasters castle in over 90 percent of their games, and nine times out of ten on the Kingside.

When should you castle? Castle when your King is endangered or when you do not have a better move, such as developing an important piece. Timing is important. Castling too soon informs your opponent of your King's permanent address and allows him to direct his pieces toward that sensitive sector. Conversely, postponing castling too long is often dangerous because you may be attacked and lose castling privileges.

Occasionally, especially when Queens and several minor pieces have been exchanged early, a King is relatively safe in the middle — and is closer to the center of action for the endgame — but such instances are rare, and castling to safeguard your King should be a standard part of the opening. A safe King is a happy King. Castle!

Hindrance

Along with controlling the center, developing all pieces, and safeguarding your King, an important fourth opening objective is to hinder your opponent from accomplishing the same goals. If a move weakens your opponent's position without harming yours, and prevents or hinders your opponent from realizing his opening objectives, the move is probably a sound idea and will gain a relative advantage (Diagram 4):

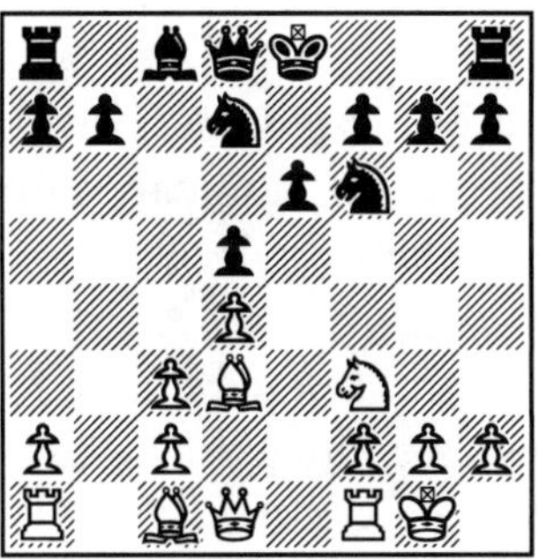

Diagram 4-White to move

White has available the obvious move 9. *Bg5*, pinning the black N/f6 to the Queen, but chose instead **9. Ba3!** to prevent Black from castling Kingside (a King cannot castle through check). Queenside castling by Black could be dangerous because of the half-open b- and c-files, which White could use later for attack. White's strong 9. *Ba3* develops a new piece and hinders Black.

In addition to the four basic principles covered above, you may find the following important guidelines helpful to your opening play.

Opening Guidelines

- *Open with* 1. e4 *or* 1. d4. On the first move, advance a center pawn two squares to occupy and attack the center and release a

Bishop, thereby preparing early castling. As Black, defending with the symmetrical *1... e5* or *1... d5* on the first move is excellent for the same reasons. Flank openings and defenses are no sounder, and can be experimented with later in your development as a player.

- *Make only a few pawn moves.* Pawn moves in the opening have four purposes: to control the center, release pieces, defend your piece-and pawn-formation, and hinder or restrain opposing pieces and pawns. Two or three pawn moves in the opening can accomplish these tasks.
- *Maintain a center pawn.* A center pawn, preferably on the fourth rank, restricts your opponent's central piece-and-pawn activity and prevents your position from being overrun in the center.
- *Develop with a threat when possible.* Developing with threats limits your opponent's replies and can seize or maintain the initiative. If your opponent is busy defending, he cannot be attacking.
- *Usually, develop Knights before Bishops.* Knights are usually developed before Bishops, since the best squares for the Knights are known first. Whenever the ideal placement of a Bishop becomes clear, develop the Bishop accordingly.
- *Do not lose material.* The side ahead in material (pieces and pawns) usually wins chess games, so do not begin by falling behind in material early. Equal exchanges of pieces and pawns may be desirable in the opening if they improve your position, but avoid unsound sacrifices and loss of material. (Opening sacrifices—gambits—are discussed later in this chapter.)

12 Common Mistakes

Chess games cannot be won in the opening against reasonable defense, but they can be lost. Avoid the following 12 common opening mistakes, which can lose outright or lead to hopeless or impoverished middlegame positions:

1. Exposing your King
2. Losing material
3. Failing to castle

4. Attacking prematurely
5. Losing control of the center
6. Moving the same piece twice
7. Not developing all pieces
8. Developing the Queen too early
9. Pawn-grabbing
10. Blocking pieces with pawns
11. Making unnecessary pawn moves
12. Giving useless checks

These miniature games illustrate how devastating these opening mistakes can be:

1.	**e4**	**e5**
2.	**f4**	**Bc5**
3.	**fxe5?**	**Qh4†**
4.	**Ke2??**	**Qxe4#**

and

1.	**e4**	**e5**
2.	**Nf3**	**Nc6**
3.	**Bc4**	**d6**
4.	**Nc3**	**Bg4**
5.	**d3**	**Nd4?**
6.	**Nxe5!**	**Bxd1??**
7.	**Bxf7†**	**Ke7**
8.	**Nd5#**	

Weakening pawn moves which expose the King and pawn-grabbing at the expense of development are often culprits:

1.	**d4**	**d5**
2.	**Nf3**	**e6**
3.	**Bg5**	**f6**
4.	**Bh4**	**g5?**
5.	**Bg3**	**Qe7**
6.	**e3**	**Qb4†**
7.	**Nbd2**	**Qxb2?**
8.	**Bxc7**	**b6**
9.	**Rb1**	**Qxa2?**
10.	**Nxg5!**	**fxg5**
11.	**Qh5†**	**Kd7**
12.	**Be5**	**Nf6**
13.	**Qf7†**	**Kc6**

If ...*Kd8, 14. Bc7 mate.*

14. Bb5 mate.

(Or *14. Qc7 mate.)*

These brief games illustrate how quickly opening mistakes can be punished. Avoid the 12 mistakes listed above, and you will play the opening well.

Your knowledge of opening principles is now sufficient to ensure strong, competent opening play. But where will you begin? Which of the chessmen at your disposal on the board will you select for your *first* move? As we proceed to look at the array of choices before you, your own preferences and style of play will enable you to make that important choice.

A Look At The Openings

Strong Versus Weak Openings

To compare strong and weak openings, consider Diagram 5:

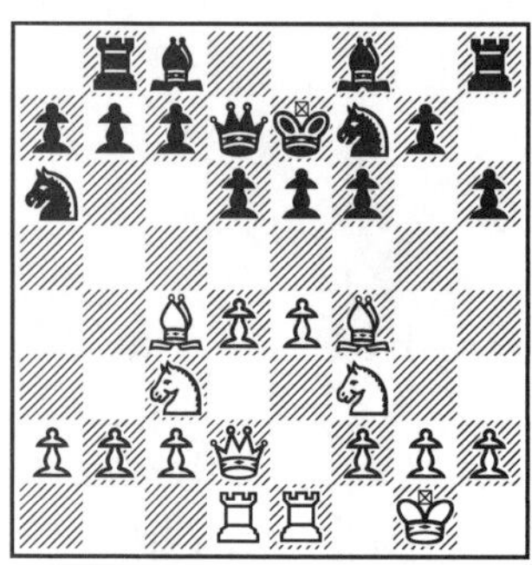

Diagram 5-White

After ten moves, White clearly stands better; he controls the center, has developed all his pieces to effective central squares, and has castled to safeguard his King. Black exerts minimal center control, his pieces are scattered and not well-posted (three have not even moved), and the permanently uncastled black King is stranded precariously in the middle — a dangerous omen. Black has committed several opening mistakes, and an unpromising middlegame is his legacy.

White's strategy will be to open the central files with pawn exchanges and attack the black King. White has no corresponding weaknesses, so Black's prospects for victory are bleak and hinge on later mistakes by White.

This example illustrates the importance of playing a strong opening. Let us explore some options for this critical choice in your own play.

Standard Openings

Over the centuries, Master chessplayers (and many strong amateurs) have developed and analyzed numerous sequences of opening moves, and created systems of White openings and Black defenses. These standard (referred to as "book") openings insure a reasonable beginning in a chess game. A chessplayer can always play the opening solely by general principles, but unless he intends to "reinvent the wheel" he should study and play standard chess openings, choosing variations to suit his style. Ample room for chess originality exists in the middlegame, and even Grandmasters find that the proven openings are best. All standard openings are based on the sound opening principles elaborated earlier; only the application of these principles differs. In any event, how *well* a chessplayer plays the opening is much more important than which opening he plays.

Chess opening nomenclature has a myriad background. Some current openings were named for chess pieces (e.g., Bishop's Opening, Queen's Gambit, King's Indian Defense), some for strong chessplayers (Alekhine's Defense, Réti Opening, Pirc Defense), and some for locations where the openings were first developed or popularized (English Opening, French Defense, Dutch Defense). Until a standardized classification system is developed, these romantic names will linger.

As an introduction to standard chess openings and defenses (over 70 exist), 25 of the most popular are presented. Play through the opening moves of all these standard openings, then try your choices of openings and defenses in practice games with worthy opponents or against your computer.

Note: If an opponent as White opens with any move other than *1. e4* or *1. d4*, simply advance the appropriate Black center pawn two squares and just "play chess" according to the key opening principles of center control, rapid development, King safety, and hindrance, and you will achieve at least an even game.

1. e4

Giuoco Piano

1.	e4	e5
2.	Nf3	Nc6
3.	Bc4	Bc5

Vienna Game

1.	e4	e5
2.	Nc3	Nf6
3.	Bc4	Nc6
4.	d3	

Ruy Lopez

1.	e4	e5
2.	Nf3	Nc6
3.	Bb5	

King's Gambit

1.	e4	e5
2.	f4	exf4
3.	Nf3	

Smith-Morra's Gambit

1.	e4	c5
2.	d4	cxd4
3.	c3	dxc3
4.	Nxc3	

Göring's Gambit

1.	e4	e5
2.	Nf3	Nc6
3.	d4	exd4
4.	c3	dxc3
5.	Bc4	cxb2
6.	Bxb2	

1. d4

Queen's Gambit Declined

1.	d4	d5
2.	c4	e6
3.	Nc3	Nf6
4.	Bg5	Be7
5.	e3	0–0
6.	Nf3	Nbd7
7.	Rc1	

Queen's Gambit Accepted

1.	d4	d5
2.	c4	dxc4
3.	Nf3	Nf6

Colle's Opening

1.	d4	d5
2.	Nf3	Nf6
3.	e3	e6
4.	Bd3	c5
5.	c3	Nbd7
6.	Nbd2	Be7
7.	0–0	0–0
8.	Re1	Qc7
9.	e4	

Curry's Opening

1.	d4	d5
2.	Nf3	Nf6
3.	Bg5	e6
4.	e3	Be7
5.	Bd3	Nbd7
6.	Nbd2	0–0
7.	c3	b6
8.	Qc2	Bb7
9.	0–0–0	c5
10.	h4	

Blackmar-Diemer's Gambit

1.	d4	d5
2.	e4	dxe4
3.	Nc3	Nf6
4.	f3	exf3
5.	Nxf3	

1. c4

English Opening

1.	c4	e5
2.	Nc3	Nf6
3.	g3	Bb4
4.	Bg2	

Defenses
To 1. e4

French Defense

1.	e4	e6
2.	d4	d5

Caro-Kann's Defense

1.	e4	c6
2.	d4	d5

Center Counter Defense

1.	e4	d5
2.	exd5	Qxd5 or Nf6

Sicilian (Najdorf) Defense

1.	e4	c5
2.	Nf3	d6
3.	d4	cxd4
4.	Nxd4	Nf6
5.	Nc3	a6
6.	Bg5	e6

Sicilian (Dragon) Defense

1. e4 c5
2. Nf3 d6
3. d4 cxd4
4. Nxd4 Nf6
5. Nc3 g6
6. Bc4 Bg7

Pirc's Defense

1. e4 d6
2. d4 Nf6
3. Nc3 g6
4. f4 Bg7
5. Nf3 0-0

To 1. d4

Tarrasch's Defense

1. d4 d5
2. c4 e6
3. Nc3 c5

Tartakower's Defense

1. d4 d5
2. c4 e6
3. Nc3 Nf6
4. Bg5 Be7
5. e3 0-0
6. Nf3 h6
7. Bh4 b6
8. Rc1 Bb7

King's Indian Defense

1. d4 Nf6
2. c4 g6
3. Nc3 Bg7
4. e4 d6
5. Nf3 0-0

Nimzo-Indian Defense

1. d4 Nf6
2. c4 e6
3. Nc3 Bb4

Gruenfeld's Defense

1. d4 Nf6
2. c4 g6
3. Nc3 d5

Queen's Indian Defense

1. d4 Nf6
2. c4 e6
3. Nf3 b6
4. g3 Bb7

Dutch Defense

1. d4 f5
2. g3 e6
3. Bg2 Nf6
4. Nf3 Be7
5. 0-0 0-0
6. c4 d6

Gambits

Gambits — sacrifices of material (usually one or two pawns, sometimes a piece) in the opening — are played to gain a lead in development, open lines, control the center, seize the initiative, and gain opportunities for attack. A gambiteer typically hopes his lead in development will result in an early attack against the enemy King. An excellent example of a gambit is the classic King's Gambit (Diagram 6):

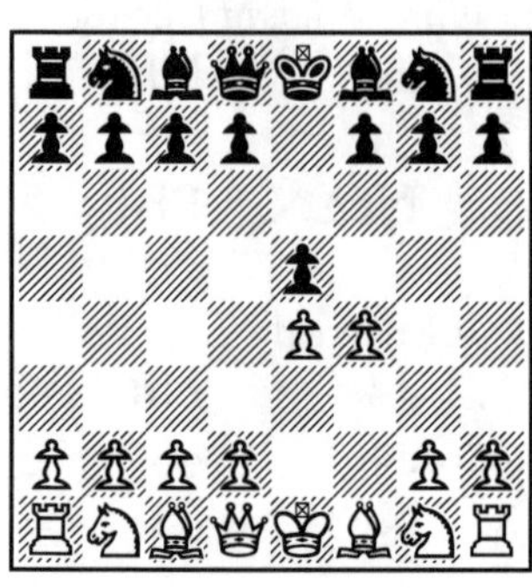

Diagram 6-Black

With **1. e4 e5 2. f4,** White offers a pawn to deflect Black's central e5-pawn (*2... exf4*). White hopes to establish an Ideal Pawn Center with an early *d2-d4* and, after *Nf3*, *Bc4* and *0–0*, exert pressure along the half-open f-file against Black's vulnerable f7-square. White will have pressure on Black's position, and Black must defend carefully if he accepts the gambit pawn.

A lead in development and early control of the center are usually only temporary advantages, and gambits can be risky or even unsound if they do not lead to an attack against the opposing King. When a *piece* is sacrificed early, an attack against the enemy King is essential!

Gambits are speculative and risky, but remain a favorite of aggressive, attacking players. Play gambits occasionally to sharpen your tactical skills — and to win games!

Defending Against Gambits

Gambits, risky for White, can be dangerous for Black. Gambits especially pose dangers for the unprepared or unwary defender. Faced with a gambit, a Black player has three options: accept the gambit, decline the gambit, or offer a countergambit.

Countergambits by Black are theoretically suspect and usually risky, since Black is one move behind. But some countergambits — such as the Falkbeer Countergambit to the King's Gambit — yield promising games.

Aside from declining a gambit, one reliable approach to defending against gambits is to accept the initial sacrifice, then return the extra material at an appropriate time for positional considerations. In the King's Gambit, for example, *1. e4 e5 2. f4 exf4 3. Nf3 d5 4. exd5 Nf6* gives Black a good game.

Most Black players prefer to either ACCEPT the gambit material and resign themselves to playing the requisite defense until equalizing in development — being prepared to return the extra material to improve or equalize their positions — or DECLINE the gambit to achieve a safe and active position with material equality. Many strong chessplayers opt to accept familiar gambits and decline unfamiliar ones.

Following are brief accepted and declined variations of three typical gambits, plus one countergambit:

King's Gambit
Accepted

1. e4 e5
2. f4 exf4
3. Nf3 g5
4. Bc4 Bg7
5. 0–0 h6
6. d4 d6
7. Nc3 Be6
8. Bxe6 fxe6

Declined

1. e4 e5
2. f4 Bc5

(Safer than *2… d6*, *2… Nf6*, or *2… Qh4†*.)

3. Nf3 d6
4. Nc3 Nf6
5. Bc4 Nc6
6. d3 Bg4

Smith-Morra's Gambit
Accepted

1. e4 c5
2. d4 cxd4
3. c3 dxc3
4. Nxc3 Nc6
5. Nf3 d6
6. Bc4 e6
7. 0–0 Nf6
8. Qe2 Be7
9. Rd1 e5
10. Be3 0–0

Declined

1. e4 c5
2. d4 cxd4
3. c3 Nf6

(Or *3… d5* or *3… d3*.)

4. e5 Nd5
5. cxd4 d6

Blackmar-Diemer's Gambit
Accepted

1. d4 d5
2. e4 dxe4
3. Nc3 Nf6
4. f3 exf3
5. Nxf3 Bf5
6. Bc4 e6
7. Bg5 Be7
8. 0–0 0–0

Declined

1. d4 d5
2. e4 e6

(French Defense) or

1. d4 d5
2. e4 c6

(Caro-Kann's Defense)

Falkbeer's Countergambit

1. e4 e5
2. f4 d5
3. exd5 e4
4. d3 Nf6
5. dxe4 Nxe4
6. Nf3 Bc5
7. Qe2 Bf5

8. Nc3 Qe7

Careful defense is required against gambits. The main ideas for the defender are to develop quickly, not become too aggressive early, and be willing to return the extra material for a sound position.

Comparison of Openings

All standard openings are sound, and the choice is a matter of style and preference, reflecting a balance of aggression (with risk) and safety (with less opportunity). For your guidance, following is a general comparison of several standard openings.

Openings	**Safe**	**Aggressive**
1. e4	Giuoco Piano Ruy Lopez	King's Gambit Smith-Morra' Gambit
1. d4	Queen's Gambit Colle's Opening	Curry's Opening Blackmar-Diemer's Gambit
Defenses	**Safe**	**Aggressive**
vs. *1. e4*	French Defense Caro-Kann Defense	Sicilian Defense Center Counter Defense
vs. *1. d4*	Tartakower's Defense Nimzo-Indian Defense	King's Indian Defense Dutch Defense

For a more detailed discussion of the ideas and themes of any particular standard opening, including specialized variations, consult an opening manual (*e.g.*, *Modern Chess Openings*, *Encyclopedia of Chess Openings*, *The Ideas Behind the Chess Openings*.)

Choosing *Your* Opening

There are three schools of chess opening theory: Classical, Modern, and Hypermodern. All three agree that control of the center is important. The Classical approach is to control the center immediately, primarily with pawns and pieces (e.g., Queen's Gambit Declined). The Modern school does the same, except that pieces, rather than pawns, play a primary role early (e.g., Nimzo-Indian Defense). The Hypermodern method is to allow the opponent to advance his center pawns uncontested in the hope that the advanced pawns will become vulnerable later (e.g., King's Indian Defense). The Classical or Modern approaches are recommended for intermediate players, since Hypermodern defenses can lead to extremely cramped positions if unsuccessful.

All three schools agree that it is more important to control the center after 15 moves than after five moves(!), and their differences reflect method and timing — style.

Playing sound openings is a big step toward victories in chess. All standard chess openings are sound and playable. Which openings and defenses should you play? The primary criteria are your playing style and the types of middlegame positions you prefer. Games beginning with *1. e4* are usually more tactical early, while in games beginning with *1. d4* tactics are usually deferred and more positional maneuvering occurs. Attacking players generally prefer to open with *1. e4*, and positional players often opt for *1. d4* (or *1. c4*).

Your openings should reflect and promote *your* style of play. Just because a strong chessplayer plays a certain opening or defense is no assurance that the same opening is right for you. Here are some guidelines to help you choose your best openings and defenses as you learn more by reading this book:

- The foremost principle is to *choose an opening that fits your style* — tactical or positional. Since the outcome of the opening strongly influences the pattern of early middlegame play, a chessplayer should select openings that lead to middlegame positions which experience has proven to be preferable.

- Another helpful guideline is to choose a desirable balance of aggression (with accompanying risk) and safety (with less opportunity). Gambits are meat to some chessplayers, poison to others. Some openings generally lead to open positions, others to semi-open or closed formations. Learn your preferences, and play openings that lead to balanced risk/safety positions you desire.
- A third principle is to choose flexible openings which provide opportunity and scope for various sound plans later. A foiled narrow, single-purpose opening leaves a player with desolate middlegame prospects.
- Finally, it is wise to select openings that can be achieved most of the time. Openings which require extensive cooperation from your opponent are generally to be shunned. You can seldom realize such openings.

Learning a New Opening

The best method to learn a new opening is to first learn the *ideas* or themes in that opening, then memorize the first few basic moves. Early memorization of extended variations is unnecessary and often confusing. Play by the *principles* of chess rather than memory.

Play the openings and defenses you know best in serious games; experiment with new openings in casual (skittles) games. Try your new opening against weaker opponents or your chess computer (at lower levels) first, to gain experience with the various types of positions, then graduate to higher levels and stronger opponents. After experimenting, specialize in a few openings and defenses, and learn them well. Be thorough — learn the standard traps for both sides in your chosen openings and defenses. Specialized books on opening traps are available. When an opponent makes an unorthodox or "non-book" move, rely on your knowledge of sound opening principles — just "play chess" — and you will achieve a successful opening. Unorthodox opening moves will not lead to an advantage against play based on sound principles.

At all times in the opening, play according to the **Master-proven** principles of *center control*, *rapid development*, *King safety*, and *hindrance*.

Recommended Openings and Defenses

Recommended openings and defenses for intermediate players are:

- *1. e4:* If *1. e4* is your favorite opening move, try these openings: 1) Giuoco Piano; 2) Ruy Lopez; 3) Vienna Game; 4) King's Gambit.
- *1. d4* (and *1. c4*)*:* If *1. d4* or *1. c4* is your preference, play these openings: 1) Queen's Gambit; 2) Colle's Opening; 3) English Opening; 4) Curry's Opening.
- Defenses to *1. e4:* In addition to the solid *1... e5*, play these defenses: 1) Sicilian Defense; 2) French Defense; 3) Caro-Kann Defense; 4) Center Counter Defense.
- Defenses to *1. d4:* In addition to the reliable *1... d5*, play these defenses: 1) Tartakower's Defense; 2) Nimzo-Indian Defense; 3) King's Indian Defense; 4) Tarrasch's Defense.

All these openings are sound, and provide a solid, flexible foundation for developing further openings to expand your opening repertoire.

You will still have to learn how to handle different defenses to your first move if Black doesn't *cooperate with your system.*

Summary

In the opening, White attempts to maintain and increase his initiative conferred by the first move. Black tries to equalize with a view toward seizing the initiative. Properly played, the opening will lead to an active and promising middlegame with aggressive prospects.

A guiding principle is to play openings and defenses which lead to the types of middlegame positions you prefer. Favor sound openings which feature *active piece play* and emphasize center control, rapid piece development, and King safety. Play open and semi-open games, and forego closed games with complicated positional maneuvering until tactics and direct attacks have been mastered.

A house without a solid foundation will crumble and fall when the later storms buffet. The opening is the foundation of your chess game — build a sound, strong opening!

Chapter 4

THE CURRY OPENING

Dare to be original. The graveyard of mankind is littered with the bones and ashes of countless men too timid to express their ideas.

Developed in 1971 by the author, the Curry Opening is a Queen Pawn opening which offers White an excellent balance of aggression and safety. The central theme of the Curry Opening is Kingside pressure against Black while maintaining a safe white King position on the Queenside. This promising opening conforms to the three most important opening principles of center control, piece development, and King safety, and offers White sound, active positions.

The ideal sequence of White moves in the Curry Opening is:

1. **d4**
2. **Nf3**
3. **Bg5**
4. **e3**
5. **Bd3**
6. **Nbd2**
7. **c3**
8. **Qc2**
9. **0-0-0**
10. **h4** (if ...*0-0* by Black).

The move order may be varied as necessary or appropriate.

Early White transpositions into the Queen's Gambit, Colle, London, and Trompovsky Openings are possible, giving the Curry Opening considerable flexibility.

In the Curry Opening, White establishes a solid position with strong Kingside pressure. Positionally sound and tactically promising, the

Curry Opening offers White excellent prospects for a Kingside attack or active central play. Experience has indicated that Black must defend carefully or counterattack energetically to survive.

Illustrative Games

To be sound and playable, a chess opening must offer a secure, flexible position from which to maneuver for middlegame attacks against a wide variety of defenses. The following games illustrate the Curry Opening against an orthodox Queen-pawn defense and the flexible, modern King's Indian Defense. Several Curry Opening wins against a variety of defenses, and an instructive loss, appear in Appendix A.

The author's first game with the Curry Opening at a local chess club yielded the following results:

	Curry	Amateur
1.	d4	d5
2.	Nf3	Nf6
3.	Bg5	e6
4.	e3	Be7
5.	Bd3	Nbd7
6.	Nbd2	0–0
7.	c3	b6
8.	Qc2	Bb7
9.	0–0–0	h6
10.	h4	

The ideal White position in the Curry Opening has been reached.

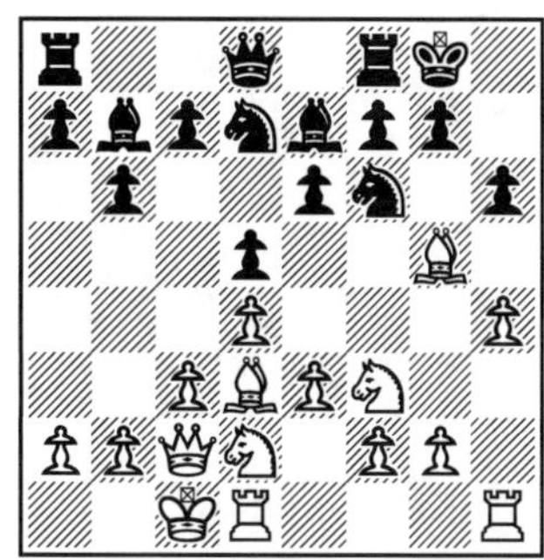

Diagram 7-Black

10.	...	hxg5
11.	hxg5	Ng4
12.	Bh7†	Kh8
13.	Bg8†	Kxg8
14.	Qh7#	

Next is an example of the Curry Opening versus the sturdy, flexible, and popular King's Indian Defense.

	Curry	Amateur
1.	d4	Nf6
2.	Nf3	g6
3.	Bg5	Bg7
4.	e3	d6
5.	Bd3	0–0
6.	Nbd2	Nbd7
7.	c3	c5
8.	Qc2	cxd4
9.	exd4	Qa5
10.	h4	b5
11.	a3	Bb7
12.	0–0–0	Rac8

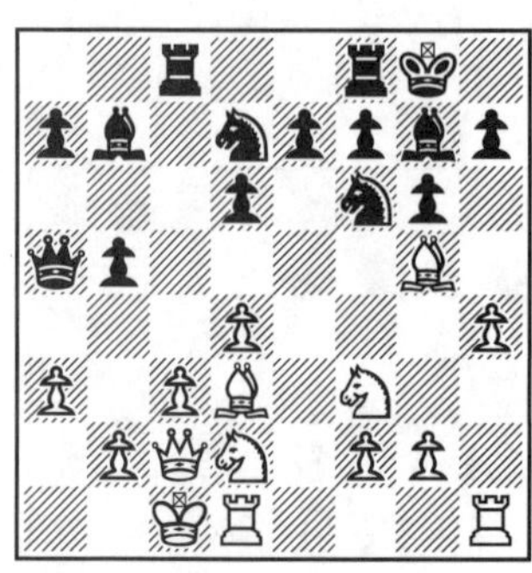

Diagram 8-White

13.	h5	Nxh5
14.	Rxh5	gxh5
15.	Bxh7†	Kh8
16.	Rh1	f6
17.	Rxh5	fxg5
18.	Bf5†	Kg8
19.	Be6†	Rf7
20.	Qg6	Rcf8
21.	Qh7#	

In both preceding games White achieved his ideal position in the Curry Opening, and White's ensuing Kingside attacks were swift and effective.

Comparisons

The only chess opening similar to the Curry Opening is the Torre Attack, developed by 20th-century Mexican Grandmaster Carlos Torre. However, the similarities between the two openings are overshadowed by four significant differences:

	Curry Opening	Torre Attack*
1.	0-0-0	0-0
2.	Qc2	Qe2
3.	h4	not played
4.	Nbd2-f3	Nbd2-c4

*Torre-Lasker, Moscow, 1925, for example.

These four key differences between the Curry Opening and the Torre Attack alter the strategy and thrusts of each opening.

Summary

The author's many successes with the Curry Opening against strong chessplayers, including Masters and Experts, are most encouraging. A Grandmaster writing in *Chess Life* has termed the Curry Opening "... a spicy, theoretical dish." The merits of this opening will be revealed with more testing at the Master and Grandmaster levels. Whatever the future holds for the Curry Opening, enterprising chessplayers — you — have a pioneering opportunity to become a part of chess history by learning, playing (surprising opponents), and *winning* with the promising new Curry Opening!

Part II

THE MIDDLEGAME

Chapter 5

THE MIDDLEGAME

Before the endgame, the gods have placed the middlegame.
— Tarrasch

After the opening, the challenging, complex, and often critical middlegame begins. It is characterized by the three elements: *strategy*, *positional play*, and *tactics*. *Strategy* is the formulation of plans to exert maximum offensive and defensive force. *Positional play* is the positioning of pieces and pawns to control important squares for optimum activity and flexibility. *Tactics*, the most powerful factor in chess, are direct threats to win material or checkmate.

Most games are decided in the middlegame by attacks against the Kings and tactics which win decisive material. Strategy and tactics dominate, and attack and defense are the main activities. Checkmate, the ultimate goal, is always first priority.

The transition from opening to middlegame often causes intermediate chessplayers considerable difficulty, for they are departing the known with its fixed plan (control the center, develop all pieces, safeguard the King) and venturing into the unknown with no clear idea of how to proceed. At this crucial, early stage of the middlegame, *planning* (strategy) becomes important. But first, is the opening really over? Have you castled and developed all your pieces, and placed both Rooks on open files (or central files likely to become open), for example? If so, then proceed to middlegame considerations.

Goals in the Middlegame

The most important middlegame principle is to establish and maintain a *safe, active position* while pursuing the following three goals:

- Checkmate the enemy King
- Win material
- Establish a winning endgame

All purposeful middlegame play is directed toward accomplishing these goals and preventing your opponent from realizing the same objectives. The details of tactics, combinations and sacrifices, attacks on the enemy King, and checkmating patterns will be covered in subsequent chapters. First, we will concentrate here on mastering a basic, systematic method to use in selecting your next move in the crowded and complex world of the middlegame.

Five-Step Approach

All that matters on the chessboard is good moves.

— Former World Champion Bobby Fischer

The goal in chess is to play the best move in *every* position. How can you find the best moves consistently? A chess game is a series of problems. Each position is a new problem to be solved, with the solution being the "best move" (determined through various processes which we will try to outline in these chapters). Repetitive problems, such as chess positions, are amenable to a systematic method of problem-solving — far preferable to a semi-random approach to each new position.

One systematic approach is the trial-and-error method, in which every reasonable move is mentally tried and the consequences evaluated. Besides being inefficient and time-consuming, this method requires that *every* move be considered to insure that the best move is included, and strong surprise moves are often overlooked.

Another systematic approach is to: a) determine your *goal* in each position; b) define the *tasks* required to achieve your goal; then c) determine specifically what the next move or sequence of moves should be to accomplish it. This goal-directed method is highly recommended as being more efficient and effective, since only relevant candidate moves need be considered.

The recommended five-step, systematic method for selecting the best move in each chess position is:

1. Analyze the position

2. Determine your goals
3. Define tasks
4. Develop candidate moves
5. Choose the best candidate move

Steps 2 and 3 are referred to as *planning*.

To play effective moves consistently, analyze the position accurately and completely (especially looking for *weaknesses)*, determine your offensive or defensive goals (what you would *like* — or what you *need* — to do), define the *essential tasks* required to realize your desired goal position, then consider only those candidate moves which accomplish the required tasks — if such moves exist, you will find them in your selective search. Finally, select and play the best move available among the relevant candidate moves (sometimes there *are* equally good "best" moves—e.g., multiple ways to checkmate).

Let us examine these five steps in detail.

1. Analyze The Position

> *Chess mastery essentially consists of analyzing chess positions accurately.*
>
> — Former World Champion Botvinnik

Chess is a game of threats, and every move in a chess game should be responsive to the *offensive opportunities* and *defensive necessities* in each position. The most certain method of recognizing these opportunities and necessities is to *analyze* the position as accurately and as completely as possible within the time constraints available. Analysis is the critical foundation for sound plans and effective moves. Your plans and moves reflect — and can be no better than — your analysis. A full analysis need not be repeated on every move. Once a complete and accurate analysis has been made, it can be *updated with the changes on each move*. Periodically, or whenever "major changes" occur, a completely new analysis of the position should be made. As always, your first concern will be a reassessment of the position's strengths and weaknesses.

The Middlegame

Seven Factors To Analyze

Considering *both* sides, you can analyze all chess positions according to these seven comprehensive factors:

- King safety
- Material status
- Possible tactics
- Piece placement and mobility
- Pawn structure
- Control of important squares
- Tempi

These important factors — especially *relative differences* — form the basis for sound plans and effective moves. Especially, look for imbalances. King safety is always first priority, with material status usually second and potential tactics third.

King Safety

As yourself these questions, for *both sides:*

Is the King safely castled behind a protective barrier of pawns, or is it exposed or restricted?

Are enemy pieces near or aimed at the King?

Are sufficient defenders available near the King?

Do open or potentially open lines lead toward the King?

Does the King have safe flight squares?

Material Status

The normal values of the chessmen (in pawn units) are: Queen – 9; Rook – 5; Bishop – 3+; Knight – 3; pawn – 1. The King is invaluable, since if the King is lost (checkmate), the game is lost.

These operating values are not absolute; they depend on the pieces' actual *power, mobility*, and *potential* in each position. The numerical values can thus be influenced or changed — a Knight on a strong outpost may be worth four pawns in strength, for example, while a "bad" Bishop restricted by its own pawns may currently be worth only two pawns.

When evaluating material status, be certain to ask:

What is the material count for both sides, *and* does each piece's activity (or lack of it) modify the point count?

Also, what is the composition of any disparity (e.g., is a two-point advantage in the form of two pawns, a Bishop or Knight for one pawn, or a Rook for a Bishop or Knight)?

Possible Tactics

Are there any immediate or potential tactical opportunities (covered in detail in Chapter 6)?

Does your opponent have any tactical weaknesses you can exploit?

Can you force or induce any weaknesses?

Do any tactical weaknesses exist in *your* position?

Piece Placement and Mobility

Are all the pieces safe, active, and mobile? Are any confined, blocked, or hindered? Are the pieces coordinated and defended, and do they cooperate? Are any pieces inactive or tied to menial defensive tasks that a pawn or less valuable piece could perform?

Pawn Structure

Are the pawn formations strong, or are there weaknesses (isolated, doubled, backward)? Do any "holes" exist in the pawn structure? Are all the pawns protected? Are there hanging pawns? Are any pawns passed? Is there a pawn majority? Are the pawns mobile or blocked?

Control of Important Squares

Which side controls the center squares and those around both Kings, or other significant squares? Is the control semi-permanent (with pawns) or temporary (with pieces)? Can controlling pawns or pieces be exchanged or deflected?

Tempi

Tempi are counted by determining the minimum number of moves required to reach the desired position. Which side has the greatest number of moves existing on the board, and how valuable are those extra moves? A lead in tempi often confers the initiative, and a sizable lead in tempi is a signal to attack.

These seven factors — signposts to guide your planning — overlap in influence, but for purposes of analyzing a position can be considered separately, then synthesized to develop an overall assessment of the position. Be thorough — do not overlook the small details, for they often contain the keys to victory. A misplaced or pinned enemy piece or pawn, a potentially overworked defender, an open line leading toward the opposing King, or even a weak square in the opponent's position may be all that is required for a successful tactic or attack.

A complete analysis yields a clear picture of the position and provides the basis for sound plans. Let us analyze a chess position, highlighting the seven characteristic features (Diagram 9).

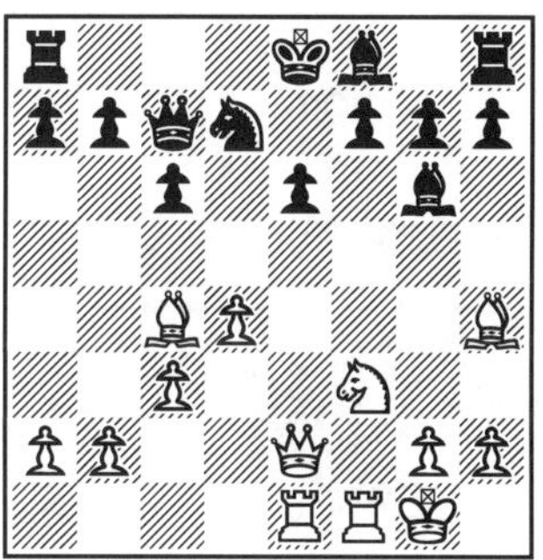

Diagram 9-White

First, a detailed analysis:

	White	**Black**
King safety	Safe	Restricted (cannot castle)
Material status	−1 pawn	+1 pawn
Possible tactics	Yes (*Bxe6!*)	No
Piece placement and mobility	Excellent	Poor (undeveloped)
Pawn structure	Sound	Adequate
Control of important squares	Superior	Inferior
Tempi	9	6

White's tremendous full development, combined with Black's undeveloped position and the restricted black King, more than compensates for White's pawn minus, and White has a promising attack starting with *1. Bxe6!*

(The game actually concluded quickly with **1. Bxe6! Nf6** [*1... fxe6* allows *2. Qxe6† Be7 3. Qxe7 checkmate*] **2. Bxf7‡! Kd7** [if *2... Kxf7, 3. Qe6 mate*] **3. Qe6† Kd8 4. Qe8 mate** — the black N/f6 is pinned.)

Another example of a complete analysis follows Diagram 10:

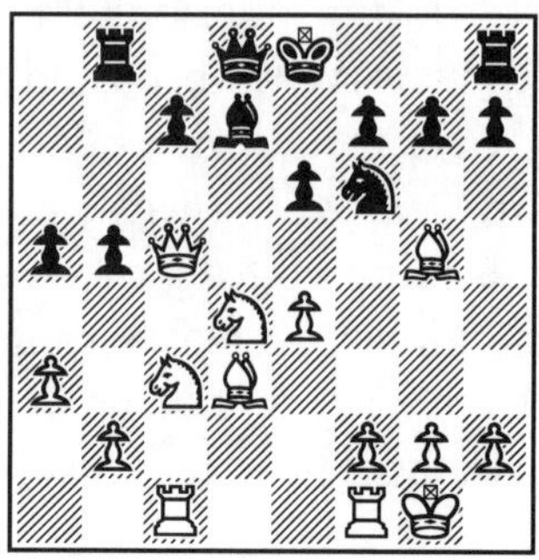

Diagram 10-White

Analysis of the position reveals the following:

	White	**Black**
King safety	Safe	Restricted (cannot castle)
Material status	+Bishop, Knight −1 pawn	-Bishop, Knight +1 pawn
Possible tactics	Yes *(Ncxb5*, *Nc6*, or *e5)*	No
Piece placement and mobility	Excellent, active	Fair
Pawn structure	Sound	Fair (no pawn on fourth rank, c-pawn backward)
Control of important squares	Superior	Inferior (...*0-0* impossible)
Tempi	11	6

White is five points ahead in material (Bishop and Knight for a pawn) and has an imposing lead in development and safe King position, while the black King is restricted and cannot castle. White clearly stands better and has a winning position. (White's material advantage and strong attacking position, combined with Black's immobile King, led to a successful checkmating attack in 12 moves, beginning with **1. Ncxb5 c6 2. Nd6†)**.

When analyzing a position, it is often helpful to minimize the similarities on both sides and concentrate on the *differences*, or imbalances, which give rise to winning opportunities (Diagram 11):

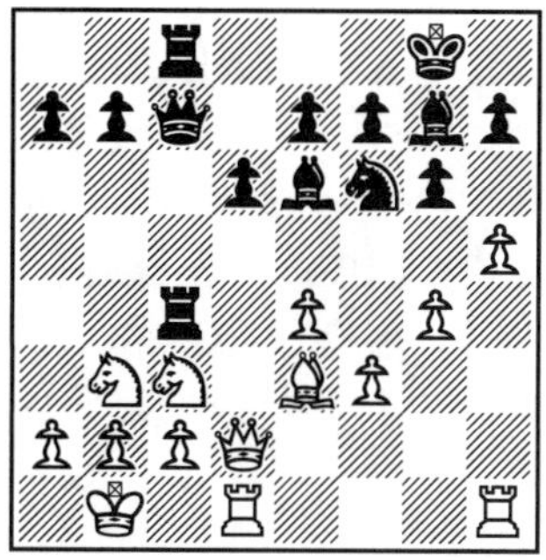

Diagram 11-White to move

Analysis of this position reveals that material is even and both Kings are under attack — Black's by a Kingside pawnstorm, and White's by a Queenside piece attack. White's pawnstorm is more advanced (he will be able to play *hxg6* next, opening the h-file for attack), but his pieces must be advanced to bolster the attack. Meanwhile, Black's pieces are aimed at the white King. Black can attempt to disrupt its defenders (*...a5-a4*) and, if the white Queen moves to the Kingside for attack, to possibly break up the white King's protection with the Exchange sacrifice *...Rxc3*. The position is dynamically unbalanced, with chances about even. Both sides should pursue their opposite wing attacks vigorously, and the side whose attack breaks through first will probably win the game.

These examples illustrate the critical information to be gained from analyzing the seven basic factors inherent in each position. An accurate assessment will invariably bring to light any imbalances which exist — and thereby expose the strengths and weaknesses of both sides.

Strengths and Weaknesses

Chess is a game of relative strengths and weaknesses, and every game reflects their interplay. Each player strives to maximize his own strengths and minimize his weaknesses, while attempting to minimize his opponent's strengths and capitalize on his weaknesses. *Every successful tactic, combination, sacrifice, and attack is based on one or more weaknesses.*

Without them, no successful tactics can occur. *Winning in chess consists of exploiting opponents' weaknesses!*

The next logical step, therefore, is to analyze the position according to the *strengths* and *weaknesses* made apparent by your previous seven-point examination.

Strengths and weaknesses are of two types: *tactical* and *positional*.

- *Tactical* strengths include:

1. Batteries (doubled or tripled pieces acting along a file, rank, or diagonal toward an enemy piece or vital square)
2. Pins of enemy chessmen

- *Tactical* weaknesses include:

1. Exposed King
2. Vulnerable back rank
3. Unguarded pieces and pawns
4. Pinned pieces and pawns
5. Pieces in a line
6. Pieces vulnerable to Knight fork
7. Pieces with no retreat
8. Overworked defenders
9. Unstable defenders
10. Vulnerable vital guards

- *Positional* strengths include:

1. Control of center
2. Center pawn on our fourth rank vs. enemy pawn on his third rank
3. Superior development
4. Greater space control
5. Strong outpost
6. Control of open file
7. Doubled Rooks
8. Rook(s) on seventh rank
9. Control of open diagonal
10. Half-open file
11. Bishop pair
12. Bishop vs. Knight
13. Mobile pawn wing
14. Offside pawn majority
15. Advanced pawn chain
16. Advanced pawn wedge
17. Advanced pawn
18. Passed pawn
19. Protected passed pawn
20. Outside passed pawn
21. Better King position
22. Available tempi

- *Positional* weaknesses include:

1. Restricted King
2. Open lines toward the King
3. Cramped position
4. "Bad" Bishop
5. Isolated pawns
6. Doubled pawns
7. Backward pawns
8. Hanging pawns
9. "Holes" in pawn structure
10. Weak-square complex

These tactical and positional strengths and weaknesses — typical central features — enable a player to formulate opportunistic plans.

2. Determine Your Goals

Strategy and Planning

Strategy is the formulation of sound plans to exert maximum offensive (and requisite defensive) force to achieve specific advantages and goals. A sound plan provides the framework for developing effective moves. Rather than play only move-to-move, play with a series of sound, purposeful, flexible plans.

Several important considerations regarding sound planning:

1. Plans can be offensive or defensive.
2. Plans should have specific goals.
3. Plans should be based on specific features in the position.
4. Plans are made for a few moves at a time; several will be made during the game.
5. Plans should be *flexible*, and modified or replaced when necessary.
6. Planning is constant — every move in a chess game should fit into a definite plan.

Sound planning involves selecting realizable goals, based on an accurate and complete analysis of the position — especially its strengths and weaknesses. Purposeful plans reflect what is both positionally desirable and tactically feasible.

Recognize that it is unlikely that any "plan" is perfect (except maybe a short-term checkmate); every move yields control of some squares as it attacks new ones. Plans need to be modified as the position changes. Stubbornly clinging to an inappropriate or ineffective plan too long is no better than abandoning a sound plan too soon. Most plans are short-range (two to five moves), progressing gradually toward the ultimate goal of checkmate.

Typical short-range plans involve minor goals: developing pieces, controlling the center, winning material, seizing an open file or diagonal, establishing a Knight outpost, doubling major pieces on an open file, posting a Rook or doubling Rooks on the seventh rank, controlling important squares, hindering the opponent, exposing the enemy King, improving the mobility of your pieces, simplifying (trading pieces) when ahead in material, strengthening your pawn formation, weakening the opposing pawn structure, and increasing your King's safety. These small advantages accumulate and win chess games. A series of successful plans with minor goals can produce a won game.

When planning, do not be plagued by self-doubt. Uncertainty and risk are an inherent part of chess which all chessplayers must abide. Whether your plan is an ambitious Kingside attack or a modest Queenside defensive consolidation, have faith in your plans and have the courage of your convictions, based on your analysis of the position, to play your chosen moves. If your analysis is accurate, your plans will be sound, and your moves will be effective.

Strategy and planning will open a panorama of more purposeful play for you, and enable you to liberate yourself from move-to-move chess. Sound planning takes practice and experience. As you improve in chess, your plans will correspondingly improve. Usually, even a faulty plan is better than no plan at all, so focus on planning in your chess games. Analyze and PLAN first, then move.

Your plan will be founded on the position's strengths and weaknesses as revealed in your analysis. If those weaknesses are yours, your plan must be defensive; if the weaknesses are your opponent's, however, you are free to formulate an attack strategy. Next we'll look at the most effective ways to exploit any weaknesses found in your opponent's position.

Tactical Vulnerability

Use your analysis to identify your opponent's weaknesses in a *hierarchy* — look for weaknesses around the King first (checkmate is highest priority), then consider Queens, Rooks, Bishops, Knights, and pawns. The effectiveness of this approach is illustrated in Diagram 12: What is White's best move?

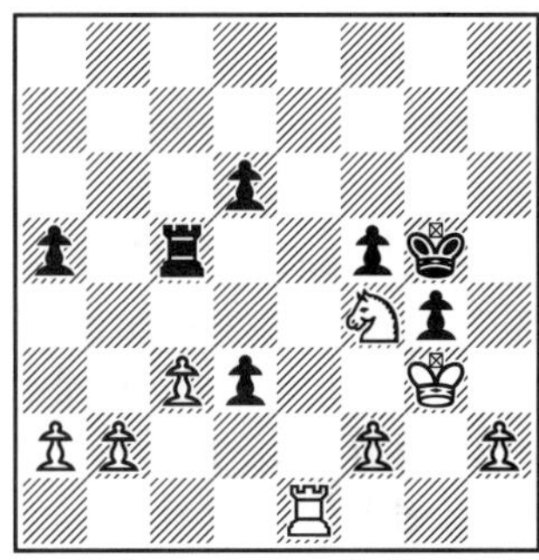

Diagram 12-White to move

A Knight ahead, White can win Black's advanced passed d3-pawn with *1. Nxd3*, or win the Exchange with *1. Ne6† Kf6 2. Nxc5 dxc5*.

But White noticed that the black King was restricted (a weakness), being able to retreat only to the sixth rank. Accordingly, White played **1. Re6!,** denying the black King access to f6 or h6. After **1... d2** (other moves do not help), White immediately concluded with **2. Rg6 checkmate!**

Analyzing for weaknesses in a hierarchy — with checkmate as the first priority — enabled White to force a swift *checkmate* in a position in which many chessplayers would have settled for a lesser gain.

Consider the strengths and weaknesses in Diagram 13:

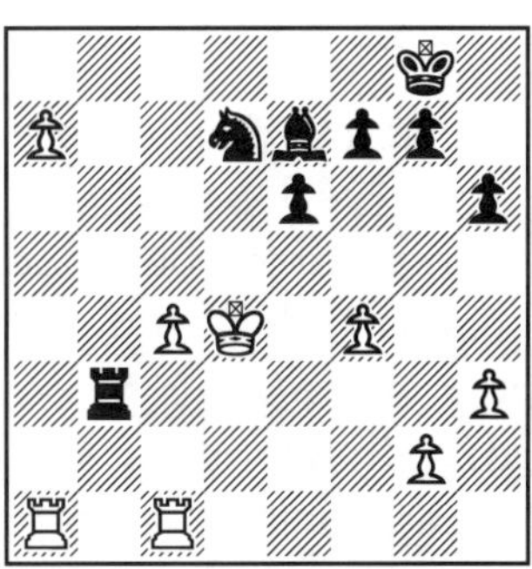

Diagram 13-Black to move

Material is even, although unbalanced, and White has an advanced outside passed a7-pawn (a strength) threatening to promote to a new Queen on the next move. Black can sacrifice his Bishop for the dangerous passed a-pawn with *1... Bc5† 2. Ke4 Bxa7 3. Rxa7*, but the sacrifice would leave him two points behind in material, and White would still have a passed c-pawn supported by a Rook. What is Black to do?

Black saw a significant weakness in White's position: the white King is exposed and restricted — in fact, its only available move is to e4. Accordingly, Black ignored White's imminent queening threat and won the game immediately with **1... Bf6†! 2. Ke4 Nc5 checkmate!** Black could even have mated in two other ways: *1... Bc5† 2. Ke4 f5 checkmate* or *1... Bc5+ 2. Ke4 Re3 checkmate*. The weakness of the exposed and restricted white King was decisive.

This dramatic example highlights the importance of searching for weaknesses near the enemy King *first*.

For another example of a weakness near a King and a swift finish, consider Diagram 14:

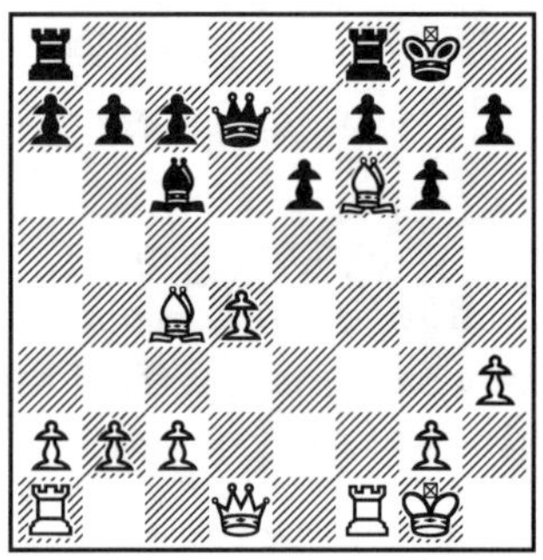

Diagram 14-White to move

Black has exchanged his former fianchettoed B/g7 for a white Knight, so the dark squares (f6, g7, h6) around the black King are weak. White immediately exploited the weak dark-square complex around the black King with **1. Qd2!,** threatening *2. Qh6* and *3. Qg7 checkmate*. Black can only delay this early mate by surrendering his Queen (*1... Qd8*, *1... Qe7*, or *...Qxd4†*), so Black resigned. Look for weaknesses near the enemy King first!

Your hierarchical search for weaknesses won't always stop with the King, however. Sometimes, the search goes all the way down the line to a lowly pawn, but can be just as deadly. Diagram 15 illustrates:

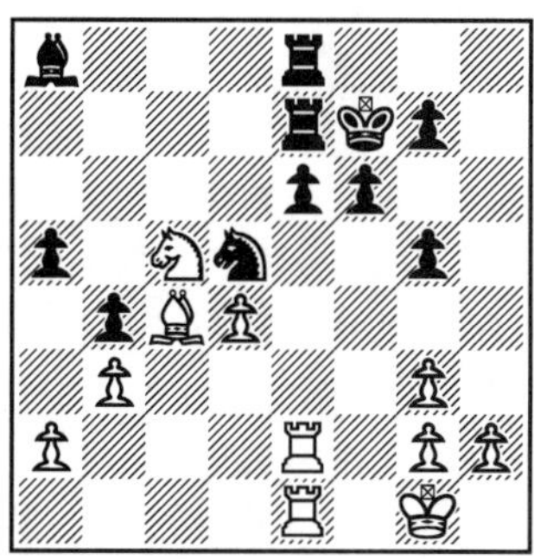

Diagram 15-White to move

Material is even, and both sides have strengths and weaknesses — White has a supported N/c5 on a strong outpost and doubled Rooks attacking the weak black e6-pawn; but the white d4-pawn is isolated, and White's g2- and g3-pawns are doubled. Black has a supported, centralized N/d5 which can move to an advanced supported outpost (c3) with a threat on the white R/e2, also opening the long diagonal for the black B/a8; but Black has a weak e6-pawn and doubled g5- and g7-pawns. The *most* sensitive weakness in the Black position is the weak e6-pawn, currently equally attacked and defended, and White's plan is to undermine the protection of that weak black pawn.

Surprisingly, the game concluded quickly with **1. Bb5!** (attacking one defender of the black e6-pawn) **Rb8** (counterattacking the white Bishop) **2. Bd7** (attacking the weak black e6-pawn a fourth time!) **Nc3** (counterattacking the white R/e2) **3. Bxe6† Ke8 4. Bd7†!** and Black resigned, for he must lose a Rook.

Black's weak e6-pawn was his downfall — attempting to protect this weakness cost him the game. Black would have been wiser to let his weak e-pawn be captured and seek counterplay. ***Defending a weakness too stubbornly might cost more material or cause a position to deteriorate.***

The most important weaknesses are those near the Kings — if you can *checkmate* your opponent, little value accrues in playing to win a pawn, Knight, Bishop, Rook, or even Queen. Keep this *tactical hierarchy* in mind at all times, and look for weaknesses near the enemy King first. If no weaknesses exist near the opposing King, consider possible ways to win a Queen, Rook, Bishop, Knight, or pawn, in that order. Play to win *all* you *safely* can!

Positional Vulnerability

Superior positions involve positional *strengths* in your position and positional *weaknesses* in the opponent's. Superior positions allow you to seize and maintain the initiative (ability to create threats), control the play, and impose your will on the game. Your opponent's positional weaknesses allow you to post your pieces and pawns on strong squares, control vital squares and lines, and execute effective tactics (Diagram 16):

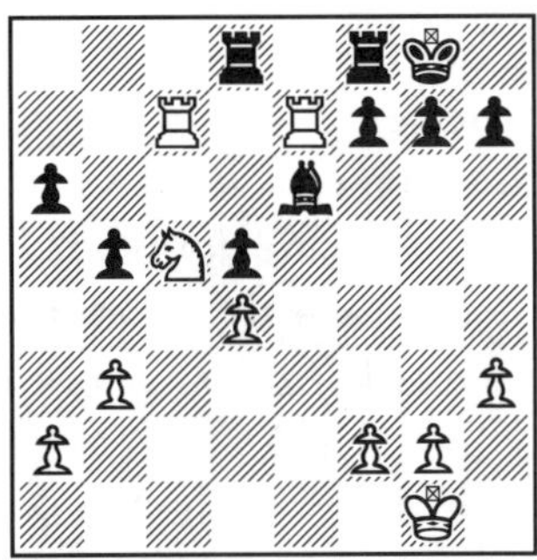

Diagram 16-White to move

Material is even, and both sides have isolated d-pawns (a weakness); but White has a Knight outpost at c5 and doubled Rooks on c7 and e7 (the seventh rank — positional strengths). White capitalized on his positional advantages to initiate game-winning tactics with **1. Nxe6!,** capturing the black Bishop and forking the black Rooks. Facing material ruin, Black responded **1... fxe6.** White concluded with checkmate on the seventh rank: **2. Rxg7† Kh8 3. Rxh7† Kg8 4. Rcg7 mate.** This example demonstrates the impressive power of doubled Rooks on the seventh rank.

Another example of positional strengths and weaknesses is shown in Diagram 17:

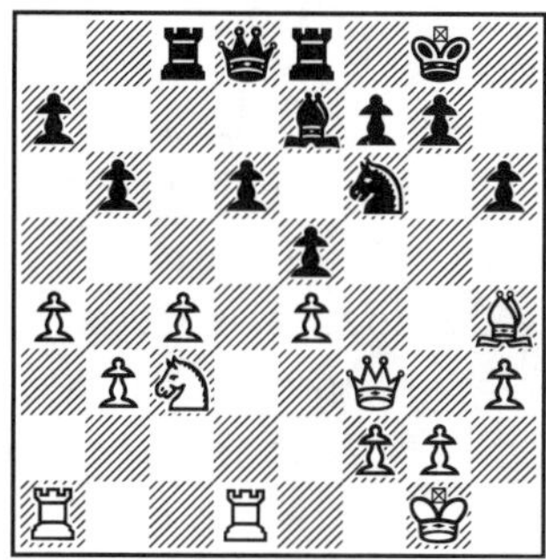

Diagram 17-White to move

Black has two positional weaknesses: a backward d6-pawn and a hole in his pawn structure at d5 — a potential outpost for the white N/c3. Currently, the black N/f6 is defending this hole. White removed the guardian Knight with **1. Bxf6! Bxf6,** then occupied the outpost with **2. Nd5.** The powerful white N/d5 radiates control in all directions, while Black's pieces are cramped and have little mobility. White has a bind (a clamp on the position) and a strong initiative; his outpost N/d5 later participated in a winning Kingside attack.

Positional strengths win chess games, and positional weaknesses lose chess games. Tactical weaknesses usually lose material or the game more quickly, but positional weaknesses lose just as surely — avoid them in your position, and seek (and create) them in your opponent's.

3. Define Your Tasks

After an accurate analysis has mapped the position's strengths and weaknesses, and thus provided you with the goal (offensive or defensive) toward which to plan, the next step is to determine which changes on the board would bring your plan to fruition.

Imagination is valuable at this stage — it is helpful to *visualize* your specific goal. Ask yourself, "What would I *like* to do?" Imagine your pieces and pawns in "the" IDEAL POSITION, with obstructing or defending enemy chessmen eliminated, moved, or pinned. Then try to *define the tasks* (moves) necessary to achieve that desired position.

The changes in the current position required to achieve your IDEAL POSITION represent your *general* tasks. To define your *specific* tasks, first determine the ideal squares and paths necessary for your pieces and pawns to reach your IDEAL POSITION, then ask, "What is *preventing* me from achieving my IDEAL POSITION?" — determine which obstructive defenders must be eliminated, deflected, blocked, or immobilized to reach your goal position.

Whether your goal is checkmate, material gain, a positional advantage, or an effective defensive formation, first visualizing your pieces and pawns in the IDEAL POSITION is an excellent start.

4. Develop Candidate Moves

The key criterion in developing candidate moves is that they must perform or contribute toward the specific tasks defined in Step 3. In developing candidate moves, first consider *forcing moves* (checks, captures, and threats to check and capture), since they limit your opponent's replies, render his moves more predictable, and deny him time for effective counterplay.

Do not be satisfied with the first good move you find — there may be a better one—look until you have several from which to choose.

5. Choose the "Best" Move

In a typical middlegame position, there will be several plausible candidate moves. Once identified, they should be analyzed *separately*, then evaluated *comparatively*.

Selecting the best move involves choosing from among the relevant candidate moves the one which best promotes your goals: accomplishes the required tasks, wins the most material, or gains the greatest positional advantage.

Many chessplayers shift back and forth among candidate moves when analyzing them. This widespread practice is usually confusing, and always inefficient. Candidate moves (say A, B, and C) should be analyzed completely and sequentially in separate "*watertight compartments*," the door to each compartment clanging shut once that move's advantages and disadvantages have been analyzed. Then, after all the candidate moves have been carefully analyzed separately (in your head), their relative merits can be compared.

No absolute scale exists for evaluating chess moves — every move can only be evaluated against alternatives. We will examine two methods for doing this; choose the one with which you are most comfortable.

Grading Moves

To evaluate a candidate move, it is often helpful to assign a numerical "grade" based on its merits and drawbacks. A suggested grading scale is -10 (blunder, loses outright) to +10 (outstanding, wins outright), with zero being a neutral (balanced advantages and disadvantages) move. After all candidate moves have been thoroughly analyzed and carefully graded, a comparison of their respective "grades" will reveal the best move.

Analyze the position in Diagram 18, and identify and grade responsive candidate moves for Black:

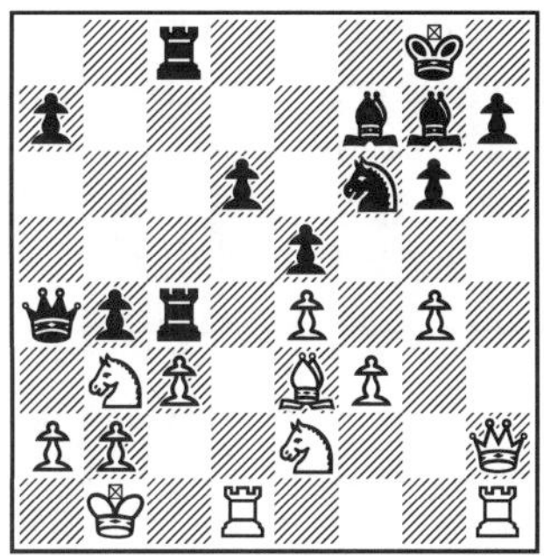

Diagram 18-Black to move

Material is even, and opposite wing attacks are in progress. On the previous move Black played **1... e5,** and White withdrew his attacked Bishop with **2. B/d4-e3.** The white R/d1 now attacks the black d6-pawn. How should Black respond?

Black's plausible defensive candidate moves to save his threatened d6-pawn include *2... Qa6*, *...Qc6*, *...Qd7*, *...Bf8*, *...Ne8*, *...Rd8*, *...R8c6*, and *...R4c6*. All eight moves defend the threatened d-pawn, but which move in this bewildering array of defensive responses is best? *Remember*: when meeting short-term threats, play moves that promote your long-term goals!

Let us analyze and evaluate the eight Black candidate moves and assign "grades":

2... Qa6	Queen is a very expensive guard. Also removes black Queen from the vicinity of the white King.	+3
2... Qc6	Same as 2... Qa6, plus loses the Exchange (3. Na5!).	−4
2... Qd7	Same drawbacks as 2... Qa6, plus pins black d-pawn.	+1
2... Bf8	Cheaper guard, but leaves N/f6 unguarded; and, is the Bishop more active at f8?	+4
2... Ne8	Cheapest guard available, but allows 3. Qxh7† losing a pawn and rendering black's King less secure.	−3
2... Rd8	Undoubles attacking Rooks and diminishes Black's attack, plus pins the black d-pawn.	−1
2... R8c6	Keeps Rooks doubled, does not pin d-pawn, Rook at c6 can swing to a6 for attack, but cramps Rook at c4 and creates possible vulnerable back rank.	+5
2... R4c6	All the benefits of 2... R8c6 without the drawbacks. Improves the mobility of Rook, provides flexibility in maneuvering Rooks, and also uncovers attack on white N/b3 by the black B/f7.	+8

Conclusion: Other moves such as moving away from d6 (*2... d5*) being ineffective, and counterattack (*2... bxc3 3. Nxc3*) merely delaying and allowing White to reinforce his weak P/a2, Black's best defensive move is **2... R4c6** with a grade of "+8." *2... R4c6* meets White's short-term threat (*3. Rxd6*) and promotes Black's long-term goals (*3... Ra6* to support an attack against the white King).

"King of the Mountain"

An alternative practical method of evaluating candidate moves is the "King of the Mountain" approach. Start by analyzing the advantages and disadvantages of any candidate move (preferably an apparently promising one), consider it the initial standard, then successively analyze and compare the other candidate moves to the standard, replacing the current "King of the Mountain" with any better move until all have been analyzed and evaluated. The move remaining as "King of the Mountain" is the best move in the position. This method is simple and, if the analysis of each candidate move is thorough, can be quite effective.

The numerical method is more precise, but the "King on the

Mountain" approach is simpler and equally effective. Once the best move has been found, re-analyze it thoroughly (as time allows) for insurance, and check it carefully for SAFETY.

Adopting either of these systematic methods of analyzing and evaluating responsive candidate moves — whether in the opening, middlegame, or endgame — will pay dividends immediately.

The goal-directed, five-step method given above for navigating the middlegame saves time and avoids confusion by narrowing the search for, and improving the evaluation of, goals and plans, thus insuring more consistently purposeful moves. Whether attacking, defending against threats, improving your position, or hindering your opponent, this recommended method offers a systematic approach for selecting the best move in every position. With practice, you can learn to apply this logical system consistently, and play more effective middlegames.

The improvement in your planning skills will be immediately apparent — but remember, there are *two* players on the board. In addition to formulating and executing your own plans, you must also remain aware of your opponent's, and be able to adjust your plans as necessary to stay abreast of new developments.

Four Key Questions

An apocryphal story concerns a famous Greek philosopher who, while walking in a field one day pondering the sky, fell into a well. Avoid becoming so involved in long-range plans that you overlook immediate threats from your opponent.

Every move alters the position on the chessboard, so pay particular attention to your opponent's last move. Immediately after *each* of your opponent's moves, ask yourself:

1. What is the THREAT?
2. What has CHANGED?

Before each of *your* moves, ask yourself:

3. Does this move IMPROVE MY POSITION?
4. Is this move SAFE?

Consistently asking and correctly answering these four critical questions before every move will enable you to avoid many serious mistakes, recognize more opportunities, and improve the effectiveness of your moves. Let us examine each of them them in greater detail, with examples.

Each of your moves should be *responsive* and *safe*. To insure this, every time your opponent makes a move ask yourself the first two vital questions: "What is the THREAT?" and "What has CHANGED?" This will unerringly identify any threats or new opportunities created by your opponent's last move. If a threat is discovered, decide whether you should parry it immediately or if you can safely continue with your own plans.

The following examples will illustrate.

1. What Is The Threat?

Was my opponent's last move a check or capture?

Does it threaten a check or capture on the next move?

Does it attack or pin any of my pieces or pawns?

Does it threaten to improve the position of any of his pieces or pawns?

Is there a positional threat (e.g., occupying an outpost, doubling Rooks on an open file, securing a Rook on the seventh rank, creating a passed pawn, isolating or doubling any of my pawns)?

Does his last move portend and prepare any long-term threats (such as a Kingside attack)?

Whatever the position, it is necessary — sometimes crucial — to determine the *purpose* of your opponent's last move, even if it does not involve an immediate threat. What is he up to? And what can he do next?

Consider Diagram 19:

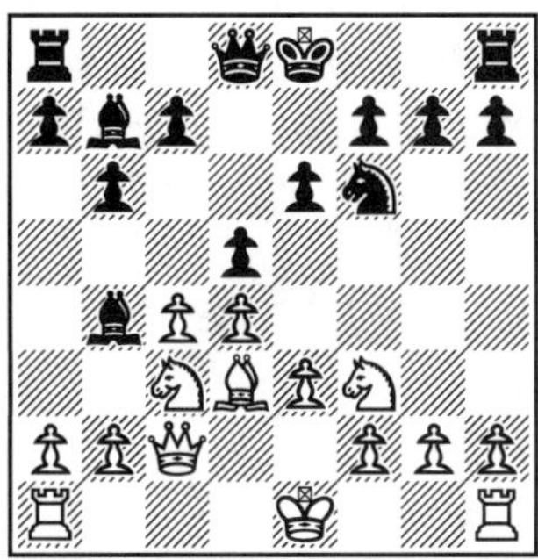

Diagram 19-Black to move

White has just played **1. Q/e2-c2.** What is White's THREAT? Answer: *2. Qa4†!* winning the black B/b4, with a double attack on the black Bishop and King. Responsive Black defenses to White's threat include 12 candidate moves:

1... Bxc3† (counterattack)
1... c6, ...Bc6, ...Qd7, or *...Nd7* (interpose against check)
1... Qd6, ...Qe7, ...a5, or *...c5* (guard Bishop)
1... Bd6 or *...Be7* (move away)
1... 0-0 (move away)

In the game, Black chose **1... Qe7** (flexibly preparing either *2... 0-0* or *2... 0-0-0)* to parry White's threat.

For another example, consider Diagram 20:

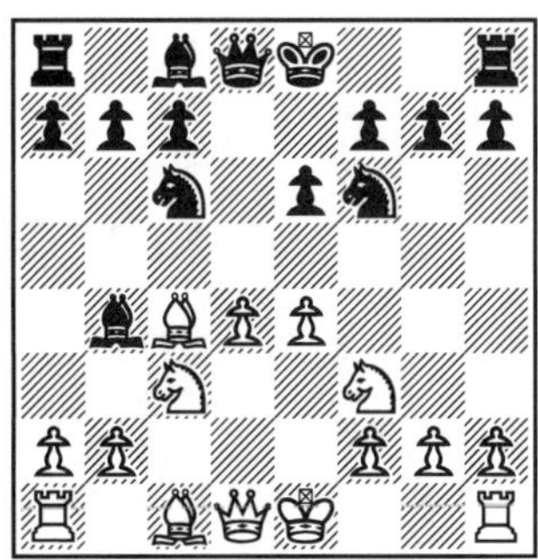

Diagram 20-White to move

Black has just played **1... Bb4.** What is Black's THREAT? Answer: Black threatens *2... Nxe4*, winning a valuable center pawn, since White's defending N/c3 was pinned by Black's last Bishop move. White's candidate defenses to Black's threat are:

2. Bg5 (pin attacker)
2. Bd3 or *Qd3* (guard pawn)
2. e5 (move away)

(*Note*: Defending the white e4-pawn with *2. Qc2*, *Qe2*, or *Nd2* will lose White's d4-pawn to *2... Nxd4*. And *2. a3*, attacking the black Bishop, or *2. Bd2* or *2. 0–0*, unpinning the defending white Knight, would be ineffective against *2... Bxc3* followed by *3... Nxe4* and Black has won White's e-pawn.)

In the game, White decided on **2. Bd3** to neutralize Black's threat (the d4-pawn is indirectly defended—see Diagram 27).

2. What Has Changed?

Does my opponent's last move create any new weaknesses with tactical or positional possibilities for him or me?

Is he concentrating his forces?

Has he pinned or unpinned any of his or my pieces or pawns?

Are any pieces, pawns, or important squares in his or my position now unguarded, or inadequately guarded?

Has he created, removed, or attacked any vital guards?

Is the protection of weak points in his or my position still adequate?

Has his last move left any pieces *en prise?*

Created any weak pawns?

Exposed or restricted his King?

Created a vulnerable back rank?

Learn to recognize what has CHANGED with each move.

Examine Diagram 21:

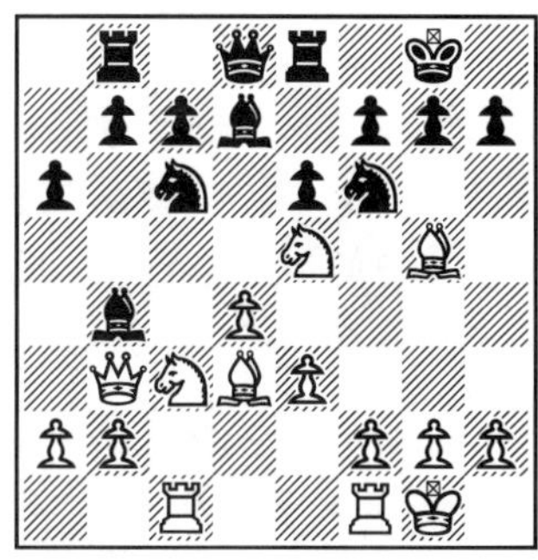

Diagram 21-Black to move

White has just played **1. N/f3-e5.** What has CHANGED? Answer: Black's B/b4 is now endangered, since White's last move (*1. Ne5)* threatens to capture the black N/c6, removing the black Bishop's defender (e.g., *2. Nxc6 Bxc6* [*...Bxc3 3. Nxd8* is unthinkable] *3. Qxb4*, and Black has lost a Bishop). Plausible Black defenses to White's threat include:

1... Bxc3 (counterattack)
1... Nxe5 (capture attacker)
1... a5 or *...Qe7* (guard Bishop)
1... Ba5, *...Bd6*, *...Be7*, or *...Bf8* (move away)

In the game, Black chose to meet White's threat to his Bishop with **1... Be7,** unpinning his N/f6.

If an opponent inflicts no immediate threats and defense is not required, a chessplayer has a "free" move, and should strive to create threats of his own, increase the pressure on his opponent's position, win material, or prepare or launch attacks in the furtherance of his plan.

To develop threats, look first at *forcing moves* — checks, captures, and threats to check or capture — on the next move. Look for *weaknesses* in your opponent's position, and for tactical opportunities to checkmate, attack, or win material. Weaknesses DO exist in all chess games — a chessplayer just has to learn to recognize them.

Examine Diagram 22:

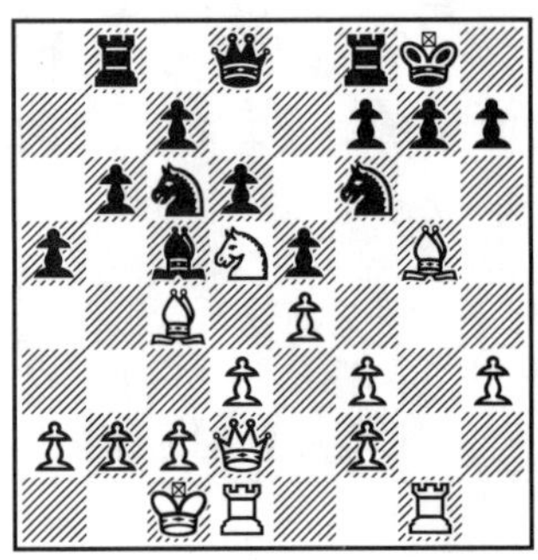

Diagram 22-White to move

Black has just played **1... 0–0,** which poses no immediate threat to White; so White has a "free" move, and seeks tactical opportunities as a first priority. Black's N/f6 is pinned, and Black's last move (*1... 0–0*) created a new weakness — Black's g7-pawn is now potentially pinned to the black King by the white R/g1 if the white B/g5 moves ("What has CHANGED?"). White took advantage of the changed circumstances in Black's position by playing **2. Bxf6! Qd7** (the black g7-pawn is pinned, and if *2... Qxf6, 3. Nxf6†)* **3. Rxg7† Kh8 4. Rg5 mate.** White recognized and quickly exploited the new weakness in the Black position after *1... 0–0.*

Tactical opportunities frequently occur when *weaknesses* exist, so be alert to recognize and exploit weaknesses — remedy your own weaknesses promptly.

In this next example (Diagram 23), find a winning plan for White:

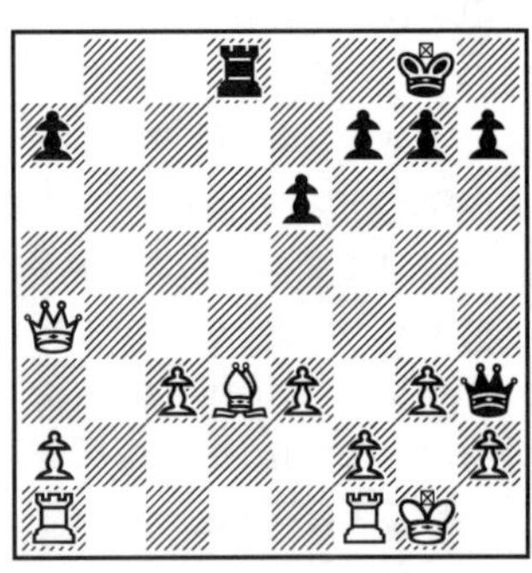

Diagram 23-White to move

White is a Rook, Bishop, and pawn (9 points) ahead in material, and his strategy is to simplify (trade pieces) to achieve a winning endgame, even returning some material if necessary. White therefore played **1. Qh4!,** with the double threat of *2. Qxd8 checkmate* and *2. Qxh3*. Black was forced to exchange Queens with **1... Qxh4.** After **2. gxh4 Rxd3** (winning the white Bishop), **3. Rfd1!** pinned the black Rook to the open d-file because of Black's vulnerable back rank. So Black reluctantly traded Rooks with **3... Rxd1†.** After **4. Rxd1 Kf8 5. c4 Ke7 6. c5** Black resigned, for the white Rook restricts the black King from the c-file, and the white c-pawn will queen.

3. Does This Move Improve My Position?

The essential criterion for a chess move is whether it strengthens your position and promotes your goals and objectives. Each move can be viewed as a transaction — hopefully, you gain something on each move, and you must give up something. The strong chessplayer seeks to make consistently favorable transactions — chess "bargains" — in which he always gains more than he loses *on every move*. Consequently, his advantages accumulate.

If defense is not required and no immediate tactical or attacking opportunities exist, try to IMPROVE YOUR POSITION by activating dormant pieces, opening key lines for attack, seizing outposts, contesting open files and diagonals, doubling Rooks on important files, posting a Rook strongly on the seventh rank, shifting pieces toward the major attacking sector, or increasing the scope of blocked or immobile pieces. Consider Diagram 24:

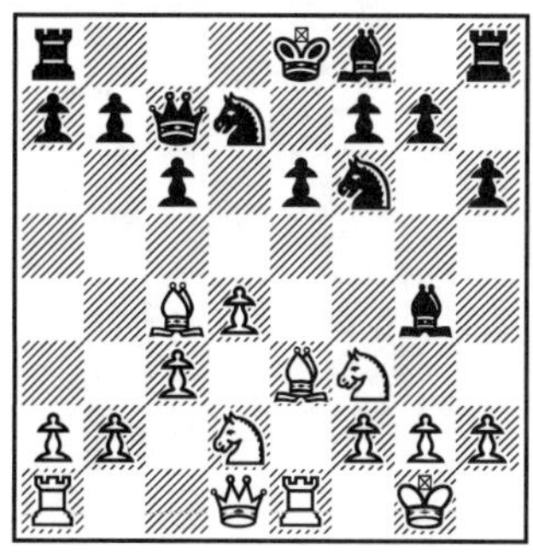

Diagram 24-Black

On the previous move White played **1. Re1,** which poses no immediate threats. Black sees no exploitable weaknesses in the White position, and therefore seeks to IMPROVE HIS POSITION. To that end, Black is considering the candidate moves *1... Bxf3*, *1... Nb6*, *1... 0-0-0*, and *1... Bd6*. Do any of these moves improve Black's position? Let us analyze:

...Bxf3 would move a well-developed piece twice in the opening (generally a poor idea), relieve a strong pin, and bring a new white piece (Knight or Queen) to f3, giving White a lead in development.

...Nb6, attacking the white B/c4, is likewise undesirable because *...Nb6* would also move a developed piece twice in the opening, and, after the white Bishop retreats to b3, d3, or e2 (breaking Black's strong pin), the black Knight is not well-posted on the Queenside (if *...Nbd5* later, *c4* evicts the Knight).

Neither *...Bxf3* nor *...Nb6* improves Black's position, even temporarily.

...0-0-0 is strategically desirable, but tactically unfeasible. After *...0-0-0, 2. Qa4 Kb8 3. d5!* threatens *Qxa7†*, and the black King is insecure. *...0-0-0* is unsafe, and would not improve Black's position.

...Bd6 develops a new piece, prepares for Kingside castling, and threatens to win a pawn (*2... Bxh2†*), since White's N/f3 is pinned. Of the four candidate moves, *...Bd6* IMPROVES BLACK'S POSITION the most. In the game, Black continued with **1... Bd6.**

An excellent way to IMPROVE YOUR POSITION is to activate your least active pieces first (Diagram 25):

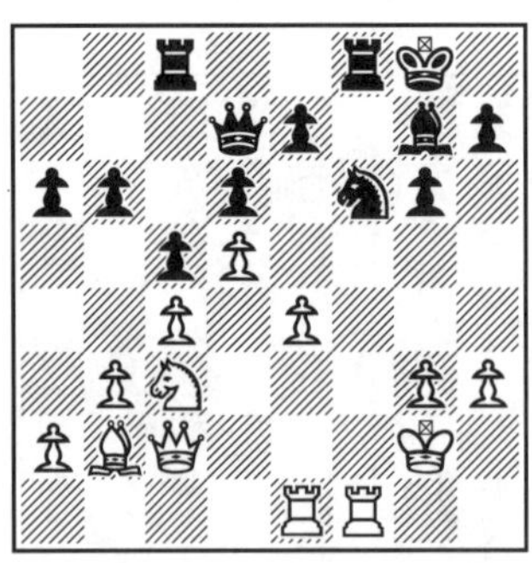

Diagram 25-White to move

Material is even in this position, and Black's last move **(1... Qd7)** poses no immediate tactical or positional threats. White also has no immediate tactical opportunities, and thus seeks to IMPROVE HIS POSITION. His least active pieces are his N/c3 and B/b2. With this in mind, White played **2. Ne2,** after which the fianchettoed white B/b2's long attacking diagonal is unblocked, and the Knight heads for f4 to assist in a Kingside attack. The quiet move *2. Ne2* IMPROVED WHITE'S POSITION.

For another example, consider Diagram 26:

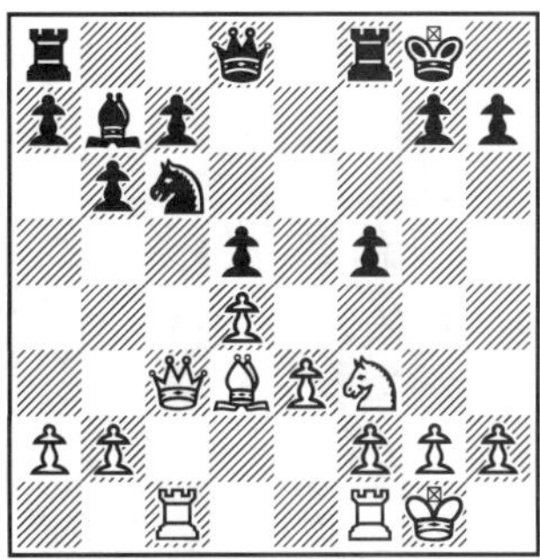

Diagram 26-White to move

Material is even, but White's pieces are more active, a hole exists in the black pawn structure at e5 (a weakness), and Black's c7-pawn is backward (another weakness). White would like to IMPROVE HIS POSITION by establishing a Knight outpost on e5 (*1. Ne5*), but Black could simply capture *1... Nxe5*. If *2. dxe5*, then *... c5!*, would eliminate both Black weaknesses (although White would have a passed e5-pawn). Before playing *Ne5* (plan), White must first eliminate the black N/c6 (task). Therefore White played **1. Bb5!,** soon capturing the black N/c6 with the Bishop and occupying the e5 outpost with *Ne5* as planned. White's strong N/e5 outpost proved valuable in his later successful winning attack.

4. Is This Move Safe?

Last, but emphatically not least, we will examine the fourth critical question: "Is this move SAFE?"

Every chess move should pass a primary SAFETY test: if I make this contemplated move, does my opponent have any move which can hurt me (cost me material or position) immediately or soon?

After my move, would my King and all my pieces and pawns be adequately defended?

Would my opponent have any dangerous checks or captures?

Would my move create any weaknesses?

Would (or could) my move lose material?

What is my opponent's *best* reply to my contemplated move?

Would it refute my move?

Which side would stand better after my opponent's best reply to my move?

Avoid playing moves which help your opponent — refer to Diagram 27:

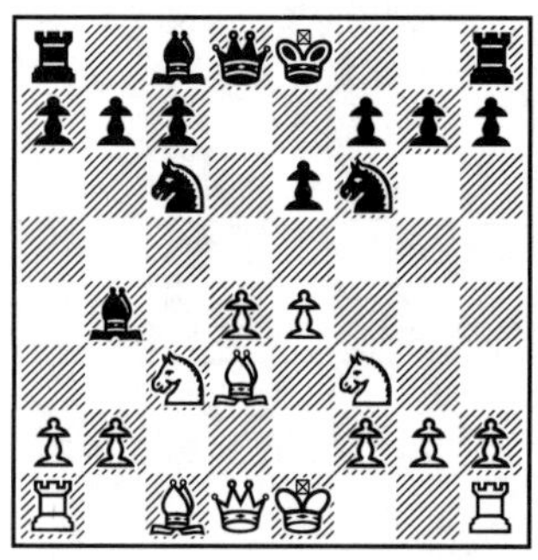

Diagram 27-Black to move

White has just played **1. B/c4-d3** to defend his threatened e4-pawn, and Black is considering the candidate move *1... Nxd4* apparently winning a valuable center pawn (if *2. Nxd4 Qxd4* and Black remains a pawn ahead). The question is: is *1... Nxd4* a SAFE move? Answer: absolutely NOT! If *1... Nxd4?, 2. Nxd4 Qxd4?? 3. Bb5+!*, and Black loses his Queen to the discovered attack. Even if Black does not recapture on d4 with his Queen after *1... Nxd4? 2. Nxd4*, he has lost a powerful Knight for a pawn. The conclusion: *1... Nxd4* is not SAFE. Do not draw the curtain too soon — analyze to a quiet position.

In the game, Black continued with **1... 0–0,** now safely threatening *2... Nxd4*.

Consistently asking and correctly answering the previous FOUR KEY QUESTIONS will enable you to avoid fatal mistakes and recognize winning opportunities.

Remember the three general situations which may exist after your opponent's last move:

1. Opponent made a threat
2. Opponent made no threat and has weaknesses
3. Opponent made no threat and has no weaknesses

Defining which type of position exists will help narrow your search for the best move, as schematically illustrated in the following flow chart.

"YOUR MOVE"

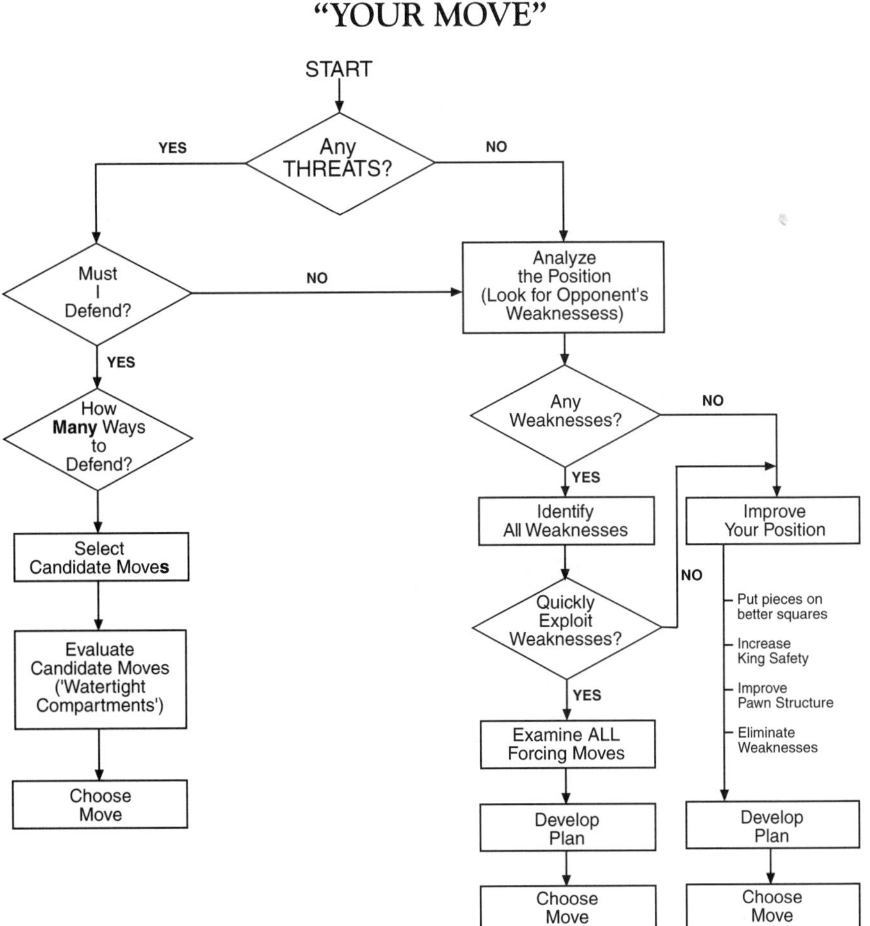

• FOLLOW THIS PROCEDURE ON **EVERY** MOVE!

If your opponent's last move created a threat that you must parry, play a responsive *defensive* move. If there is no significant threat, *look for weaknesses* in your opponent's position and for tactical and positional opportunities. If no significant threat was created by your opponent's last move and no weaknesses exist in his position, try to *improve your position*.

Follow this procedure on *every* move to ensure that a solid, flexible position is maintained — a critical activity in the middlegame.

Positional Play

Positional play is a means to an end — effective tactics. Winning tactics do not spontaneously occur in chess. Barring unforced errors by the opponent, successful tactics are the deserving fruits of a superior position established by sound positional play. Positional play, the control of significant offensive and defensive squares and lines, involves active piece placement and sound pawn structures. Specific positional goals in the middlegame are to maintain control of the center, establish outposts for pieces, open files and diagonals for penetration and attack, and gain control of the seventh rank.

Inferior positional play is seldom redeemed by tactical salvation. Seek positional superiority first — do not gamble on recovering from inferior positions with later game-saving tactics.

Diagram 28 offers an example of superior positional play.

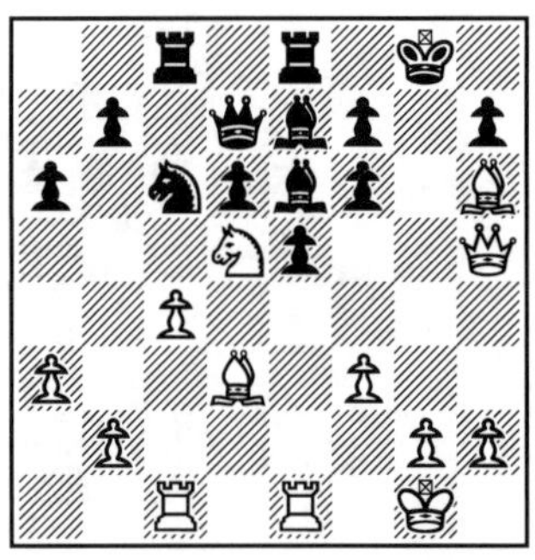

Diagram 28-White to move

White's King is safe, the white pawn structure is sound, all white pieces are in play, and White has four extremely active pieces (Q/h5, B/h6, N/d5, and B/d3). The black King, on the other hand, is exposed and restricted, the black pieces are cramped and have limited scope, plus Black has doubled f-pawns and a backward d6-pawn. White has clear positional superiority, which he converted into win with the surprising tactical sacrifice **1. Bg7!** (threatening *2. Qxh7 checkmate*). If Black captures *1... Kxg7, 2. Qxh7† Kf8 3. Qh8* would be mate, so Black declined White's Greek gift offer and tried **1... f5** to close the supporting white B/d3's diagonal leading to h7. White continued **2. Nf6†!,** forking the black King and Queen. After **2... Bxf6 3. Bxf6** Black resigned, as *4. Qg5†* (or *Qh6*) and *5. Qg7 checkmate* was unavoidable.

Tactics are the payoff for superior positional play. White capitalized on his superior position — the result of previous sound positional play — to force checkmate with a swift sacrificial attack. Such stunning examples of converting positional superiority into quick tactical wins are frequent.

Positional play — what some chessplayers jocularly refer to as "what to do when there is nothing to do" — involves improving your offensive or defensive position and hindering your opponent, often by the control of important squares and lines, especially central squares and squares around both Kings. Control of these significant squares enables you to post your pieces aggressively and deny your opponent's pieces access to these key squares; controlling open lines allows your pieces to attack and penetrate from long range. Two significant aspects of positional play which facilitate these conditions are outposts and pawn play, which we will now examine in detail.

Outposts

An important middlegame goal is to establish and maintain outposts for your pieces, especially Knights and Bishops. (An *outpost* is a square in or near enemy territory on which a piece can be safely placed and not be easily evicted or profitably exchanged.) Following are some significant facts and guidelines regarding outposts:

- The best outpost squares are those near the enemy King or the center.
- Pieces, not pawns, should occupy outposts.
- A Knight is generally the best piece to occupy an outpost, followed by a Bishop.
- The eventual payoff for occupying an outpost is tactics, while the

immediate benefits are the attack and defense of nearby squares.

- An occupied outpost removes both offensive and defensive squares from the enemy, and restricts enemy pieces and pawns.
- Occupy an outpost when it can be supported by another piece (preferably) or a pawn. Occupy the outpost without support if the enemy cannot attack it.
- Avoid, contest, and neutralize (undermine or exchange) enemy pieces on outposts.
- Outposts are created by pawn weaknesses, and are often the squares in front of weak pawns—look for the isolated, doubled, and backward pawns for potential outposts.

For an example of an effective outpost, refer to Diagram 29:

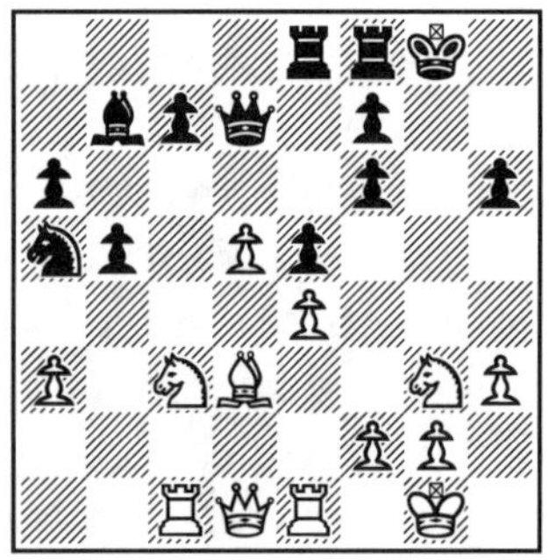

Diagram 29-White to move

Black has doubled f-pawns; consequently, the weak square f5 is a potential outpost for the white N/g3. Furthermore, if the white N/g3 were on f5 (attacking g7 and shielding the white Queen's checking square g4 from the black Q/d7), White could play *Qg4†* followed by *Qg7 checkmate*. Accordingly, White played **1. Nf5!,** seizing the important outpost. Black responded **1... Kh7** to allow *2... Rg8* to guard the sensitive g7 mating square. White continued **2. Qh5,** threatening *3. Qxh6†* (supported by the N/f5) *Kg8 4. Qg7 checkmate*. Black's intended *2... Rg8* is now ineffective (if *2... Rg8, 3. Qxh6 mate)*. Black must now surrender his Queen (*2... Qxf5)* to avoid checkmate, so Black resigned.

White's strong Knight outpost played a decisive role in his swift, convincing attack against Black's exposed and restricted King, while Black's doubled pawns in front of his castled King proved a fatal weakness.

Strong outposts are a critical advantage in middlegame play, and should be pursued at every safe opportunity — their absence can cripple your game. Outposts are often gained and held with the support of pawns, so effective pawn play must also comprise one of your major positional considerations.

Pawn Play

If tactics are the heart of chess, pawn play is its soul. Because pawns move so slowly, and their position changes gradually, pawn structure — the skeleton of chess positions — is the most permanent feature of the game. As such, it influences — and sometimes dictates — strategy and tactics by defining available squares and lines for pieces, and is thus the primary constraint on their activity. The goal, therefore, is to develop pawn formations which allow your pieces maximum scope and stability while restricting your opponent. Sound pawn formations combined with active pieces are the cornerstone of effective positional play and tactics.

A vanguard for pieces, pawns can:

control the center and other important squares;
attack, block, and hinder opposing chessmen;
defend friendly chessmen;
be exchanged or sacrificed to open lines for attack; and
promote to Queens, (or, rarely, other pieces).

Some pawn formations are strong (chains, phalanxes, passed pawns, pawn majorities), and others are weak (isolated, doubled, backward). Two restrictive weaknesses of weak pawns are: 1) they can only be defended by pieces, costly defenders; and 2) the square immediately ahead of the weak pawn is a potential enemy outpost. Pawn weaknesses should be avoided or remedied.

Pawn structure affects the outcome of every game. Often, one pawn (promoted to a Queen) proves decisive. Half of the chessmen are pawns — pawns count!

Various types of pawn structures are illustrated in Diagram 30:

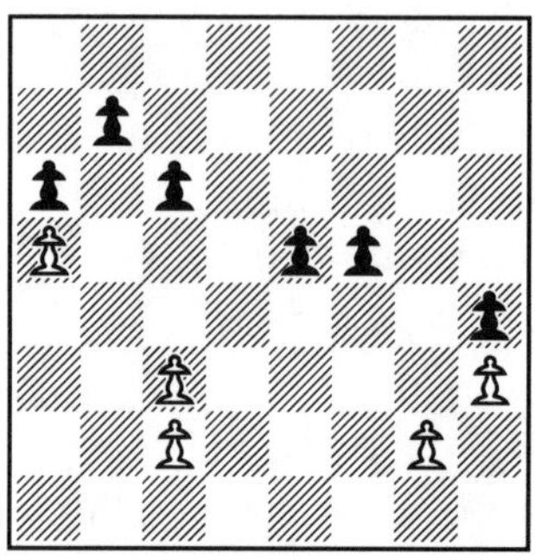

Diagram 30

White's a5-pawn is isolated, his c2- and c3-pawns are isolated and doubled, and his g2-pawn is backward. Black's b7-pawn is backward, his e5-pawn is a passed pawn, his e5- and f5-pawns are hanging pawns, and his h4-pawn is isolated. Overall, Black has the superior pawn structure because of his extra passed e5-pawn.

For an example of the cramping effect pawns can exert in the middlegame, examine Diagram 31:

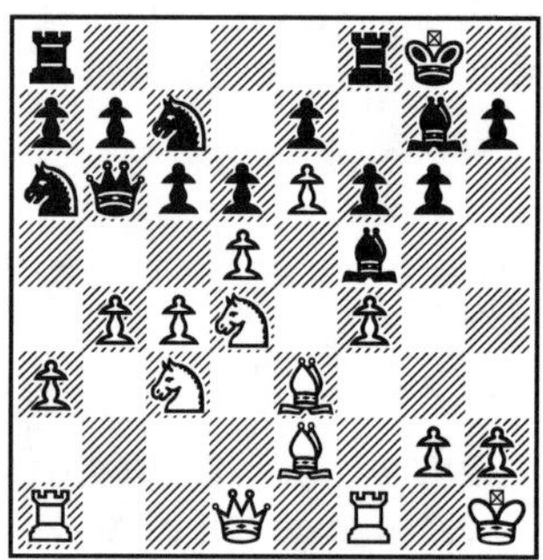

Diagram 31-White

The choked black pieces can hardly move, being severely restricted by the formidable white central pawn mass. In fact, White shortly trapped and won the black Queen with the aid of his pawns: **1. Nxf5! c5** (to protect the black Queen from the white B/e3) **2. Nxe7† Kh8 3. Na4!** and the black Queen is lost. A stunning example of superior pawn play!

For another example of superior pawn play, consider Diagram 32:

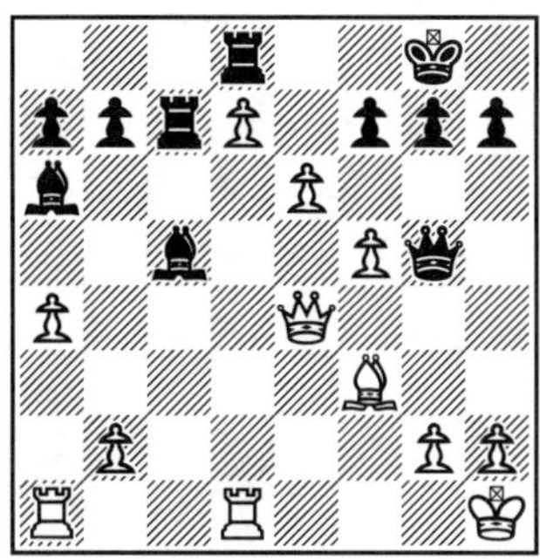

Diagram 32-White to move

Earlier White sacrificed a Knight for two pawns to achieve a central pawn majority and a passed d-pawn. White's strategy was to promote a central pawn; following several well-timed white pawn advances, White played **1. Qe5!,** attacking the trapped black R/c7. Black responded **1... Bb6** to protect the Rook, and White continued **2. e7!** Black resigned, for a white pawn will queen or Black must suffer ruinous loss of material (e.g., *2... Qxe7 3. Qxe7 Rcxd7 4. Rxd7*).

Pawn weaknesses should be remedied whenever possible, preferably by advancing and exchanging the weak pawns. For flexibility and mutual protection, the fewer pawn "islands," or clusters of connected pawns, the stronger the pawn formation, generally. Since pawn moves are irreversible, improper pawn advances may leave irreparable weaknesses. Think carefully of the consequences before moving a pawn.

As you improve and play stronger opponents, pawn play will become a greater factor in deciding the outcomes of your games. Understanding the important role of pawns and developing skill in proper pawn play are essential steps in strengthening your middlegame — and can directly affect the endgame, if a pawn advantage allows you to "simplify."

Simplifying

If you have a winning material or positional advantage in pawn structure or King position, or both, eliminate all pieces and simplify into a winning King-and-pawn endgame, even sacrificing slight material if necessary. Pure King-and-pawn endgames are the easiest to win — with no enemy pieces to complicate matters, endgame goals are clarified and play is generally quite straightforward. The side ahead in pawns or position, therefore, will seek to simplify — exchange remaining pieces — to make his win simpler and more certain. Exchanging pieces will also reduce the opponent's chances for counterplay and surprise tactics.

In Diagram 33, for example, what is Black's best move?

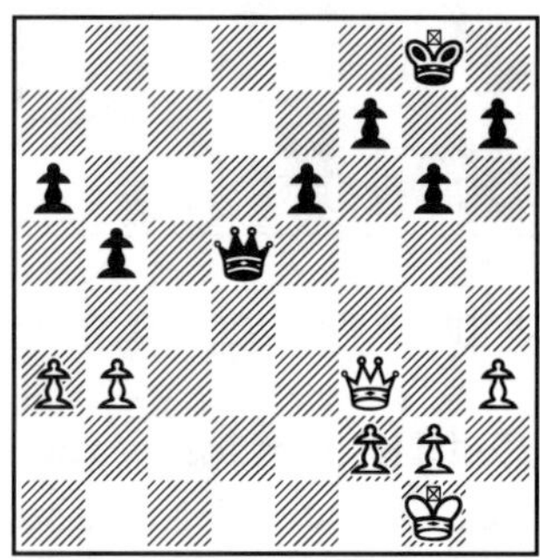

Diagram 33-Black to move

Black has an extra pawn, but White's pawn structure is sound. With the powerful white Queen on the board, Black's win is problematic. Prospects of checkmate or further win of material are not imminent, so Black seeks a more favorable endgame.

To establish a more certain win, Black seized the opportunity to simplify and disrupt White's Kingside pawn structure by trading Queens with **1... Qxf3!** After **2. gxf3,** White had an isolated h-pawn and isolated and doubled f-pawns. The white Kingside pawns cannot defend each other, and must look to the white King for protection. This crippled pawn structure proved no match for Black's healthy Kingside pawn majority and incursive King: **2... Kg7 3. Kg2 Kf6 4. f4 Kf5 5. Kg3 e5 6. fxe5 Kxe5 7. f4† Ke4 8. h4 h5 9. b4 f5 10. Kg2 Kxf4 11. Kh3 Kf3 12. Kh2 Kg4 13. Resigns.**

Black's simplifying *1... Qxf3!* achieved winning positional (White's weak Kingside pawns) and material (Black's extra pawn) advantages in the resulting King-and-pawn endgame.

Another example is illustrated in Diagram 34:

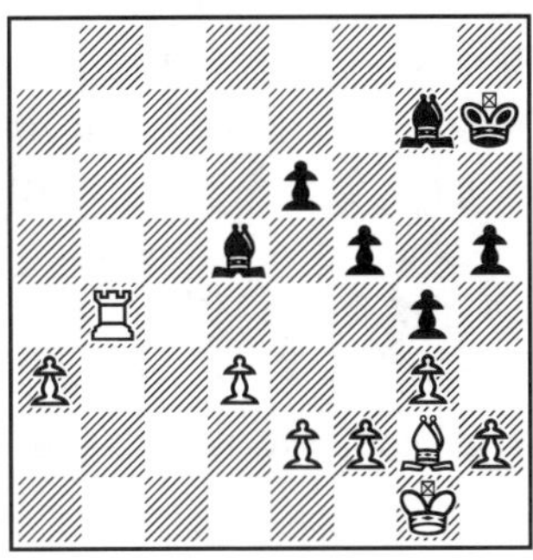

Diagram 34–White to move

White is the Exchange and two pawns ahead, but almost certainly will be unable to checkmate Black without a new Queen. White has a potential new Queen in his outside passed a3-pawn. So White simplified into a winning endgame: **1. Bxd5!** (removing the black Bishop defending a8, the white a-pawn's promotion square) **exd5 2. Rb7** (pinning and immobilizing the remaining black B/g7) **Kg8 3. Rxg7†!** (removing the last Black defending piece) **Kxg7 4. a4 Kf7 5. a5** and the white pawn will queen, winning the game. Simple and effective, trading pieces when ahead can quickly produce a won game.

Extensive simplifying to achieve a winning endgame is shown in Diagram 35:

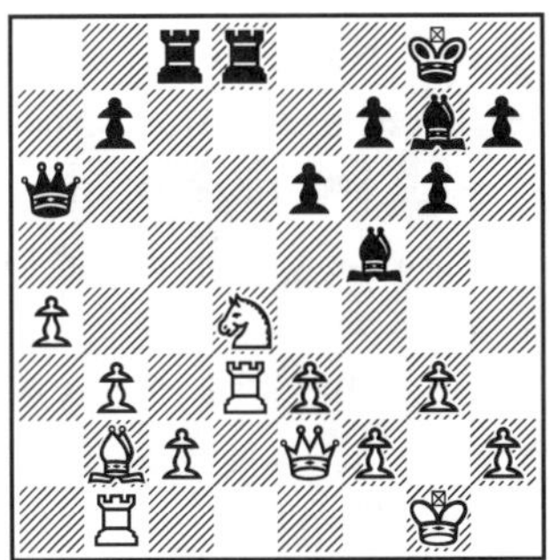

Diagram 35-White to move

In this middlegame position, White is two pawns ahead and has a 3:1 Queenside pawn majority, a winning endgame advantage. But with so many black pieces remaining on the board, White's task of exploiting his Queenside pawn majority is difficult. Therefore, White simplified into a winning endgame by exchanging several pieces: **1. Nxf5!** (threatening *2. Ne7+*, forking the black King and Rook) **exf5 2. Rxd8† Rxd8 3. Qxa6 bxa6 4. Bxg7 Kxg7.** White retains his two-pawn surplus and Queenside pawn majority, and now has a passed c-pawn.

Next, **5. b4 Rb8 6. c4** mobilized White's Queenside pawn majority and, after White transferred his King to the Queenside to assist his pawns' progress against the black Rook and King, White later queened a Queenside pawn and won.

Another exemplary illustration is shown in Diagram 36:

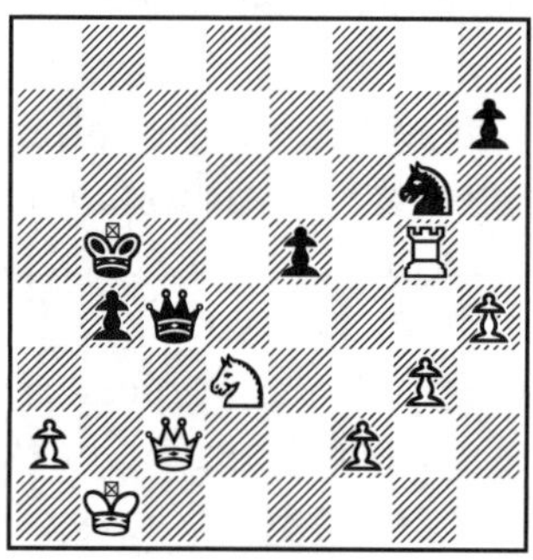

Diagram 36-White to move

White is a Rook and pawn ahead, but Black has an active Q/c4 and pesky N/g6 to generate counterplay and complicate matters. To simplify, White played **1. Qxc4† Kxc4 2. Nxe5† Nxe5 3. Rxe5 Kd4 4. Rd8 Resigns.** In this simplified endgame position, White has an easy win by advancing his Kingside pawns. Note how quickly White transformed a somewhat complicated middlegame position into a straightforward endgame win by simplifying.

For a final convincing example of efficient simplifying, examine Diagram 37:

Diagram 37-Black to move

Black is 5 points ahead in material (Queen for Bishop and pawn), but White has a dangerous advanced passed d6-pawn. White's B/d2 is *en prise* to the black R/b2, but the black Q/b1 is attacked by the white R/f1. What is Black's most certain route to victory?

Black simplified with **1... Qxf1†!** After **2. Kxf1 Rxd2 3. Ke1 Rxd6** (removing White's last threat) White resigned, as the black R/d6 barricades the white King from the d-file, and Black's passed c-pawn will queen. Black's timely simplification forced a simple and certain endgame win.

Strong chessplayers play for the *certain* win, even if more lengthy. They seldom take risks when ahead, and they seek the surest route to victory. Simplifying when ahead is often a brutally effective winning technique.

As the end of the middlegame approaches with no checkmate imminent, both sides should project the type of endgame which may ensue as material is further reduced. To evaluate your potential endgame prospects, *imagine all pieces off the board* (except any surplus) and examine the relative pawn structures and King positions. With an advantage in pawn formation or King position, or both, you may wish to simplify to reach a winning endgame by trading pieces, although your material advantage is slight or nonexistent. Under certain circumstances — such as a superior pawn structure and highly favorable King position — a sacrifice to eliminate all pieces can be an effective and safe winning procedure. Conversely, the side facing a losing endgame should avoid trades, and keep the play in the middlegame.

You now have a formidable array of methods and techniques at your disposal with which to conduct an aggressive and dangerous middle-game. One essential area of expertise remains to be explored, however — defense. Without it, you may not survive the middlegame. This critical topic is at least as important as the rest, and will be examined before we move on to the attacking techniques covered in the following chapters.

Defense

Chess is not Solitaire — to win a chess game, you must first avoid losing it! Defense is an integral part of every game, and opponents' plans, moves, and threats must be respected. Even weaker players typically make several major, and numerous minor, threats during a game.

Four cardinal principles of effective defenses are:

1. Defend only as required (save moves for offense)
2. Defend economically (with minimum force)
3. Defend actively, rather than passively
4. Defend against short-term threats with moves that promote your long-term goals

To minimize defense — the goal — defend only against present or potential direct threats. The key to effective defense is to defend simply, economically, and actively.

Meet short-term threats with moves that *promote your long-term goals*. When defending, try to disturb your active pieces the least. A pawn is the cheapest defender, and should be considered first. Any defensive pieces should not be pinned, unstable (easily driven away), overworked, or too valuable. Take special care when defending with your King, because of the King's vulnerability.

Diagram 38 illustrates using active-versus-passive defense and defending with moves that promote your long-term goals:

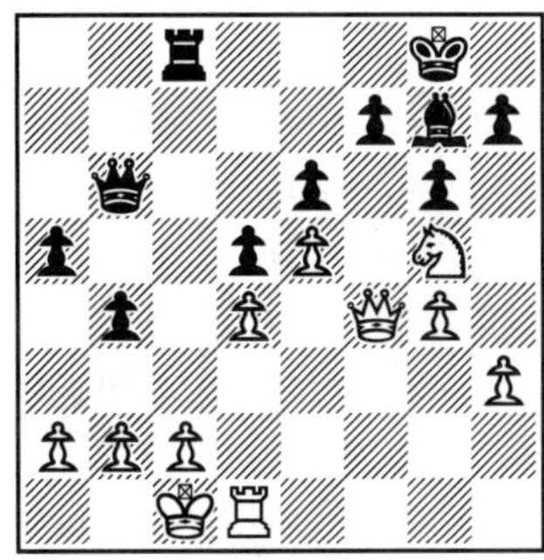

Diagram 38-Black to move

White has just played **1. Q/d2-f4,** doubly attacking the black f7-pawn, which is only defended by the black King. Black can defend his threatened f7-pawn with *1... Rf8*, but that defensive move would remove the black Rook from the attack toward the white King along the half-open c-file and leave the black Rook in a passive position at f8 behind a confining pawn. Better is *1... Rc7*, guarding the f7-pawn and maintaining attacking pressure along the c-file. Best is **1... Qc7,** which Black played in the game, defending the f7-pawn and threatening *2... Qxc2 checkmate*. The active move *1... Qc7* defends against White's short-term threat and promotes Black's long-term goal — an attack against the white King.

Meet each threat by yielding the least possible concession to secure your position. Solid, permanent defense is preferable to temporary, patchwork resistance. A defender must maintain his composure — panic routs orderly thought and invites disaster on the chessboard. Remain calm and logical. Defend carefully, and with determination — many pitfalls await the over-anxious or careless attacker. Punish unsound "gambles" by your opponent with precise tactics, and play for traps only as a last resort. Finally, a defender should seek counterplay, and the best response to a wing attack is usually a counterattack in the center.

Identifying The Threat

As previously stated, the proper first response to an opponent's every move is to immediately ask yourself, "What is the THREAT?" If you do not see the threat, you cannot defend against it. Threats can be classified in five major categories:

1. *Mating* — Directed toward checkmating your King
2. *Tactical* — Intending to win material
3. *Positional* — Aimed at seizing important squares and lines
4. *Preparatory* — Initiating an attack
5. *Preventive* — Designed to thwart your plans

Learn to recognize all five types so that you can play resourceful and tenacious defense. An excellent method of recognizing threats is to ask yourself the probing question, "What move would my opponent play next if he could?" Determine his present and potential threats and plans.

Defensive Methods

The six general methods to parry an attack are:

1. Counterattack
2. Capture attacker
3. Pin attacker
4. Interpose
5. Guard
6. Move away

When attacked, first consider counterattack. When feasible, it is often the best defense. Of course, the threats generated by the counter-attack must equal or exceed the opponent's original threats (Diagram 39):

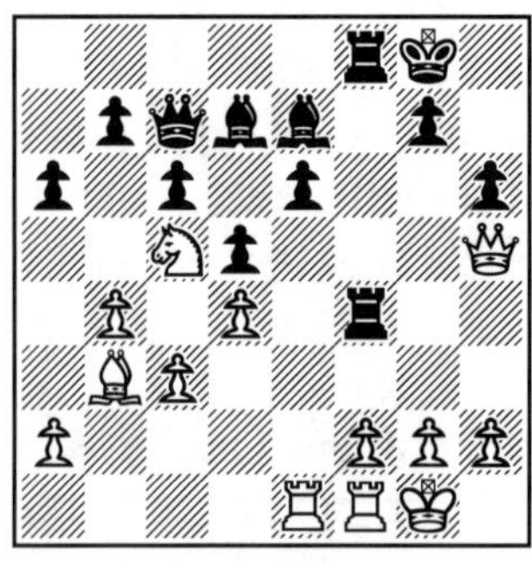

Diagram 39-Black to move

White has just played **1. R/a1-e1,** twice attacking Black's backward e6-pawn, which is guarded only once by the black B/d7. What is Black's best defense?

Black resourcefully played the counterattacking **1... Rh4!,** simultaneously threatening *2... Qxh2 checkmate* and *2... Rxh5* winning the white Queen. White responded **2. Qe5** to protect against both threats, and Black continued his counterattack with **2... Bd6,** again attacking the white Queen and, after the Queen moves, the white h2-pawn. After **3. Qe3 Bxh2† 4. Kh1 Bg1†!** (now if *5. Kxg1, Qh2 mate)* **5. Qh3** (desperation) **Rxh3† 6. gxh3** Black concluded his effective counterattack with **6... Qh2 checkmate.**

Most counterattacks are not so dramatically effective, but they remain a primary form of defense. Diagram 40 presents another example:

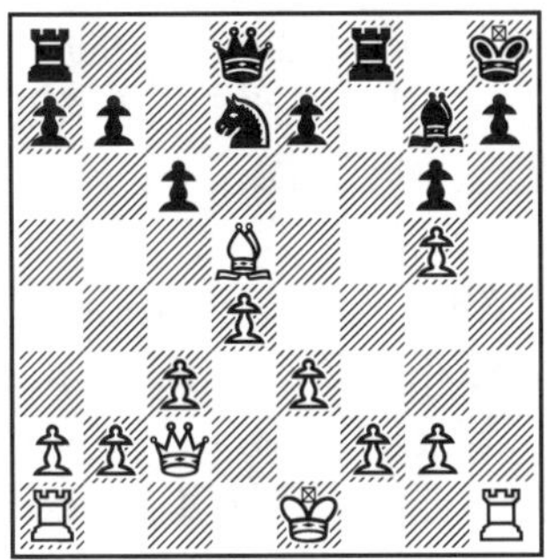

Diagram 40-White to move

Black has just played the threatening **1... c6,** attacking the white B/d5. What is White's best response? Answer: **2. Qxg6!,** counterattacking by threatening *3. Qxh7 checkmate* (Black's h7-pawn is pinned). Black's only defense to prevent immediate mate is **2... h6** (if *2... h5, 3. Rxh5* mates). After *2... h6* White continued **3. Rxh6†! Bxh6 4. Qxh6 checkmate!** White's sudden, strong counterattack was the best answer to Black's threat.

An example of a more complex counterattack appears in Diagram 41:

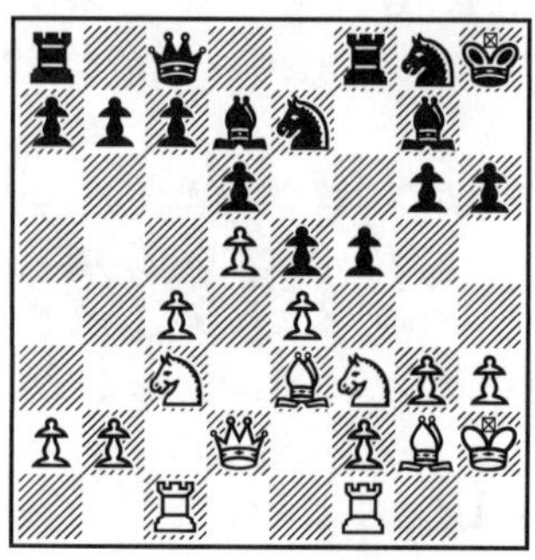

Diagram 41-White

All material is still on the board; Black is attacking on the Kingside, but White is well defended. Since the center is locked, White decided on the strategy of a Queenside counterattack and played **1. c5** to open a Queenside line. White's *1. c5* will disrupt Black's formidable Queenside pawn structure and improve the activity of White's Queenside pieces. If Black captures *1... dxc5*, then *2. Bxc5* pins the black N/e7 and creates a half-open c-file for the white R/c1. On other Black moves not involving direct threats, White will continue *2. cxd6* to open the c-file, with tactical opportunities after *2... cxd6* because of the possibility of a discovered attack on the black Q/c8.

Preparing *c5* by first playing *1. Ne1* (to free the fianchettoed white B/g2), then *2. Nd3* (to capture *4. Nxc5* after *3. c5 dxc5)* may even strengthen White's plan.

In the game, Black's Kingside attack finally stalled, and White's eventual breakthrough on the Queenside was successful. White won.

The other five defensive methods are illustrated in Diagram 42:

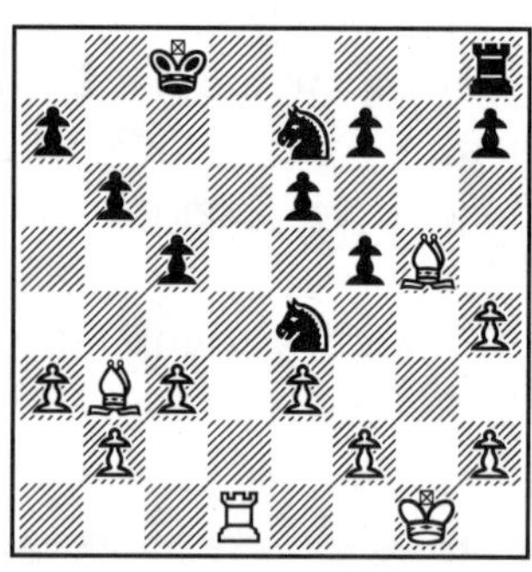

Diagram 42-Black to move

The white B/g5 attacks the unguarded black N/e7. Black's defensive resources include capturing the attacker *(...N/e4xg5)*, pinning the attacking Bishop *(...Rg8)*, interposing *(...f6)*, guarding the threatened Knight *(...Re8)*, and moving away (*...Ng6*, *...Nd5*, or *...Nc6)*. However, *...Re8* places the black Rook in a passive position, and *...Nd5* loses a pawn (if *1... Nd5, 2. Bxd5 exd5 3. Rxd5)*. In the game, Black chose **1... Rg8,** pinning the attacking B/g5 to the white K/g1 and threatening *2... h6* winning the pinned Bishop. After **2. Kf1** Black was again obliged to save his threatened Knight, and played **2... Nxg5 3. hxg5 Rxg5,** winning a pawn.

Proper *timing* is often the key to effective defense: defending too soon dissipates initiative, while defending too late is ineffective. Stop opponents' threats before they become dangerous. Defend as economically and permanently as possible. Attackers seek open lines for attack, whereas a defender attempts to keep lines near his King closed. Pawn formations often play an important role in keeping lines closed around a King (Diagram 43):

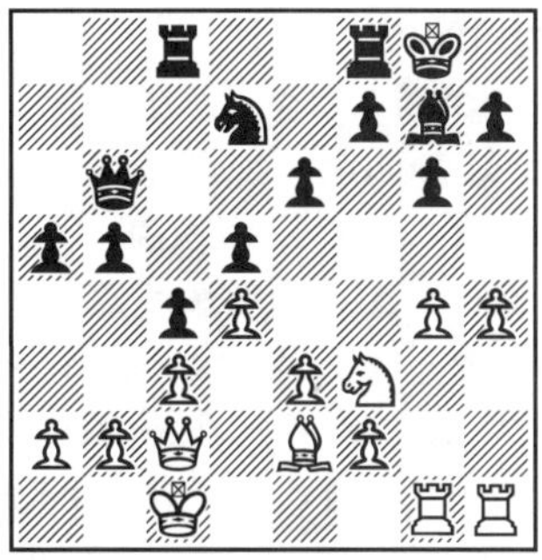

Diagram 43-Black to move

White is threatening *h5* followed by *hxg6* to open the h-file for attack. After *h5* by White, bypassing with *...g5* would not avail Black because of *Nxg5*. Black played the timely defensive move **1... h6!** to keep the lines toward the black King closed. If White now tries *2. h5*, *...g5!* keeps the g- and h-files closed; or if *2. g5*, *...h5!* closes the lines.

Preventive defense is preferable to corrective defense, and *hindering* your opponent prevents or diminishes his threats. A constant goal is to improve your relative position, and hindering moves reduce your opponent's possibilities. Cramp opposing pieces, restrict them from important squares, prevent the opponent from castling, and block or contest open files and diagonals. Above all, avoid moves which help your opponent more than you.

For a clear example of hindrance, refer to Diagram 44:

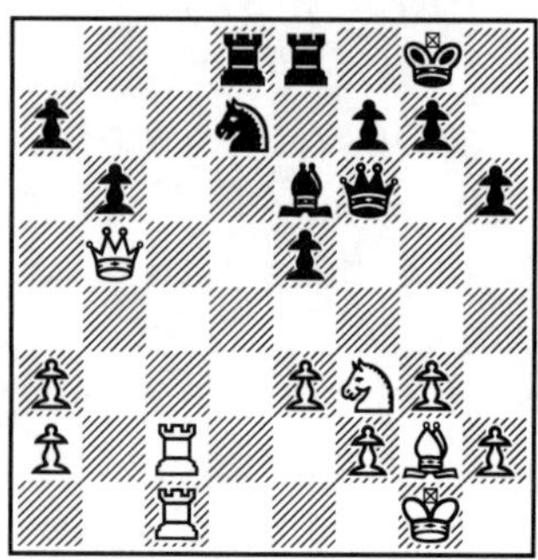

Diagram 44-Black to move

White's imposing doubled Rooks control the open c-file, with the threat of *Rc7* controlling the seventh rank with attacks against the black N/d7 and a7-pawn. Black neatly nullified the influence of the doubled white Rooks with the defensive hindrance move **...Nc5!** The white Rooks are now blocked and cannot penetrate into Black's position, and the black N/c5 is secure on a central outpost. The black N/c5 also guards against an incursion by the white Queen (*Qa4* or *Qa6)* to attack the undefended black a7-pawn. The black R/d8 is also now unblocked. Black has improved his position and hindered White.

When in a winning position, a useful technique is to ask yourself the relevant question, "How could my *opponent* win or draw this game?" Then proceed to eliminate or minimize his winning and drawing opportunities, usually by exchanging his active pieces. Simplifying for safety usually involves trading Queens and Rooks, as well as opposing minor pieces near your King. If you are significantly ahead, returning some material with a slight sacrifice can eliminate active or dangerous enemy pieces and reduce your opponent's counterplay. Simplifying for safety when ahead in material is nearly always advantageous, and may be necessary or desirable although material is even. As long as your opponent has a Queen, for example, he has mating and drawing possibilities. Be alert to your opponent's winning and drawing possibilities, and simplify as necessary.

Even when far behind, your opponent will be energetically — perhaps desperately — seeking to win or draw the game; so find his winning or drawing possibilities first, and thwart them. Carefully watch for and avoid opponents' tactics and mating attacks. Chessplayers who become overconfident and careless when ahead are often surprised by a determined, resourceful opponent, with the unpleasant result of snatching defeat from the jaws of victory.

Some specific things to avoid defensively are back-rank mates and perpetual checks (provide your King a safe flight square), Knight forks, unguarded pieces (subject to double attacks), and aligning your King and Queen on the same file as enemy Rooks or on the same diagonal as enemy Bishops, even with intervening pieces (because of discovered attacks).

When in check, remember the *three* ways to escape check: capture the attacker, interpose, or move your King. Do not automatically move your King. Generally, only in response to a double-check must the King be moved.

The major cause of "involuntary sacrifices" — losing material by overlooking opponents' threats — is becoming too involved in your own plans and overlooking or ignoring your opponent's possibilities. Every move alters the position on the chessboard — a move that was safe and effective just one move ago may now be unsafe, even disastrous. Eternal vigilance is the price of victory in chess.

Finally, play difficult and inferior positions with determination, perseverance, and optimism (your opponent may err), and seek counterplay. Faced with inevitable loss of material, lose the least possible. Play resilient, resourceful, and tenacious defense, and become tough to defeat. Active, effective, and timely defense can save many chess games and convert potential losses into draws, or even wins!

Middlegame Guidelines

Important additional guidelines for playing effective middlegames are:

- *Make purposeful moves.* In most middlegame positions, each of your moves will: defend against a threat, attack a weakness, hinder your opponent, or improve your position, depending on the requirements and opportunities in the position. Aimless moves are to be avoided, since they lose time and give your opponent extra moves to carry out his plans.

- *Centralize and coordinate pieces.* Pieces exert their maximum power near the center, and control of the center is usually necessary to launch a successful central or wing attack. Coordinated pieces create more threats. Centralized pieces should be defended by pawns and other pieces.
- *Create and seize open lines.* Open lines are the pathways into the opponent's position, and favor the better-developed side. Controlling open files and diagonals enables a player to attack from long range and penetrate with pieces. Lines are opened with pawn exchanges and, sometimes, sacrifices. Rooks should control open files, and Bishops should control open diagonals.
- *If ahead in development, open the game and attack; if behind in development, keep the game closed.* Attackers seek open lines, defenders attempt to keep lines closed, especially near the King.
- *Avoid pawn weaknesses.* Weak pawns (isolated, doubled, backward) have two primary weaknesses: 1) if attacked, they must be defended by pieces, tying valuable pieces to defense; and 2) the square in front of a weak pawn is a potential outpost for enemy pieces. Both weaknesses are restrictive. Sound pawn structures (chains, phalanxes — supported pawns abreast on the same rank) are self-supporting, mobile, and desirable.
- *Double Rooks on open files.* Rooks doubled on an open file are more than twice as strong as one Rook on the file. Doubled Rooks can penetrate decisively into the enemy position, and also deny enemy pieces access to the file.
- *Use exchanges to free cramped positions and reduce attacks.* Trade passive pieces for your opponent's active ones to gain freedom. Sometimes, especially when significantly ahead in material, a small sacrifice to free your position is appropriate. Exchange defensive pieces for your opponent's attacking pieces to diminish an attack.

Five Common Mistakes

Mistakes to avoid in the middlegame include:

- Unguarded pieces and pawns
- Exposure to checks, pins, skewers, Knight forks, doubled attacks, and discovered attacks
- Weak (isolated, doubled, backward) pawns
- "Holes" in pawn structure (potential enemy outposts)
- Moving pawns in front of your castled King (except for flight squares or to safely attack)

Summary

The middlegame is the most important — often critical — and difficult phase of chess. Most chess games are decided in the middlegame by checkmating attacks and decisive tactics. Eight essential keys to effective middlegame play are:

1. Playing the opening well
2. Building a superior position early
3. Avoiding weaknesses
4. Recognizing, creating, and attacking opponents' weaknesses with effective tactics
5. Attacking the enemy King when justified
6. Improving your own position constantly, including keeping your King safe
7. Using sound and flexible planning — short- and long-range — including preparing for an endgame
8. Playing active, effective, and timely defense

These eight basic principles, incorporating sound positional and effective tactical play, form the basis for successful middlegames.

Playing the best move in each position is a worthwhile and essential goal in all phases of chess. Choosing the best move involves five sequential steps:

1. Analyze the position
2. Determine your goal
3. Define the tasks
4. Develop and evaluate candidate moves
5. Select the "best" move

When analyzing a position, look for relative strengths and *weaknesses*. Then, imagine your pieces and pawns in IDEAL POSITION and define the tasks and moves required to achieve your IDEAL POSITION, including eliminating, deflecting, pinning, or blocking enemy chessmen. Seek candidate moves that perform the necessary tasks, evaluate the various candidate moves, then select and play the best move. For more on selecting "best" moves see Heisman's *Evaluation of Positional Elements*.

Analyze candidate moves separately in "watertight compartments," and evaluate candidate moves by comparison (numerical "grading" or "King of the Mountain" approach). Analyze *forcing moves first,* since they limit your opponent's replies, thus making the variations easier to foresee and calculate. On each move, *always* examine every possible *check* and *capture* — both yours *and* your opponent's!

It is often beneficial to find an "adequate" move first, to have a "move in your pocket" to reduce the tension of the search and against which other moves can be compared. Remember, the only move to play in each position is the ***strongest*** move within the time available. Be thorough — when you find a good move, always look for a better one (if you have the time)!

Chess is a game of threats, and every move in a chess game should be responsive to the *offensive opportunities* and *defensive necessities* in each position, as well as be *safe*.

Finally, when the decision is close and you are in doubt, choose the more *active* move. Active positions offer more winning opportunities than passive positions (passive positions contain the germs of defeat). Active piece and pawn placement can seize or maintain the initiative, develop decisive tactical and positional options, and lead directly to winning attacks.

Exercise: Find The Best Move

Sound chess judgment involves logical analysis, positional awareness, intuition, imagination, and experience. Accurate calculation of tactical variations is an essential element. Practice your chess judgment in these interesting exercises by selecting the best move for the side to play in the following two positions (Diagrams 45 and 46). Several candidate moves are given for your guidance.

Answers and explanations are provided at the end of the exercises.

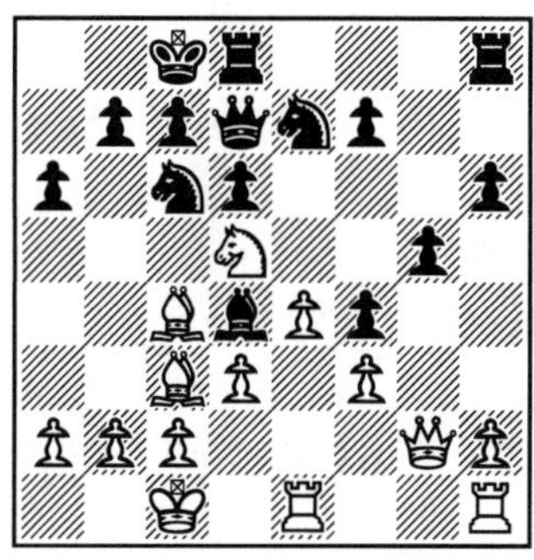

Diagram 45-Black to move

a) White has just played **1. B/d2-c3.** Candidate Black moves are *1... Bxc3*, *...Be3+*, *...Nxd5*, *...Ng6*, *...f5*, *...b5*, *...Rde8*, and *...Rhe8*.

Evaluate these candidate moves, and select the best move for Black.

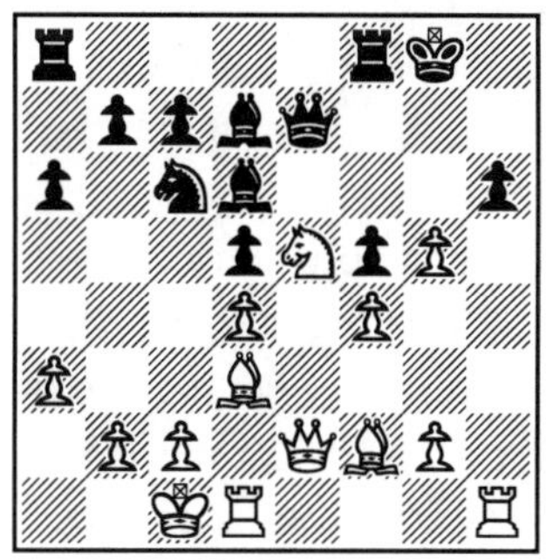

Diagram 46-White to move

b) Black has just played **1... f7-f5.** Candidate White moves are *2. gxf6 e.p.*, *gxh6*, *Rxh6*, *Ng6*, *Nxc6*, *Nxd7*, *Qh5*, and *Rde1*.

Evaluate these candidate moves, and select the best move for White.

Answers

a) Diagram 45:

1... Bxc3 is the best move (to force the retreating *2. Nxc3*, or *2. bxc3* doubling Queenside pawns in front of the white King).

1... Nxd5? loses a piece to *2. exd5 Bxc3 3. dxc6! Qxc6 4. bxc3*.

1... Be3†? loses a pawn: *2. Rxe3! fxe3 3. Bxh8 Rxh8 4. Qe2* followed by *5. Qxe3.*

1... f5, 1... Rde8, or *1... Rhe8* allows *2. Nf6 Bxf6 3. Bxf6* with White pressure.

1... Ng6 allows *2. Nf6 Qe7* (if *2... Bxf6?, 3. Bxf6* wins the Exchange) *3. Bxd4 Nxd4 4. Nh5,* blocking the black Kingside pawn majority.

1... b5 weakens the black King's pawn protection.

b) Diagram 46:

1. Rxh6 is the best move (wins a pawn and opens the h-file for attack against the black King).

1. Ng6 is refuted by *1... Qxe2 2. Bxe2 Rfe8.*

1. gxf6 e.p. allows *1... Qxf6,* guarding the black h6-pawn and attacking the white f4-pawn.

1. gxh6 wins a pawn, but closes attacking lines toward the black King.

1. Nxc6 dissipates White's attack: *1... Qxe2 2. Bxe2 Bxc6.*

1. Nxd7 trades an attacking piece for a passive defender, and allows *1... Qxd7* followed by *2... Rae8* to control the e-file.

1. Qh5 is premature. After *1... Qg7,* to win the black h-pawn, White must allow the trade of Queens (*2. Qxh6 Qxh6*) or close attacking lines (*2. gxh6*) — in either case reducing White's attack.

1. Rde1 does not win a pawn, does not contribute to White's Kingside attack, and allows Black too much defensive freedom (*1... Bxe5, ...Qg7,* or *...Rae8*).

Exercise: Win All You Safely Can

The side ahead in material usually wins, so cover the moves below and win *all* you safely can for *White* in this early Queen's Gambit position. Tally your correct moves.

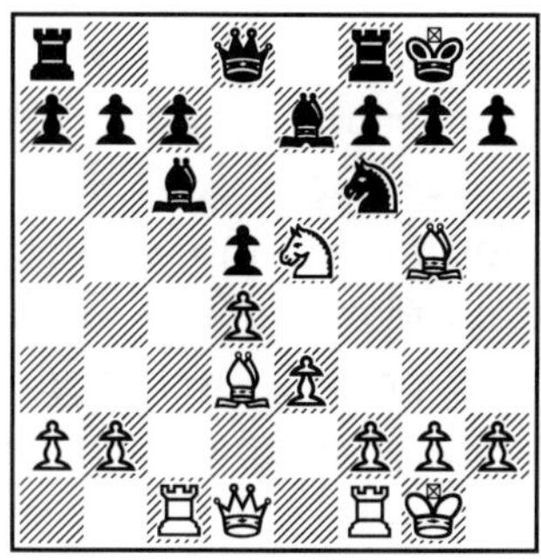

Diagram 47-White to move

COVER UP — FIND WHITE'S BEST MOVES

1. Nxc6!

Wins a pawn next move.

1. ... bxc6

2. Rxc6

White has won a pawn.

2. ... Qd7

3. Qc2!

Defends R/c6, attacks the black c7-pawn and h7-pawn twice.

3. ... Rfc8

4. Bxf6!

Removes a defender of the h7-pawn.

4. ... Bxf6

5. Bxh7†

Wins a second pawn.

5. ... Kf8

6. Bf5!

Wins the Exchange.

6. ... Qe7

7. Bxc8

White is the Exchange plus two pawns ahead.

7. ... Rxc8

8. Qc5

Simplifies — 4 points ahead, White forces a Queen trade.

8. ... Ke8

9. Qxe7†

Eliminates Queens with winning material advantage.

9. ... Bxe7

10. Rfc1

Threatens the c7-pawn.

10. ... Bd6

11. Rxd6!

Wins the Bishop (*11... cxd6 12. Rxc8†*).

11. ... Resigns

Black is hopelessly behind in material.

Correct Moves	Strength
10-11	Outstanding
8-9	Superior
6-7	Excellent
4-5	Good
1-3	Fair

Practice Games

You will improve your ability to select the best move in each position through experience. For your practice in analyzing positions and evaluating candidate moves, following are three practice games. Three candidate moves are given for each position, and your task is to select the best move in each position. The practice games are self-grading, so you can measure your skill and progress.

Practice Game #1

Following is a Queen's Gambit game. After **1. d4 d5 2. c4 e6 3. Nc3 Nf6,** cover the remaining moves in both the *Correct White Move* and *Black Move* columns (to the far right) and select the best move (A, B, or C) for *WHITE* on each move. Points for each correct White move are indicated in the *Correct White Move* column. Compare your final score with the table to determine your strength in this game.

QUEEN'S GAMBIT

	WHITE candidates			Correct	
White	A	B	C	White Move (COVER UP)	Black Move (COVER UP)
4.	e3	Bg5	Qa4†	Bg5 (5)	...Be7
5.	Nf3	cxd5	e3	e3 (5)	...Nbd7
6.	Nf3	Bd3	Bxf6	Nf3 (5)	...0–0
7.	Bd3	Be2	Rc1	Rc1 (5)	...c6
8.	c5	cxd5	Be2	cxd5 (5)	...cxd5
9.	Bd3	Nb5	Bb5	Bd3 (6)	...Qa5
10.	a3	Qb3	0–0	0–0 (5)	...a6
11.	Qc2	Ne5	Bxf6	Ne5 (6)	...h6
12.	Bxf6	Bf4	Bh4	Bh4 (5)	...Re8
13.	f4	Nxd7	Qc2	f4 (6)	...Nxe5
14.	dxe5	fxe5	Bxf6	fxe5 (6)	...Nd7
15.	Bxe7	Qh5	Qf3	Qh5 (8)	...Qd8
16.	Rxf7	Bxe7	Qxf7†	Qxf7† (7)	...Kh8
17.	Bxe7	Bg6	Qg6	Qg6 (10)	...Nf8
18.	Qh5	Rxf8†	Bxe7	Rxf8† (10)	...Rxf8
19.	Qh7†	Bxe7	Rf1	Qh7# (6)	

Points	*Your Strength:*
86-100	Outstanding
71-85	Excellent
41-70	Average
21-40	Fair
0-20	Novice

Practice Game #2

Following is a Réti Opening game. After **1. Nf3 d5 2. c4 e6 3. g3 Nf6,** cover the remaining moves in both the *Correct White Move* and *Black Move* columns (to the far right) and select the best move (A, B, or C) for *WHITE* on each move. Points for each correct White move are indicated in the *Correct White Move* column. Compare your final score with the table to determine your strength.

RÉTI'S OPENING

White	WHITE candidates A	B	C	Correct White Move (COVER UP)	Black Move (COVER UP)
4.	d3	Nc3	Bg2	Bg2 (4)	...Be7
5.	Nc3	d3	0–0	0–0 (4)	...0–0
6.	e3	b3	Nc3	b3 (4)	...c5
7.	Nc3	Bb2	d4	Bb2 (4)	...Nc6
8.	d4	Nc3	e3	e3 (4)	...b6
9.	Nc3	Re1	Qc2	Nc3 (4)	...Bb7
10.	cxd5	Rc1	d4	cxd5 (4)	...Nxd5
11.	d4	Nxd5	Rc1	Nxd5 (4)	...Qxd5
12.	Rc1	d4	Nh4	d4 (4)	...cxd4
13.	Nxd4	exd4	Bxd4	Nxd4 (5)	...Qc5
14.	Rc1	Nxc6	Bxc6	Rc1 (7)	...Qd6
15.	Bxc6	Rxc6	Nxc6	Nxc6 (7)	...Rac8
16.	Nd4	Nxe7†	Nxa7	Nxe7† (6)	...Qxe7
17.	Rxc8	Bxb7	Qd4	Bxb7 (6)	...Qxb7
18.	Qd4	Rxc8	Ba3	Qd4 (7)	...f5
19.	Rxc8	Rfd1	Qe5	Qe5 (7)	...Rfe8
20.	Rxc8	Rc4	Rfd1	Rxc8 (7)	...Rxc8
21.	Rc1	Qxe6†	Rd1	Qxe6† (7)	...Kh8
22.	Rd1	Rc1	Qxf5	Rd1 (7)	...h6
23.	Qxf5	Qd5	Rd7	Rd7 (8)	...Qf3
24.	Qf7	Bxg7†	Rxg7	Bxg7† (9)	...Kh7
25.	Qxh6†	Bxh6†	Bd4†	Bd4# (6)	

Points .... *Your Strength:*
106-125 .... Outstanding
86-105 .... Excellent

51-85 .... Average
26-50 .... Fair
0-25 .... Novice

Practice Game #3

Following is a Sicilian (Dragon) Defense game. After the opening moves **1. e4 c5 2. Nf3 d6 3. d4 cxd4 4. Nxd4 Nf6 5. Nc3 g6 6. Be2,** cover the remaining White moves and the *Correct Black Move* column (to the far right) and select the best move (A, B, or C) for *BLACK* on each move. Points for each correct Black move are indicated in the *Correct Black Move* column. Compare your final score with the table to determine your strength in this game.

White Black SICILIAN DRAGON Correct

Black Move

	BLACK candidates		A	B	C	(COVER UP)
6.	Be2	...	e5	Bg7	Nc6	Bg7 (4)
7.	0–0	...	Nc6	0–0	Bd7	0–0 (4)
8.	Nb3	...	Nbd7	b6	Nc6	Nc6 (4)
9.	f4	...	Qb6†	e6	Bd7	Bd7 (4)
10.	h3	...	Rc8	Qb6†	a6	Rc8 (4)
11.	Bf3	...	Qb6†	a6	Qc7	a6 (4)
12.	Kh2	...	b5	Qc7	Re8	Qc7 (4)
13.	Nd5	...	Nxd5	Qb8	Qd8	Nxd5 (5)
14.	exd5	...	Nb4	Nd4	Na5	Na5 (5)
15.	c3	...	Nxb3	Bb5	b5	b5 (5)
16.	Nxa5	...	Qxa5	b4	e6	Qxa5 (5)
17.	b4	...	Qc7	Qa4	Qb6	Qb6 (6)
18.	Bb2	...	Bf5	Bxc3	Qe3	Bxc3 (6)
19.	Bxc3	...	Rxc3	Qe3	Rc4	Rxc3 (5)
20.	a3	...	Bf5	Rfc8	Qe3	Rfc8 (6)
21.	Re1	...	e6	Kf8	Re3	Re3 (6)
22.	Rxe3	...	Qxe3	e6	Kf8	Qxe3 (5)
23.	g3	...	Rc3	Qf2†	Bf5	Rc3 (6)

24.	Bg2	...	Rd3	Rxa3	Qxg3†	Qxg3† (6)
25.	Kh1	...	Qxf4	Bxh3	Rxa3	Bxh3 (7)
26.	Qe2	...	Qxg2†	Bxg2†	Rxa3	Bxg2† (7)
27.	Qxg2	...	Qxf4	Qxg2†	Qh4†	Qh4† (9)
28.	Kg1	...	Qg3	Rg3	Qxf4	Rg3 (8)
29.	Resigns					

Points .... *Your Strength:*
106-125 .... Outstanding
86-105 .... Excellent
51-85 .... Average
26-50 .... Fair
0-25 .... Novice

Chapter 6

MIDDLEGAME TACTICS

Chess is 90 percent tactics!

— Teichmann

Tactics — forcing moves to win material and checkmate — win chess games. All games are ultimately decided by tactics, and strong chessplayers are sharp tacticians.

Twenty tactics comprise the vast majority of tactical play. The following six are the most common:

- Superior force
- Pin
- Skewer
- Knight fork
- Double attack
- Discovered attack

Fourteen less frequent tactics are:

- Overworked defenders
- Vital guards
- Removing defenders
- Deflecting defenders
- Sacrifices
- Back-rank mate
- In-between move
- Interference
- No retreat
- Trapping pieces
- Desperado
- *Zugzwang*
- Queening combinations
- Underpromotion

To improve, a chessplayer must become skilled in these tactics, which are illustrated in the following examples. Learn and *apply* these important tactics to win more chess games.

Major Tactics

Superior Force

Superior force involves attacking a piece or pawn more times than it is defended (Diagram 48):

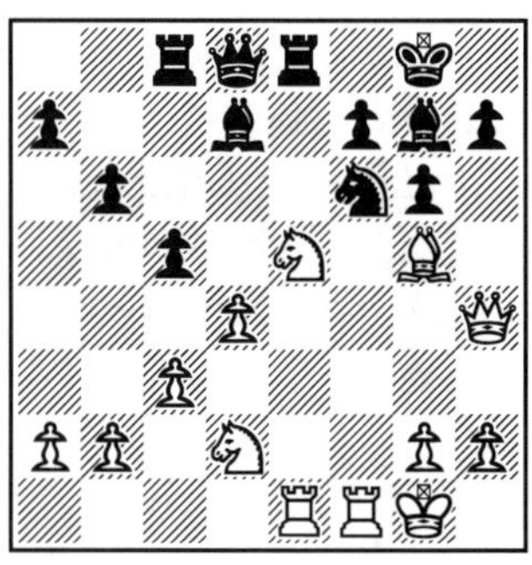

Diagram 48-White to move

Black's N/f6 is attacked three times (white B/g5, R/f1, and Q/h4) and defended only twice (black B/g7, Q/d8). White won the Knight by playing **1. Bxf6 Bxf6 2. Qxf6.** Now Black's protective f7-pawn is attacked three times (white N/e5, Q/f6, and R/f1) and defended only once (black K/g8). Black avoided further immediate material loss by exchanging Queens, **2... Qxf6 3. Rxf6 Be6,** but Black has lost a Knight.

Note: The *number*, *value*, and *sequence* of attackers and defenders must be considered before making a capture. For example, a pawn defended only by a pawn is normally safe from capture, even if attacked by several pieces.

Pin

A pin occurs when a piece attacks along the same line an enemy chessman aligned on a file, rank, or diagonal with a *more* valuable enemy chessman (Diag. 49):

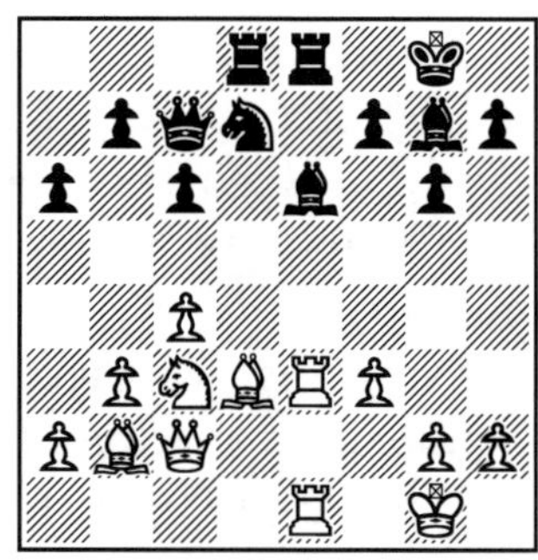

Diagram 49-Black to move

The white R/e3 and K/g1 are aligned on the same diagonal (a weakness). Black simply played **1... Bd4!,** pinning the white Rook to the King, and after **2. Kh1** captured **...Bxe3,** winning the Exchange.

One tactical weakness, a pinned pawn (resulting in "false" protection), is illustrated in Diagram 50:

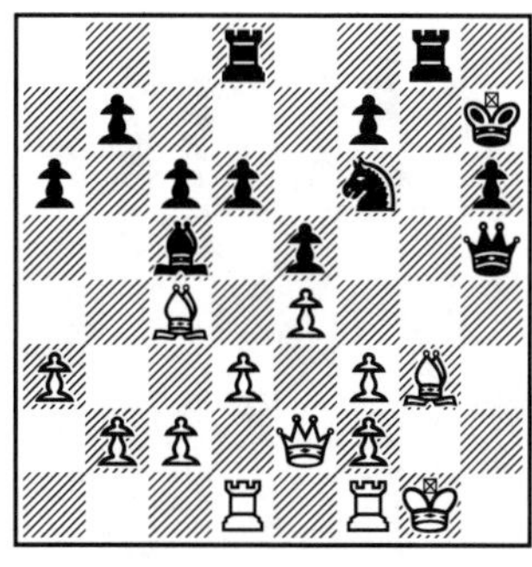

Diagram 50-Black to move

Black's Queen and Rook attack the white King, and the major

tactical weakness in White's position is the pinned (by B/c5) f2-pawn "guarding" the interposed B/g3 — false protection. Black simply played **1... Rxg3 checkmate!** — a simple and clear example of the dangers of tactical weaknesses.

Absolute pins are pieces or pawns pinned to a King, while *relative* pins are pieces or pawns pinned to a piece. Relative pins can sometimes be broken by counterattacking a more valuable enemy piece with a pinned piece, but absolute pins can be broken only by moving the King or, by interposing a piece or pawn.

Skewer

The skewer, reverse of a pin, occurs when a piece attacks along the same line an enemy chessman aligned on a file, rank, or diagonal, with a *less* valuable enemy chessman (Diagram 51):

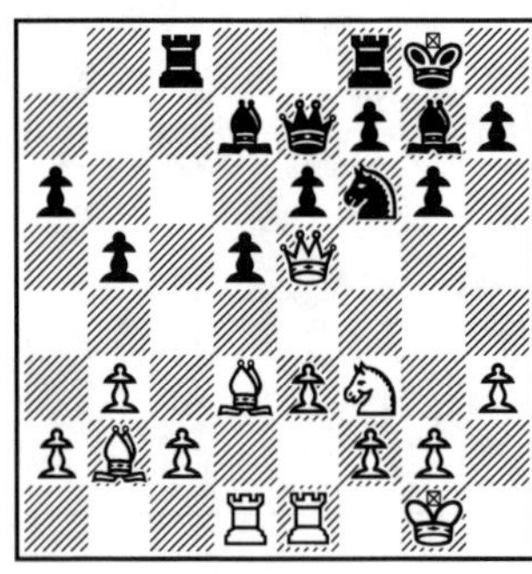

Diagram 51-Black to move

The white Q/e5 and B/b2 are aligned on a diagonal. Black exploited this weakness promptly with **1... Ne8!,** skewering the white Queen and Bishop (and defending against *2. Qxg7 checkmate)*. After **2. Qf4 Bxb2** Black has won a Bishop.

Knight Fork

A Knight fork is a simultaneous attack by a Knight on two or more enemy chessmen (Diagram 52):

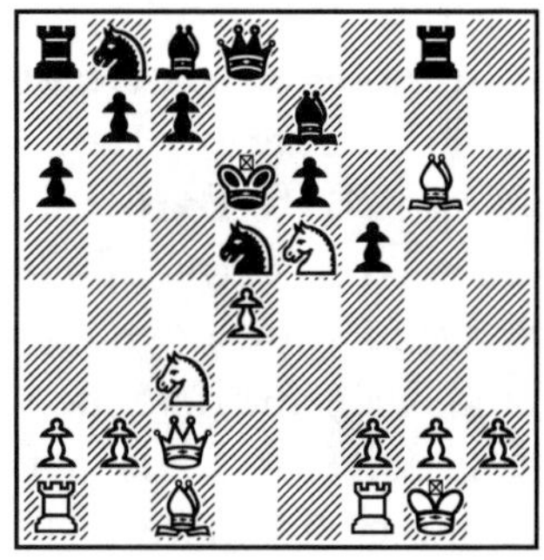

Diagram 52-White to move

White played **1. Nf7+!,** forking the black King and Queen. After **1... Kd7 2. Nxd8 Kxd8** White, significant material ahead, eventually won the game.

Note: When you find a good move, always look for a better one (if you have the time)! The black King is exposed and restricted, and White could have checkmated Black immediately with the forcing line-clearing sacrifice *1. Nb5†!!* (or *1. Ne4†!!) axb5* (forced) (or

...fxe4 forced) *2. Qc5 checkmate!* White played an obvious and strong Knight fork, but missed an opportunity to checkmate. Do not settle for crumbs, or even a large slice, when you can have the whole cake!

Double Attack

A double attack is a simultaneous attack by a piece or pawn on two enemy chessmen. Double attacks are aimed at unguarded or inadequately defended pieces and pawns (Diagram 53):

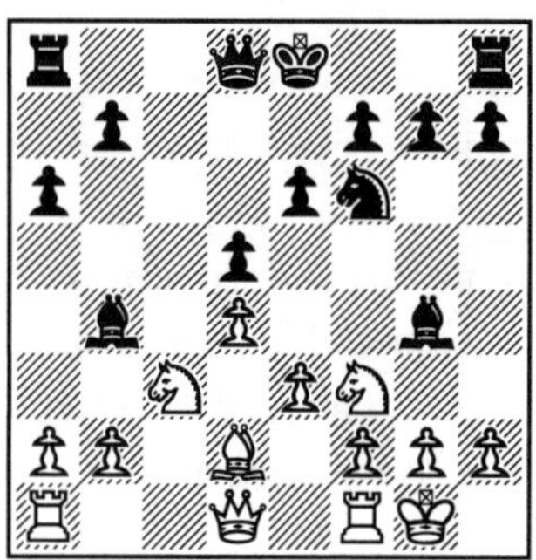

Diagram 53-White to move

Black's B/b4 is unguarded, so White played **1. Qa4†!** with a double attack on the black King and hapless Bishop. After **1... Qd7 2. Qxb4** White has won a Bishop.

Discovered Attack

Discovered attacks occur when two pieces of the same color are aligned on a file, rank, or diagonal with an enemy chessman, and the forward piece moves off the line to "discover" an attack by the remaining piece (Diagram 54):

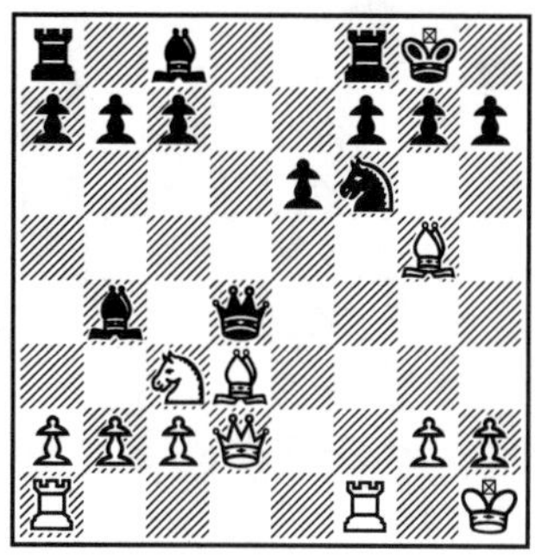

Diagram 54-White to move

Black has just unwisely captured a pawn with his Queen, and the black Q/d4 is now aligned with the white B/d3 and Q/d2. White played **1. Bxh7†!,** discovering an attack on the greedy black Queen. Following **1... Nxh7 2. Qxd4,** White has won the black Queen. (Black minimized his material loss with **2... Bxc3 3. Qxc3 Nxg5,** but White continued **4. Qxc7** and, with a sizable material advantage, won easily.)

Sometimes the forward piece in a double attack does the damage (Diagram 55):

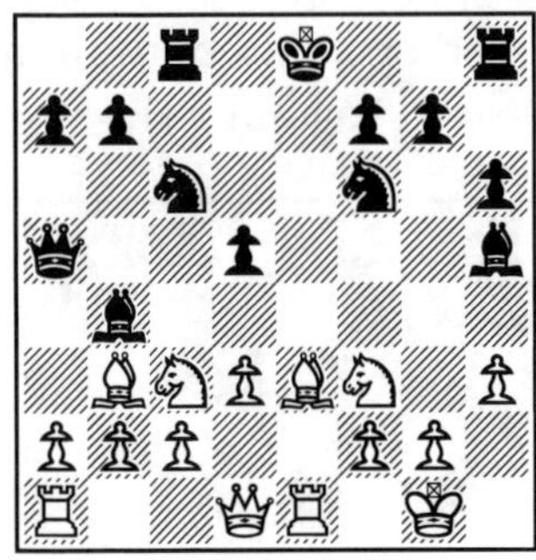

Diagram 55-White to move

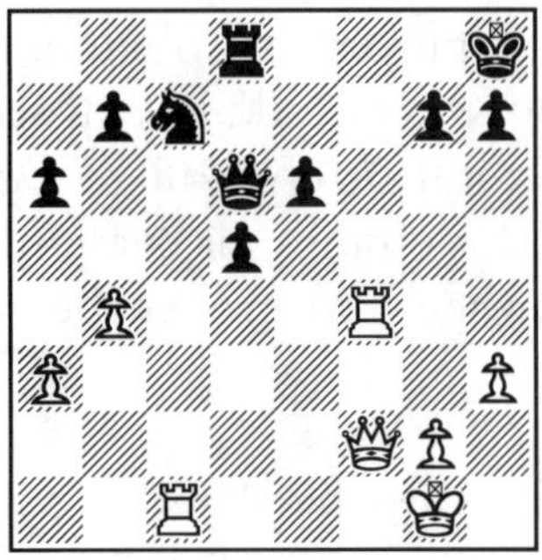

Diagram 56-White to move

Black has failed to castle, and the black King is in line with the white R/e1. White exploited this weakness to win the black Queen: **1. Bb6†! Ne7 2. Bxa5.**

Minor Tactics

Overworked Defender

An overworked defender has roo many defensive tasks. When a piece or pawn simultaneously defends two attacked chessmen or vital squares, it may be overworked. An overworked defender is exploited by capturing one chessman it defends, then capturing the other or occupying the vital square (Diagram 56):

The overworked black Queen defends the N/c7 and also guards against checkmate on f8 (starting with *1. Rf8†)*. White captured **1. Rxc7!,** and the overworked black Queen is helpless to recapture (if *1... Qxc7, 2. Rf8† Rxf8 3. Qxf8 checkmate)*. In addition to winning a Knight, White's strong Rook on c7 later enabled White to checkmate on the seventh rank.

Vital Guards

A vital guard defends a critical piece, pawn, or square. Removing, deflecting, or immobilizing (pinning) the vital guard renders the critical piece, pawn, or square vulnerable (Diagram 57):

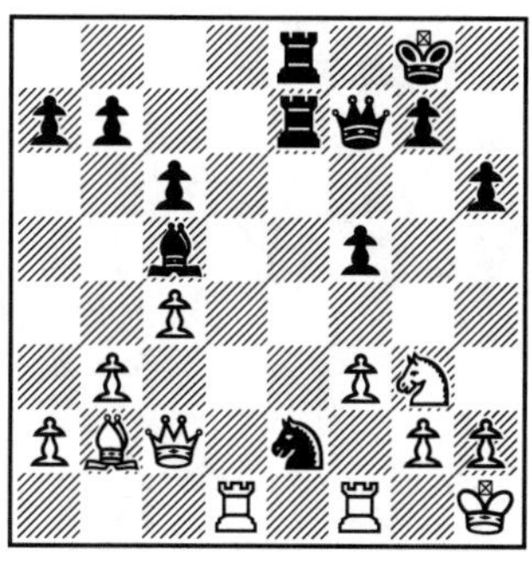

Diagram 57-Black to move

White's N/g3 and h2-pawn are vital guards preventing ...*Qh5 mate*. Black removed one vital guard and deflected the other with **1... Nxg3†!** After **2. hxg3** (forced), Black continued **2... Qh5 checkmate.**

Removing Defenders

Eliminating a defender renders the piece or pawn it was guarding vulnerable to capture (Diagram 58):

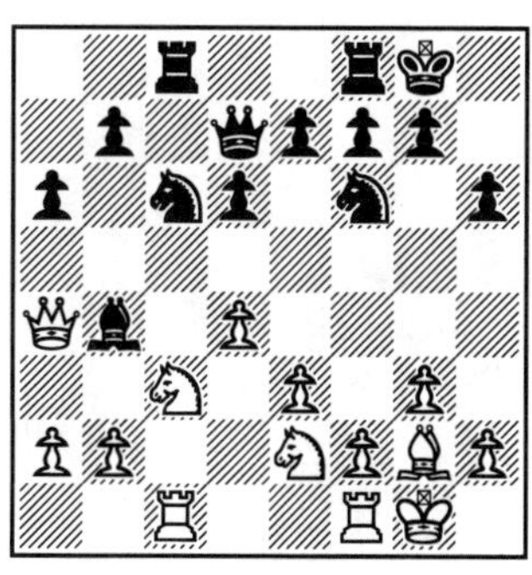

Diagram 58-White to move

The black N/c6 is defending the B/b4, which is attacked by the white Q/a4. White removed the Bishop's defender and won the Bishop with the forcing **1. Bxc6!** (capturing a piece and attacking the black Queen) **Qxc6** (...*Rxc6* or ...*bxc6* does not help) **2. Qxb4.**

Deflecting Defenders

Sometimes a defending piece or pawn can be deflected from its defensive task (Diagram 59):

Diagram 59-Black

The white K/e2 is defending the Q/f2. Black deflected the King with **1... Rd2†!** After **2. Kxd2** (if *2. Ke1* or *Kf1*, ...*Qxf2 mate*; or *2. Ke3 Qxf2†* wins) **Qxf2†,** Black won the white Queen and recovered his Rook with the double attack on the white K/d2 and R/h4.

Sacrifices

Sacrifices — our hero gives up material for anticipated tactical or positional advantages — are covered in detail in the next chapter

("Combinations and Sacrifices"). We will briefly examine them here as an element of tactical play.

Temporary sacrifices, as integral elements in tactical combinations, can force checkmate or win decisive material. Two examples will illustrate the potency of sacrificial combinations (Diagrams 60 and 61):

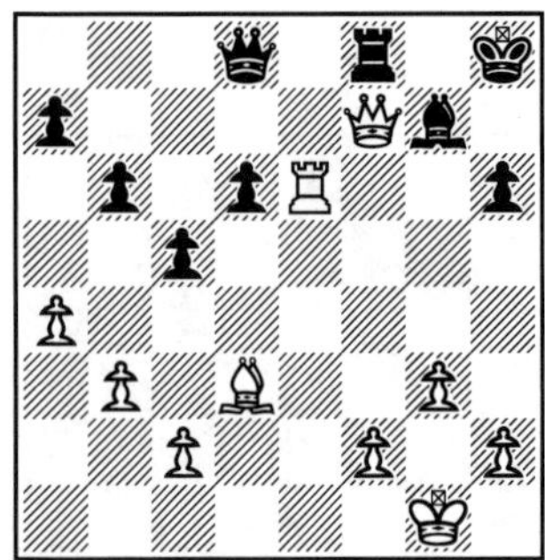

Diagram 60-White to move

Black has just played **...R/g8-f8,** attacking the white Q/f7. White ignored the threat on his Queen and played the winning sacrifice **1. Rxh6†!** Following the forced **1... Bxh6,** White continued **2. Qh7 checkmate.**

A *clearance* sacrifice is the vacating of a piece from a square with a sacrifice, so that a more effective piece can utilize the square (Diagram 61):

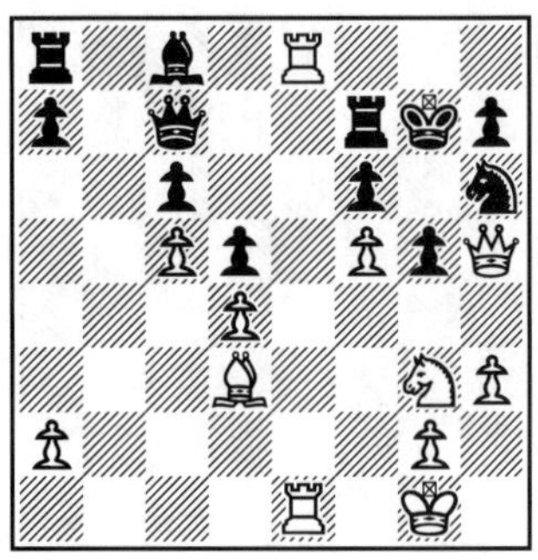

Diagram 61-White to move

The black King is severely restricted, and White exploited this tactically pregnant situation with the startling clearance sacrifice **1. Qxg5†!!,** vacating h5. After **1... fxg5** (forced), White concluded **2. Nh5 checkmate.**

Back-rank Mate

A vulnerable back rank (pawns unmoved in front of a castled King) is often susceptible to a sudden checkmate (Diagram 62):

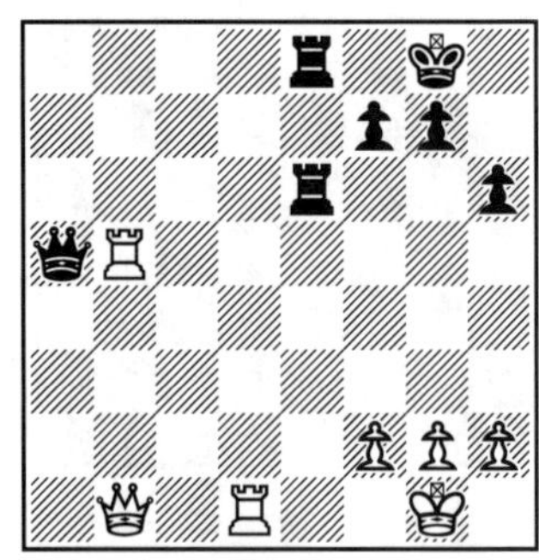

Diagram 62-Black to move

The white R/b5 is attacking

the black Queen. Black ignored the threat on his Queen and played the forcing **1... Re1†!,** and there followed **2. Rxe1 Rxe1† 3. Qxe1 Qxe1 checkmate** — a back-rank mate.

Sometimes a back-rank mate must be forced by first removing a defender, even at the cost of material (Diagram 63):

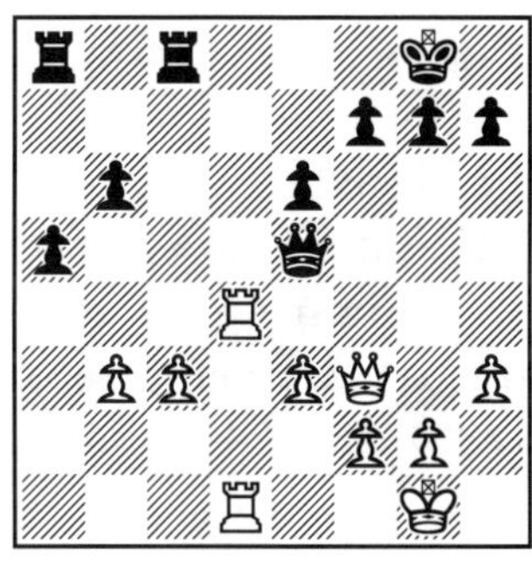

Diagram 63-White to move

Black's back rank is apparently adequately defended, for the checking square d8 is attacked and defended twice; but appearances can be deceiving. White began his assault on Black's vulnerable back rank with the amazing Queen sacrifice **1. Qxa8!!,** removing one defender of Black's back rank. There followed **1... Qc5** (*1... Rxa8 allows 2. Rd8† Rxd8 3. Rxd8 checkmate)* **2. Qxc8†! Qxc8** (*...Qf8* prolongs the agony after *3. Rd8)* **3. Rd8† Qxd8 4. Rxd8 mate.**

In-Between Move

An in-between move (also known as *zwischenzug)* is a counterattacking move interposed before responding to an opponent's threat. To be effective, the in-between threat must equal or exceed the opponent's original threat (Diagram 64):

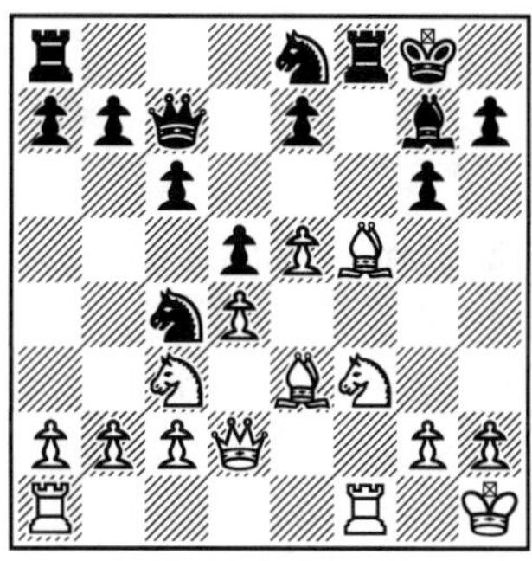

Diagram 64-White to move

Previously, Black played **1... B/c8-f5.** After White captured **2. B/d3xf5,** Black, before recapturing the white Bishop, unwisely played the in-between move **2... N/b6-c4,** attacking the white Queen. White countered with a stronger in-between move, **3. Be6†!,** attacking the black King. After **3... Kh8 4. Qc1** White has won a Bishop. In-between moves can be tricky, and should be used with great care.

Interference

Interference occurs when a piece or pawn breaks the line of

communication between an enemy piece and the piece, pawn, or square it defends (Diagram 65):

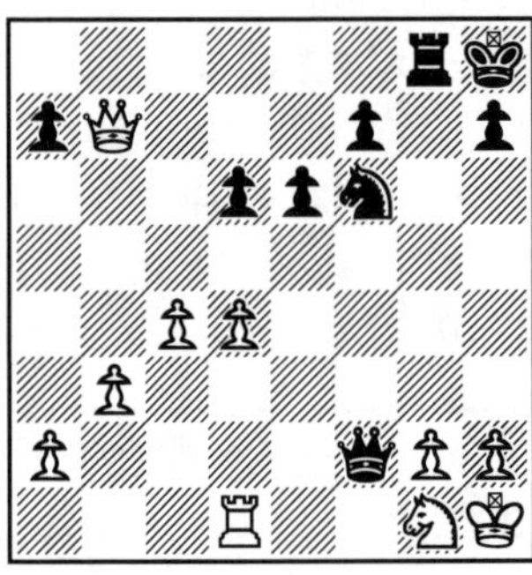

Diagram 65-Black to move

At the conclusion of an unwise pawn-grabbing expedition, the distant white Q/b7 is defending against *...Qxg2 checkmate;* so Black played **1... d5!** to interfere with the white Queen's protection of g2. Now White cannot prevent mate (if *2. g3, ...Ng4!* mates quickly).

(On his deathbed, my Grandfather shared some of his octogenarian wisdom: "Youngster," he warned, "there are five things in life to avoid: hard liquor, fast women, drugs, insulting men sporting tattoos or chain saws, and capturing your opponent's Queen-Knight pawn with your Queen." How right the old man was!)

No Retreat

A piece without safe retreat squares is vulnerable to attack (Diagram 66):

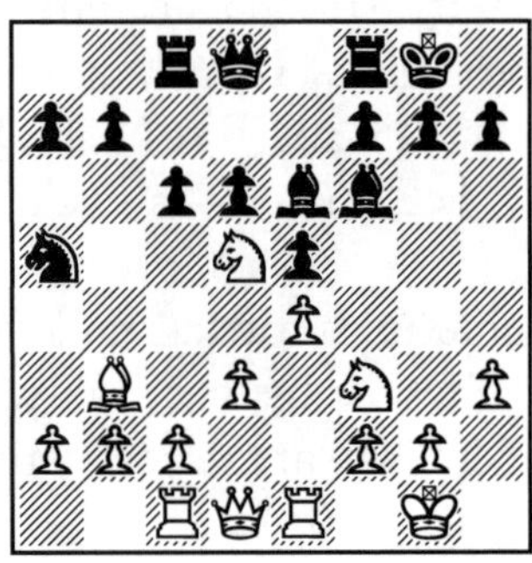

Diagram 66-White to move

The black N/a5 has no retreat squares. White began with the forcing preliminary exchanges **1. Nxf6† Qxf6 2. Bxe6 Qxe6,** then followed with **3. b4!,** winning the errant black Knight.

Trapped Pieces

Marauding pieces sometimes get trapped in enemy territory (Diagram 67):

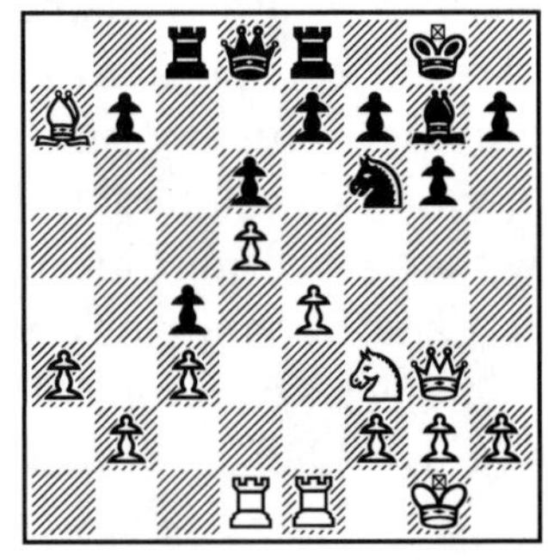

Diagram 67-Black to move

White has unwisely captured a black pawn on a7 with his Bishop.

Black responded with **1... b6!,** trapping the greedy white Bishop, and *2... Ra8* next will win the trapped Bishop.

Desperado

When a piece is inevitably lost, sacrificing it for a chessman of lesser value will minimize the material loss (Diagram 68):

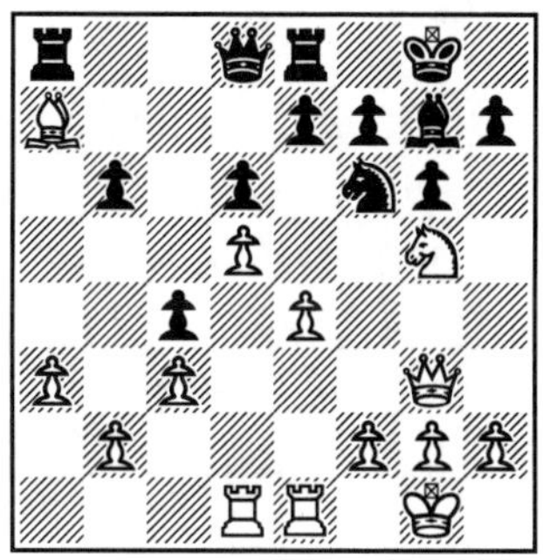

Diagram 68-White to move

This is the position from the previous diagram following two Black moves (**1... b6 2. Ng5 Ra8**). The white B/a7 is trapped and lost. Rather than lose the Bishop outright, White sacrificed the desperado Bishop for another pawn with **3. Bxb6!** After **3... Qxb6** White has gained two pawns as compensation for his lost desperado Bishop, and his 3:1 Queenside pawn majority gave him some hope for the endgame.

Zugzwang

Zugzwang (a German chess term) refers to having to move, and any move loses (Diagram 69):

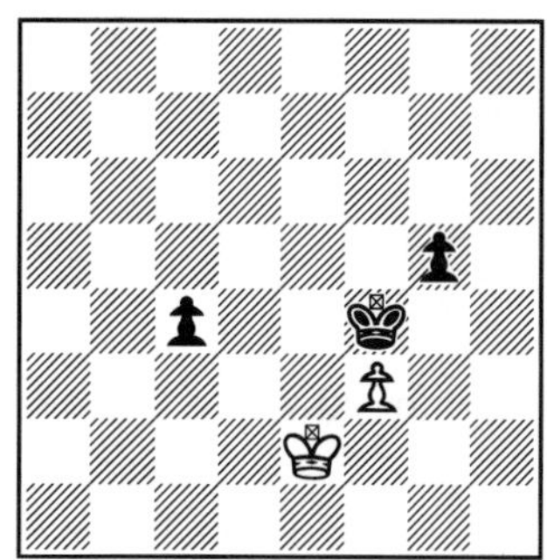

Diagram 69-Black

Black, with queening candidate pawns on both sides of the board, played **1... c3!,** placing the white King in *zugzwang:* if *2. Kd3* to capture the advanced black c-pawn, Black will play *2... Kxf3* and queen his g-pawn; if *2. Kf2* to defend the threatened f3-pawn, *2... c2* and the black c-pawn will queen.

Queening Combinations

Tactics to force the queening of a pawn often involve eliminating or deflecting blockaders or defenders (Diagram 70):

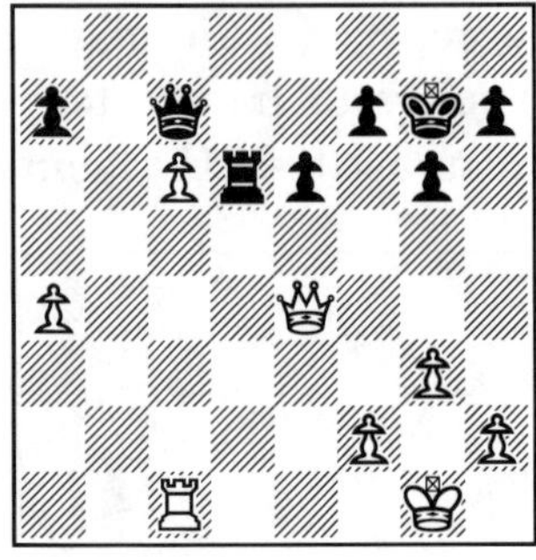

Diagram 70-White to move

White has a queening candidate in his advanced passed c6-pawn; but the pawn is blocked by the black Q/c7, and is also attacked by the black R/d6. To remove one defender and deflect the blockader, White played the preliminary **1. Qe5† Kg8,** then followed with the temporary Queen sacrifice **2. Qxd6!** After *2... Qxd6 3. c7* the c-pawn will queen, and White will emerge a Rook ahead.

Underpromotion

Pawns are underpromoted to a lesser piece than a Queen to avoid stalemate (Rook or Bishop) or give a winning check (Knight). Consider Diagram 71:

Diagram 71-White to move

1. f8=Q?? would be a draw (stalemate), so White underpromoted his pawn to a Rook with **1. f8=R!** After the forced **1... Kh6, 2. Rh8** is checkmate.

(A slower mate could have been achieved by *1. Ke7* followed by *2. f8=Q.)*

Move Sequence

In tactical positions, the *sequence* of captures can determine whether you win material, break even, or lose material (Diagram 72):

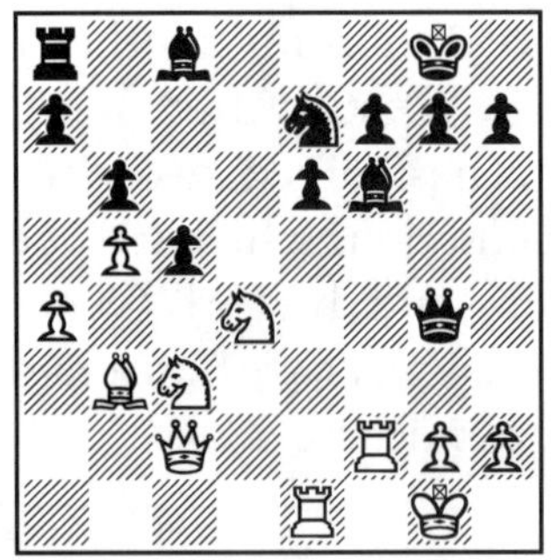

Diagram 72-Black to move

White has just captured a black Knight on d4 (**1. Nxd4**), and Black has three possible recaptures with disparate outcomes: *1... cxd4 (2. Ne4)* merely restores material; *1... Bxd4!* regains the Knight and wins the Exchange *(2... Bxf2†); 1... Qxd4?* loses the black Queen to *2. Rd1!* because of Black's vulnerable back rank.

Diagram 73 illustrates the importance of the proper sequence in multiple exchanges:

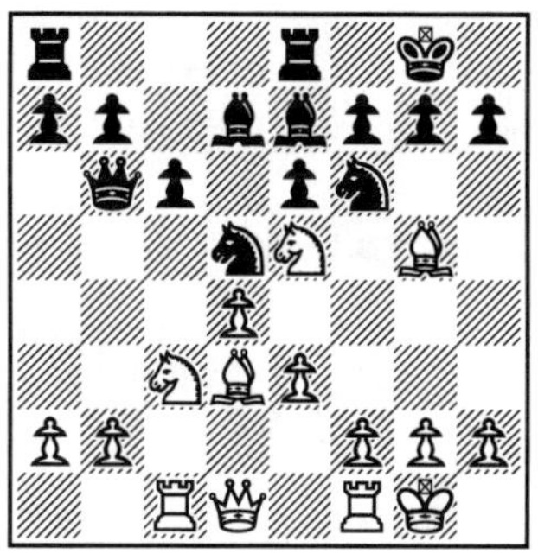

Diagram 73-White to move

Black has unwisely played **...Q/d8-b6,** and White is considering three initial captures: *1. Bxf6, 1. Nxd7*, and *1. Nxd5*. Which is best?

1. Bxf6 Nxf6 2. Nxd7 Nxd7 wins no material; *1. Nxd7 Nxd7 2. Bxe7 Rxe7 3. Nxd5 exd5* likewise wins no material; **1. Nxd5! exd5** (if *1... Nxd5, 2. Nxd7)* **2. Bxf6 Bxf6 3. Nxd7** wins a Knight.

Always carefully analyze all possible sequences of captures in tactical situations!

Summary

Tactics play a decisive role in every chess game. Tactics can checkmate, win material, and establish positional advantages.

The important tactics discussed in this chapter should be practiced and mastered. All tactics depend on one or more *weaknesses*, so learn to recognize and exploit weaknesses with appropriate tactics.

Tactical Exercises

To sharpen your tactical skill, following are eight tactical exercises for your practice. Solutions are given on the next page. Careful study of these exercises will pay dividends in your games.

WHITE TO MOVE

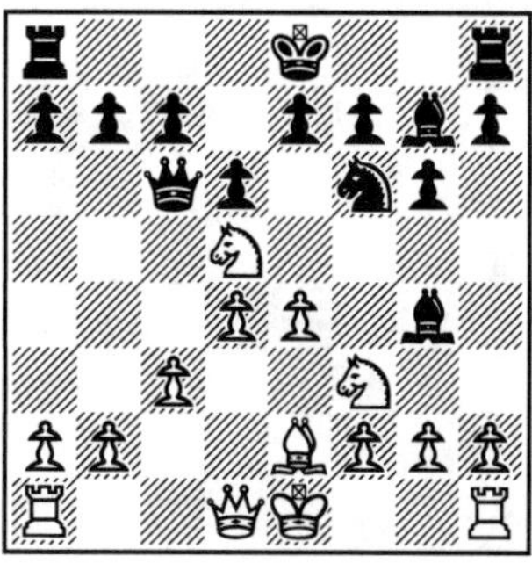

Exercise 1-White to move

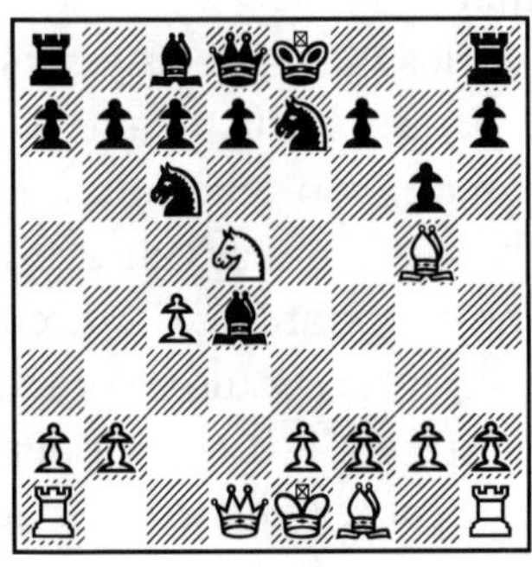

Exercise 2-White to move

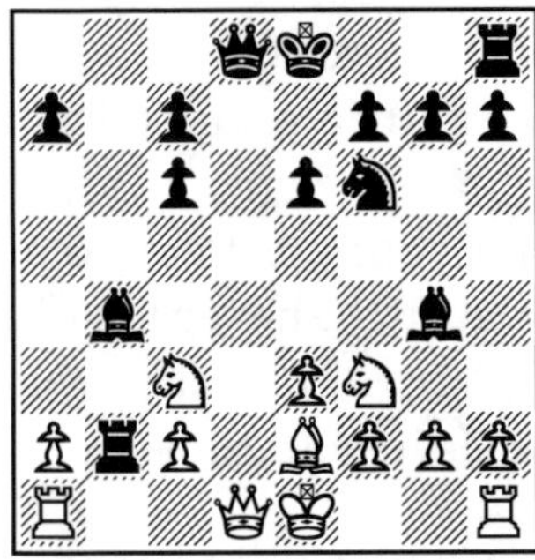

Exercise 3-White to move

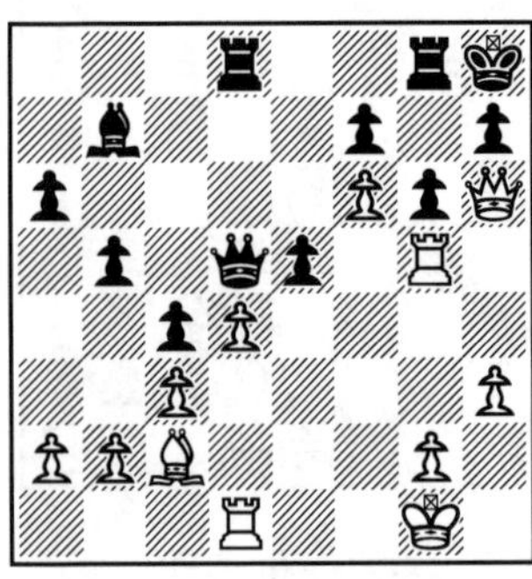

Exercise 4-White to move

Solutions:

#1. **1. Bb5! Qxb5 2. Nxc7† Kd7 3. Nxb5.**

#2. **1. Qxd4!! Nxd4 2. Nf6† Kf8 3. Bh6#.**

#3. **1. Qxd8† Kxd8 2. 0-0-0†! Ke7 3. Kxb2.**

#4. **1. Qxh7†!! Kxh7 2. Rh5#.**

BLACK TO MOVE

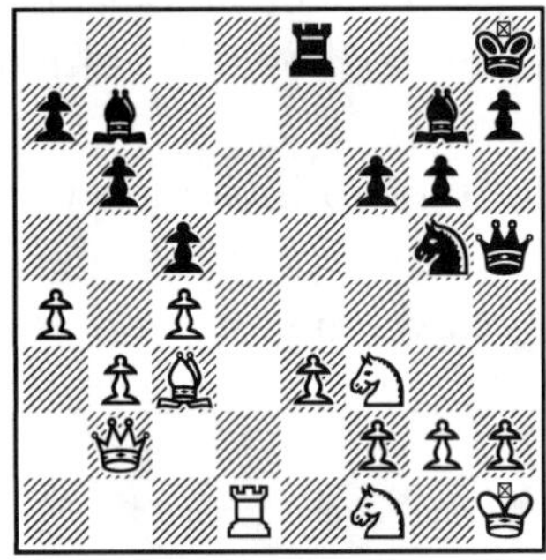

Exercise 5-Black to move

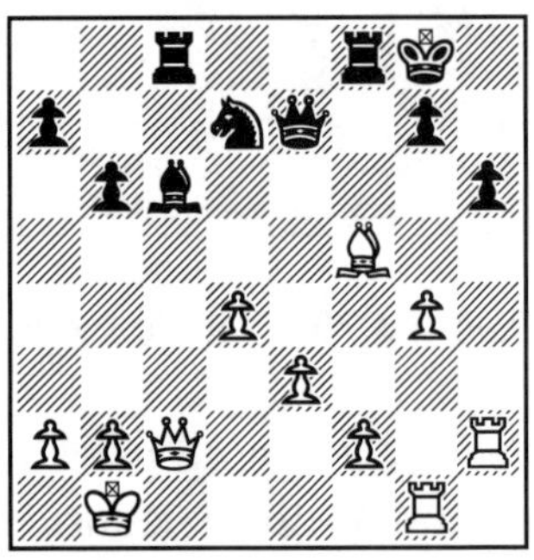

Exercise 6-Black to move

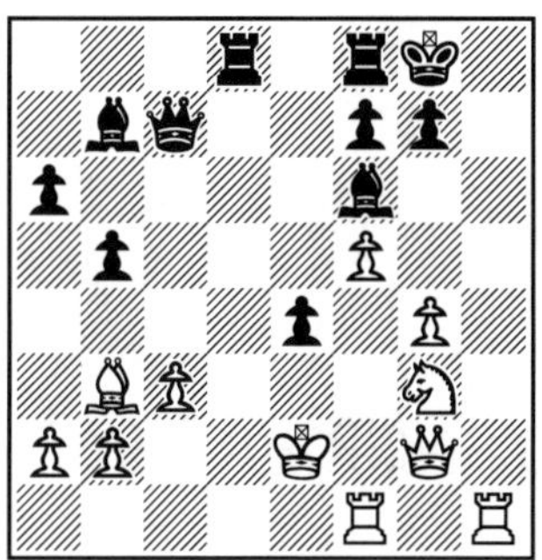

Exercise 7-Black

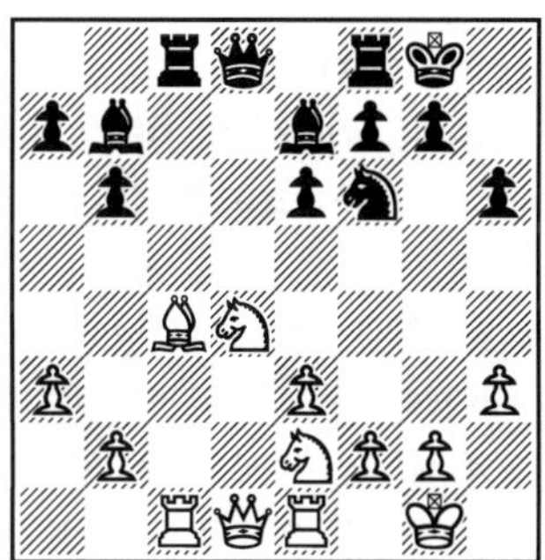

Exercise 8-Black

Solutions:

#5. **1... Qxf3!! 2. gxf3 Bxf3† 3. Kg1 Nh3#.**

#6. **1... Rxf5!** wins the Bishop (if *2. Qxf5, ...Be4†!*; or *2. gxf5 Be4!* wins the Queen).

#7. **1... Rd2†!! 2. Kxd2 e3† 3. Kxe3 Bxg2** wins Queen and Rook (14 points) for Rook, Bishop, and pawn (9 points).

#8. **1... Rxc4! 2. Rxc4 Qd5** wins the Bishop or mates (*3... Qxg2#*).

Chapter 7

COMBINATIONS AND SACRIFICES

No chessman is sacred, except the King.

Strong chessplayers seldom allow opponents to play simple, direct tactics to checkmate or win material; instead, winning tactics must usually be forced or induced. Combinations and sacrifices frequently provide the answer.

A *combination* is a series of forcing moves, often involving a temporary sacrifice of material, which leads to a tactical or positional advantage. The result of a successful combination may range from checkmate to a small positional advantage, or even defensively avoiding or minimizing a disadvantage.

Combinations employ tactical themes to exploit one or more *weaknesses* in the position, and the forcing moves in a combination are typically checks, captures, and threats to check or capture. Combinations arise in superior positions — more active piece placement and sounder pawn structure — resulting from superior positional play. The key to a successful combination, following the usual initial temporary sacrifice, is *rapid and effective follow-up* with accurate tactical moves. Combinations often produce winning advantages in chess games.

Sacrifices — yielding material for an anticipated but uncertain future advantage — are inherently riskier than combinations: the payoff of a combination is clear, immediate, and certain, while the gain from a sacrifice is speculative and long-range. Intermediate chessplayers are advised to concentrate on combinations first, because of their predictable, immediate impact and safety. It should be noted that in conversation chess players often interchange the words sacrifice and combination.

Combinations and sacrifices are played for a variety of important and *specific* purposes, including:

- To checkmate
- To win material
- To develop and maintain the initiative (ability to create threats)
- To eliminate or deflect key defenders
- To weaken or hinder the opponent
- To prevent new Queens
- To expose and restrict the enemy King
- To prevent the opposing King from castling
- To gain time for development
- To open lines for attack
- To improve mobility of pieces
- To simplify into a winning endgame
- To promote a pawn
- To avoid checkmate
- To minimize material loss ("desperado")
- To gain positional advantages, such as gaining access to vital squares, inflicting weak pawns (doubled, isolated, backward), securing a vital outpost for a Knight or other piece, posting a Rook or Rooks strongly on the seventh rank, and creating a pawn majority or passed pawn.

In the following positions, we will explore how these goals were met by successful combinations and sacrifices.

Combinations

A simple endgame combination is illustrated in Diagram 74:

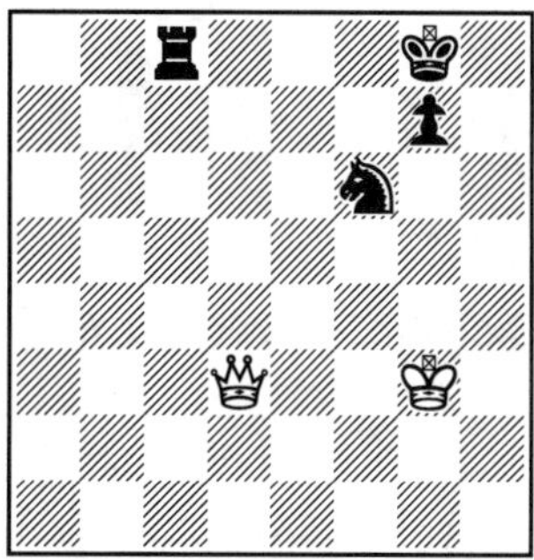

Diagram 74-Black to move

The white King and Queen are aligned on the same rank (a weakness), so Black initiated his combination by playing the forcing Rook sacrifice **1... Rc3!,** pinning the white Queen to the white King. Since Black threatened *2... Rxd3†* winning the pinned white Queen, White responded **2. Qxc3** (other moves do not help). Black continued with **2... Ne4†,** forking the white King and Queen. After the white King moves out of check, *3... Nxc3* wins the white Queen and gives Black a winning endgame (because of the pawn on g7 since a Knight is not enough to win).

A typical middlegame combination is shown in Diagram 75:

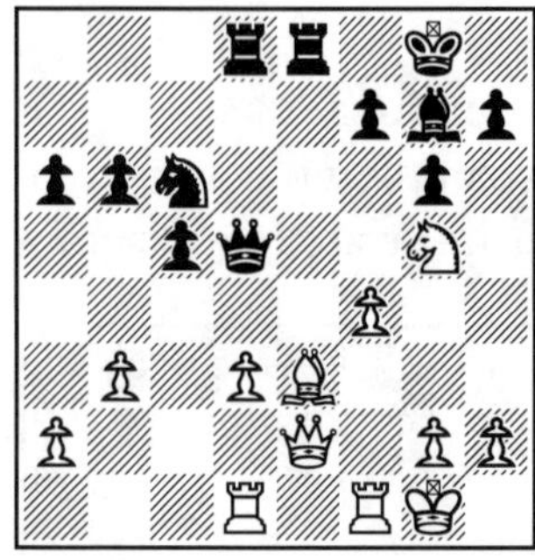

Diagram 75-Black to move

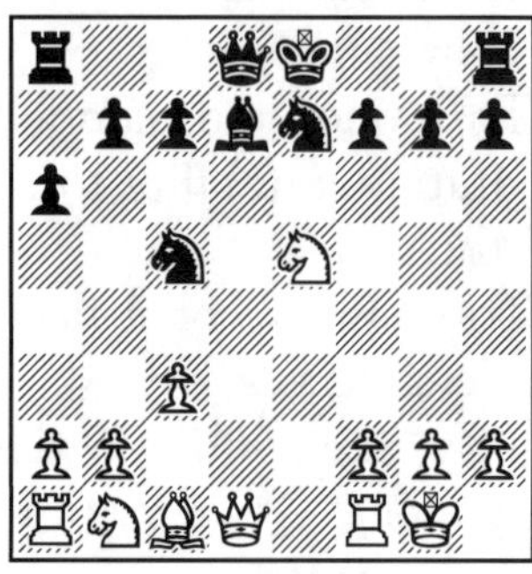

Diagram 76-White to move

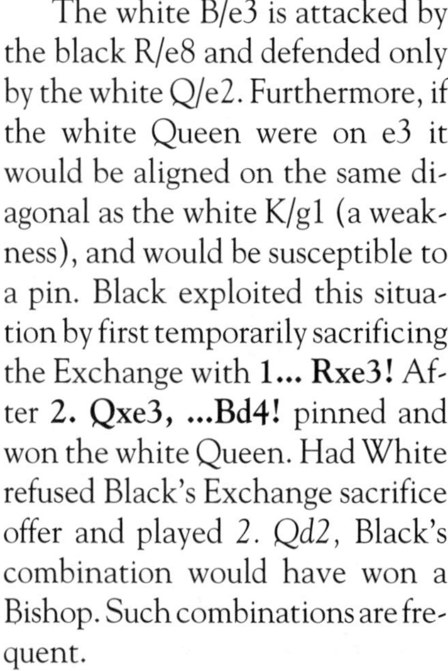

The white B/e3 is attacked by the black R/e8 and defended only by the white Q/e2. Furthermore, if the white Queen were on e3 it would be aligned on the same diagonal as the white K/g1 (a weakness), and would be susceptible to a pin. Black exploited this situation by first temporarily sacrificing the Exchange with **1... Rxe3!** After **2. Qxe3, ...Bd4!** pinned and won the white Queen. Had White refused Black's Exchange sacrifice offer and played *2. Qd2*, Black's combination would have won a Bishop. Such combinations are frequent.

(Note that *1... Bd4* first allows the defense *2. Rf3* and Black wins no material. Timing and sequence of moves are often important in combinations.)

Combinations can also occur in the opening (Diagram 76):

Following several early central exchanges, Black has an unguarded N/c5 — a weakness. White alertly played **1. Nxf7!,** capturing a pawn and threatening *2. Nxd8* (winning the black Queen) or *2. Nxh8* (winning a Rook). After **1... Kxf7 2. Qh5†** (double attack on Black's K/f7 and N/c5) **g6 3. Qxc5,** White has won a pawn and prevented the black King from castling. (Later in the game, the exposed black King was the target of a winning attack by White.)

Every successful combination is based on one or more *weaknesses* in the position. Look for weaknesses!

Specific combinational themes are illustrated in the following examples. In each position, the initial temporary sacrifice in the combination quickly forces a tactical or positional concession from the opponent, immediately gaining a significant or decisive advantage.

Checkmate

Combinations to force or hasten checkmate usually involve removing—eliminating, deflecting, pinning, or blocking — key defenders and vital guards near the enemy King. In Diagram 77, White is on the attack, but Black threatens to win a Bishop (*...Bxh4*). How should White continue to attack?

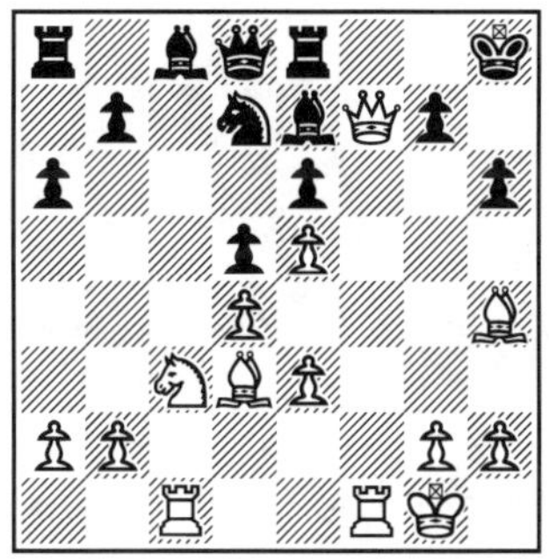

Diagram 77-White to move

White continued **1. Qg6!,** offering to sacrifice his B/h4 by threatening *2. Qh7 checkmate*. Black was forced to decline White's Greek gift offer, and played **1... Nf8,** preventing *2. Qh7 mate* and attacking the white Q/g6. Now both the white Queen and Bishop are *en prise* — what should White do?

The black N/f8 is a vital guard preventing *Qh7 checkmate*. White finished his attack strongly with **2. Rxf8†!,** sacrificing the Exchange to eliminate Black's vital Knight defender. After **2... Rxf8** (*...Bxf8* is also futile), White concluded with **3. Qh7 checkmate.**

White's timely, decisive Exchange-sacrifice combination forced an immediate checkmate.

Mating combinations sometimes follow startling paths — sacrificing the Queen is the boldest, most spectacular tactic. Hopefully decisive, a Queen sacrifice requires accurate foresight and more than a modicum of courage. For a convincing example of a successful mating combination involving a Queen sacrifice, examine Diagram 78:

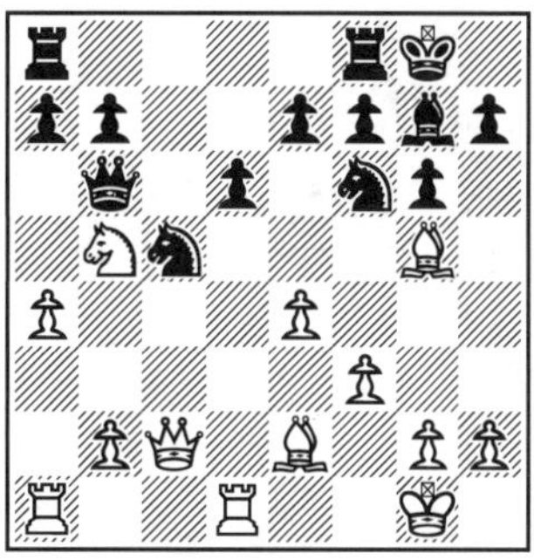

Diagram 78-Black to move

The white K/g1 is aligned on the same diagonal with the black Q/b6 (a tactical weakness). Black can win a Bishop and pawn immediately by playing the discovered check *1... Ncxe4†! 2. Nd4* (if *2. Kf1??, ...Qf2 checkmate!*) *Nxg5*. But Black saw deeper tactical possibilities in the position, and played the stronger **1... Nd3†!** (interfering with the white R/d1's protection of d4 and making *Nd4* ineffective) **2. Kh1 Nf2† 3. Kg1 Nh3‡! 4. Kh1 Qg1†!!** (sacrificing the Queen) **5. Rxg1** (forced) **Nf2 checkmate!** Remember the *tactical hierarchy*, with checkmate as the ultimate goal.

Every piece, including the Queen, is expendable if mate is achieved. Diagram 79 provides another example:

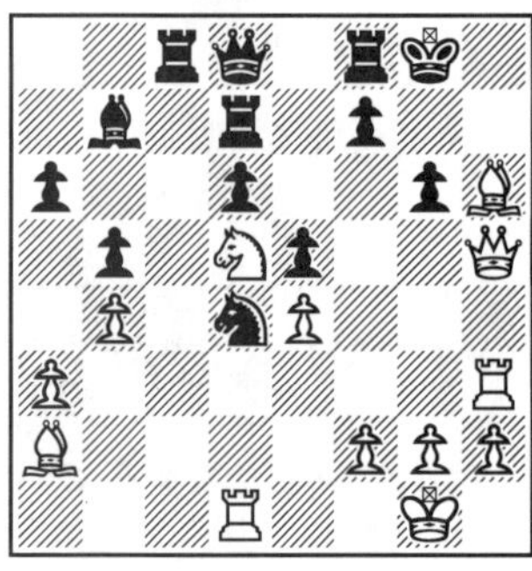

Diagram 79-White to move

Rather than retreat his attacked Queen, White played **1. Qxg6†!!** to force mate: **1... fxg6** (if *1... Kh8, 2. Qg7 mate)* **2. Nf6‡ Kh8 3. Bxf8 mate.** (The less spectacular sacrifice *1. Ne7†!* also forces mate: *1... Qxe7 2. Qxg6† Kh8 3. Qg7* [or *Bg5] mate.)* Material is a weapon to be used — sacrificed if necessary — to promote checkmate.

Win Material

Combinations to win material often require removing important defenders to enable decisive tactics. In Diagram 80, White, the Exchange behind, has just captured a black Bishop with **1. Bxb7,** and now has a double attack on the black R/c8 and a6-pawn. How should Black respond?

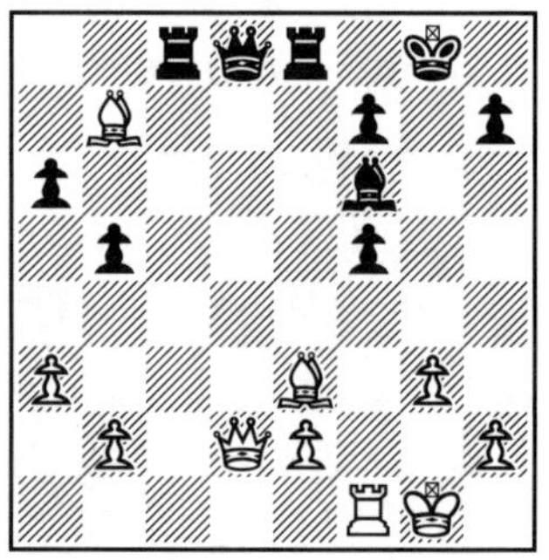

Diagram 80-Black to move

Black alertly played the surprising temporary sacrifice **1... Rxe3!,** capturing the Bishop defending the white Queen. Black is now a Rook ahead in material, and White has only three plausible replies — all lose material. If 1) *2. Bxc8, ...Qxd2* wins the white Queen; if *2) 2. Qxe3, ...Bd4!* pins and wins the white Queen; and if 3) *2. Qxd8, ...Rxd8*, and Black remains a full Rook ahead.

Black's clever and timely combination involving an Exchange sacrifice knocked the pins from under White's position and won decisive material.

Expose and Restrict Enemy King

Exposed or restricted Kings are vulnerable to attack, and combinations to denude or trap the enemy King should always be considered. In Diagram 81, Black has just played **1... Bb7** to protect his pinned N/c6. Can White expose and restrict the black King with a combination, and launch a winning attack, this early in the game?

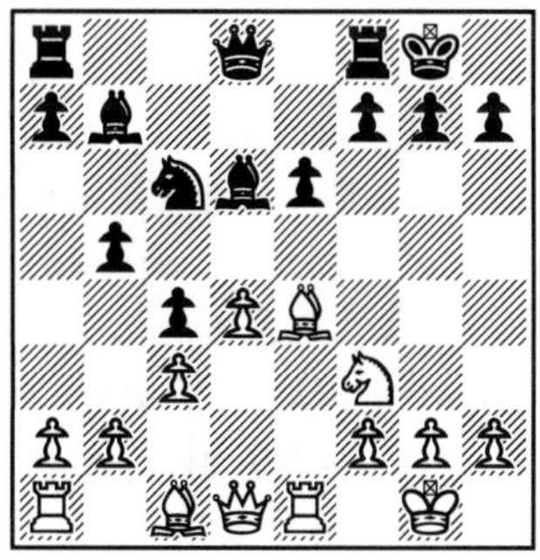

Diagram 81-White to move

Seizing the opportunity to expose the black King and follow up promptly with serious threats, White aggressively sacrificed his B/e4 with **2. Bxh7†!** The game continued **2... Kxh7** (declining the sacrifice with *2... Kh8* and losing only a pawn would have been wiser) **3. Ng5† Kg6** (*3... Kh8* or *3... Kg8* allows a quick mate after *4. Qh5!*) **4. Qg4,** and White threatened *5. Nxe6†* winning the black Queen with a discovered check. To avoid this, Black played **4... Kf6,** also giving his exposed King a safe flight square at e7.

White concluded the game neatly with a second startling sacrifice, **5. Rxe6†!!,** trapping the beleaguered black King on f6 by denying escape via e7. Black's forced reply, **5... fxe6,** enabled White to conclude with **6. Qxe6 checkmate!**

White's combination — first a Bishop sacrifice to expose the black King, then a Rook sacrifice to restrict the black monarch — sealed a convincing early win.

Prevent Castling

Kings stranded on a central file during the middlegame are generally unsafe and vulnerable to attack, so preventing your opponent from castling is usually advantageous and may be worth a pawn or more. In Diagram 82, White has sacrificed a pawn early for accelerated development and open lines, and Black has just played **1... Bg4,** pinning the white N/f3 to the white Queen. What is White's sharpest continuation?

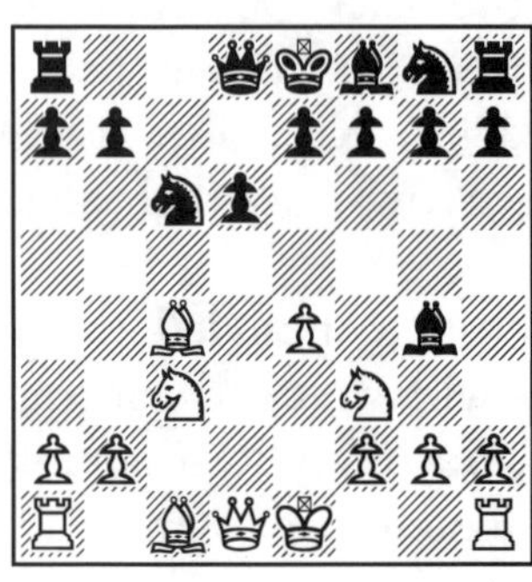

Diagram 82-White to move

White played the sharp temporary Bishop sacrifice **2. Bxf7†!,** and, whether Black recaptures the white Bishop (*2... Kxf7*) or not (*2... Kd7*), White regains his gambit pawn, thus restoring material equality, and forces Black to forfeit castling privileges. Black recaptured **2... Kxf7,** and White continued **3. Ng5† Ke8 4. Qxg4,** regaining his material and stranding the black King in the middle of the board.

White's alert combination won a pawn and denied the black King castling privileges. In the ensuing middlegame, the precarious position of the black King in the center enabled a White mating attack.

Gain Time for Development

Combinations to gain time for development usually occur in the opening, when a weak or imprecise move may allow an opponent to seize the initiative (Diagram 83):

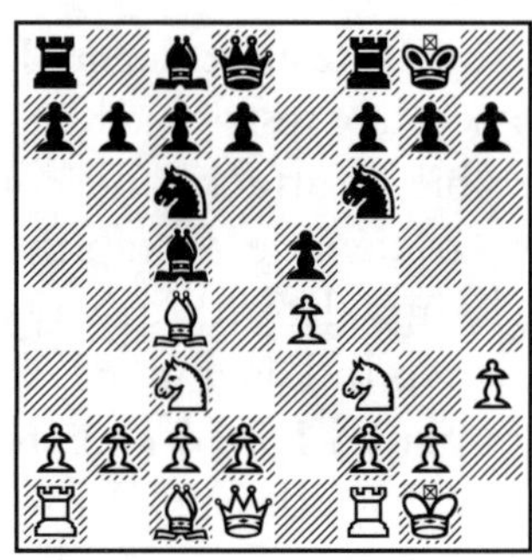

Diagram 83-Black to move

White has just played the weak **1. h3,** which gave Black the opportunity to gain a lead in development with a combination. Black initiated this promptly with **1... Nxe4!,** temporarily sacrificing a Knight for a pawn. After **2. Nxe4 d5 3. Bxd5 Qxd5** Black has regained his material, developed three pieces to White's two, placed a strong center pawn on the fourth rank, and released his B/c8 as well.

Although his combination won no material, Black leads in development and has the initiative in the game.

Open Lines for Attack

Pawns and sometimes pieces may be sacrificed to open attacking lines toward the opposing King, especially when rapid, effective follow-up is possible. In Diagram 84, Black has just played **1... h6,** attacking the white B/g5. What is

White's best reply?

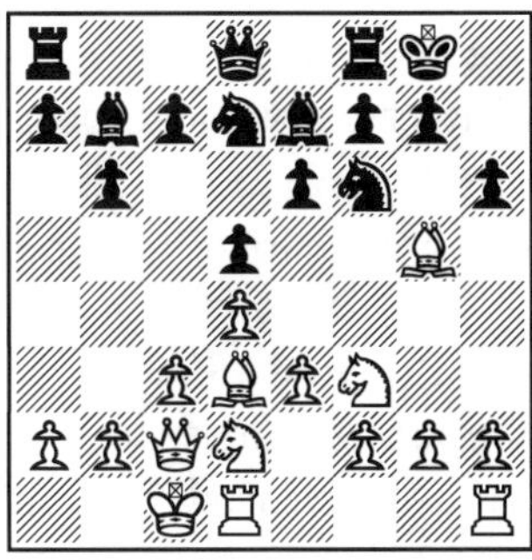

Diagram 84-White to move

White responded with the aggressive **2. h4!,** sacrificing his B/g5 to open the h-file for an attack against the black King. Black unwisely accepted White's Bishop sacrifice with **2... hxg5,** and the game concluded quickly: **3. hxg5 Ng4** (saving the threatened black Knight and threatening *4... Nxf2* winning a pawn and forking the white Rooks) **4. Bh7† Kh8 5. Bg8†! Kxg8 6. Qh7 checkmate!**

White's combination, sacrificing a Bishop, opened a vital line (the h-file) for a swift mating attack against the black King.

Improve Mobility of Pieces

Dormant or blocked pieces can often be activated by combinations that eliminate the restricting blockaders. In Diagram 85 material is even, but White has a dominant position and pressure against the black King. White needs more pieces for a successful Kingside attack, and Black has blocked the central files, immobilizing the white Rooks. In particular, the black e5-pawn blocks the white R/e1 from penetrating to e7 (supported by the white N/d5) with decisive mate threats on h7. How can White mobilize his important attacking R/e1?

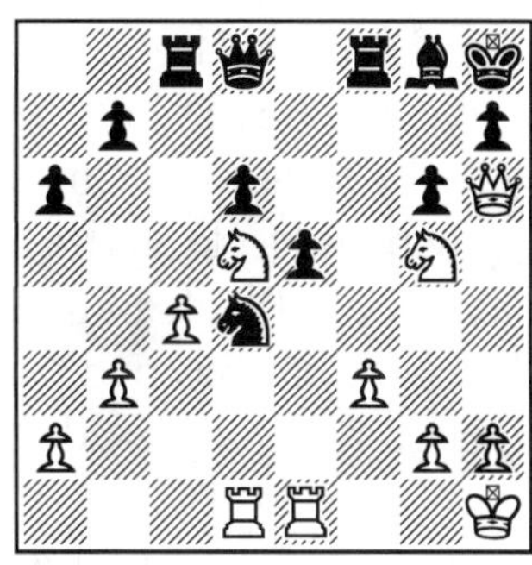

Diagram 85-White to move

White initiated his mobilizing combination with the strong Exchange sacrifice **1. Rxd4!,** winning the black N/d4 if Black does not recapture the white Rook, and mobilizing the other white R/e1 along the e-file if Black does recapture the Rook. The game continued **1... exd4 2. Re7! Qxe7** (to prevent mate on h7) **3. Nxe7 Rce8** (saves the attacked Rook and threatens *4... Re1 checkmate!* if White captures the vital guard of h7 (the black B/g8) with *4. Nxg8??*), allowing the neat finish **4. Nxg6 checkmate!**

White's combination, initiated by an Exchange sacrifice, improved the mobility of his remaining Rook and prepared a decisive attack.

Simplify Into a Winning Endgame

Simplifying combinations (to eliminate pieces or pawns to achieve a winning endgame) are frequently effective, especially when ahead in material. In Diagram 86, Black is the Exchange and a pawn ahead, but White threatens the decisive *Nxe6†!* winning a pawn and forking the black King and Rook. Black can defend with *1... Kf7*, but has two trumps in the position — his passed pawns on the a- and h-files. How can Black assure and hasten his victory?

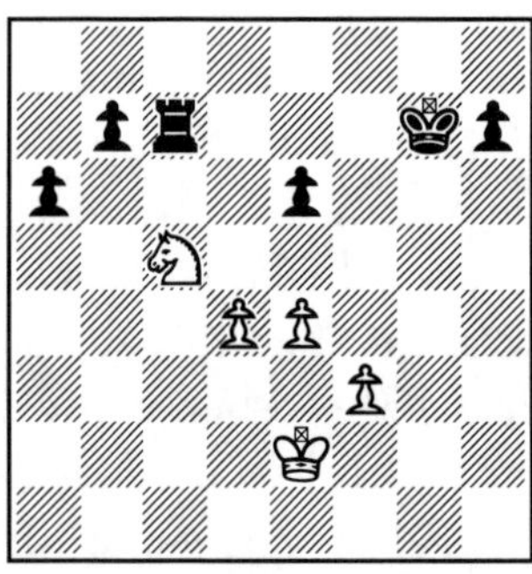

Diagram 86-Black to move

Instead of defending his threatened e-pawn, Black sacrificed his Rook for the remaining white Knight with **1... Rxc5!** After **2. dxc5 h5** White had no queening prospects, and either Black's passed a-pawn or h-pawn will soon queen, assuring Black of victory.

With a timely and appropriate Exchange sacrifice, Black simplified into a winning endgame.

Promote a Pawn

Queening paths for passed pawns may be cleared by combinations that eliminate or deflect blockaders and defenders. In Diagram 87 White has an extra pawn, but Black has a dangerous advanced passed d3-pawn. If Black advances *1... d2?* immediately, *2. Bxd2* wins the impetuous black passed pawn and protects the white R/c1. How can Black force the promotion of his advanced passed d-pawn?

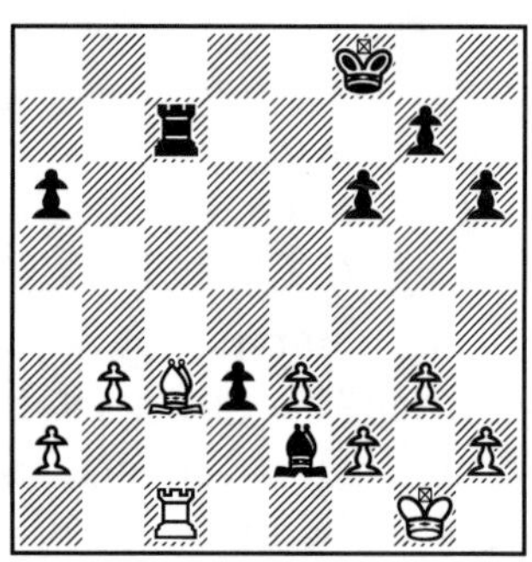

Diagram 87-Black to move

Black sacrificed the Exchange with **1... Rxc3!** to remove the guardian of d2. If White refuses Black's sacrifice (*2. Re1* or *2. Rb1*), then *2... d2* and the black d-pawn will queen. The game continued

2. Rxc3 d2 3. Rc8+ Ke7 (to guard d8) **4. Rc7+ Kd8** and White resigned, as the black passed d-pawn will queen.

Black's timely combination involving an Exchange sacrifice removed a defender and guaranteed the promotion of his passed pawn.

Avoid Checkmate

Checkmate can often be avoided by exchanging defending pieces for attacking pieces, sacrificing if necessary. In Diagram 88, Black has sacrificed his Queen for a mating attack, and threatens ... *Rfg4 checkmate*. White's defensive try *1. Re1* (to provide his King a flight square at f1) would be foiled by *1... Rfg4† 2. Kf1 Rh1 mate*. White is ten points ahead in material(!), but can he avoid checkmate?

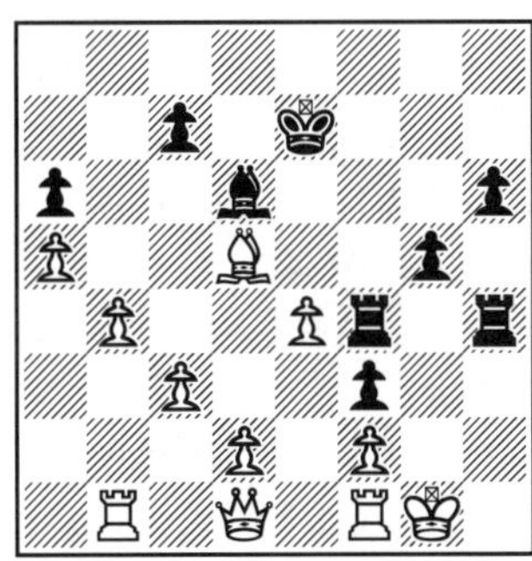

Diagram 88-White to move

White avoided checkmate by sacrificing his Queen for Black's restrictive f-pawn with **1. Qxf3!,** and the white Queen now guards g4, the black Rook's checking square. After **1... Rxf3 2. Rfe1** the white King escaped mate via f1 and e2, and White entered a Rooks-and-Bishop endgame two pawns ahead. Also, *Bb7* soon by White will snare a third black pawn, increasing White's chances for victory.

White's combination — a bold Queen sacrifice — not only avoided imminent checkmate, but also yielded White a winning material advantage in the endgame.

Minimize Material Loss

When a piece is inevitably lost, the material loss can sometimes be minimized by sacrificing the lost piece (a "desperado") for a chessman of lesser value, gaining some material as compensation. In Diagram 89, Black has just played **1... Nxe3,** capturing a Bishop, and threatens *2... Nxd1* winning a Rook or *2... Nxc4* winning a second Bishop. White realizes that if *2. Qxe3 Rxc4*, he would remain a Bishop behind. How can White minimize his material loss?

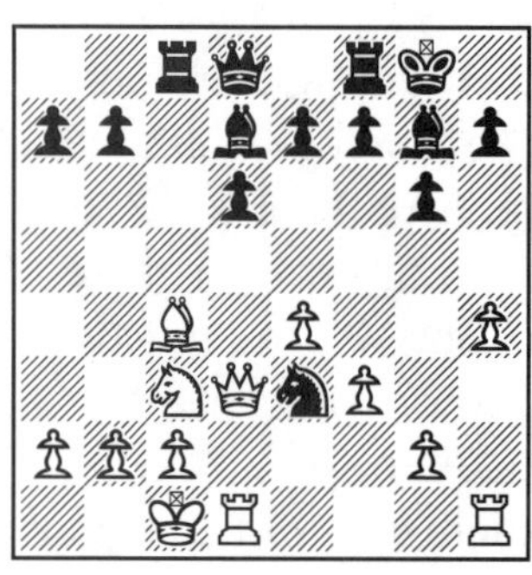

Diagram 89-White to move

White sacrificed his "desperado" B/c4 for a pawn with **2. Bxf7†!** After **2... Rxf7 3. Qxe3** White has reduced his inevitable material loss by one point, better than losing the Bishop outright.

White's combination — the "desperado" Bishop sacrifice — minimized his inevitable material loss.

Gain Positional Advantage

Forcing moves such as checks and captures may force or induce positional weaknesses (e.g., isolated, doubled, or backward pawns). In Diagram 90, White, a pawn behind and his e5-pawn threatened, has just played **1. B/e3-b6,** attacking the black Queen and discovering an attack on the unguarded black N/e4. If *1... Qxb6, 2. Qxe4* regains the piece for White and defends the white e5-pawn. How can Black, a pawn ahead, gain a positional advantage with a combination?

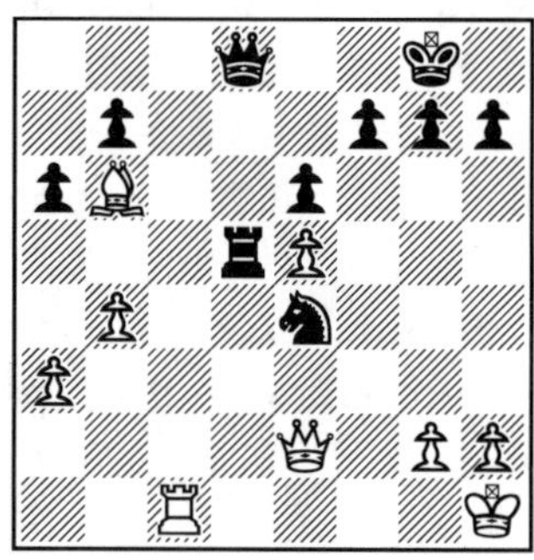

Diagram 90-Black to move

Black temporarily sacrificed his Knight with the in-between move **1... Ng3†!,** forking the white King and Queen and forcing **2. hxg3.** Then Black regained his piece with **2... Qxb6,** leaving White with weak (doubled) Kingside pawns for the endgame.

Black's alert combination — a temporary Knight sacrifice — gained an important positional advantage, as Black remains a pawn ahead in a simplified position and White's weakened Kingside pawn structure will be a serious liability in the endgame.

Sacrifices

Sacrifices — yielding material for anticipated but uncertain future advantages — are speculative and risky, and require excellent judgment, keen foresight, and often superior skill to succeed. For those reasons, sacrifices are more common in the Master domain and are relatively rare at the amateur level ("involuntary" sacrifices — losing material by overlooking opponents' threats — occur more frequently).

The following examples of sacrifices will illustrate their often promising, but always uncertain, nature.

Gain Time for Development (Gambits)

Sacrifices to gain time for development usually occur in the opening, and are called *gambits*. Speculative, gambits (early sacrifices of a pawn or more) are played to gain a lead in development, open lines, control the center, gain the initiative, and create early opportunities for attack (Diagram 91):

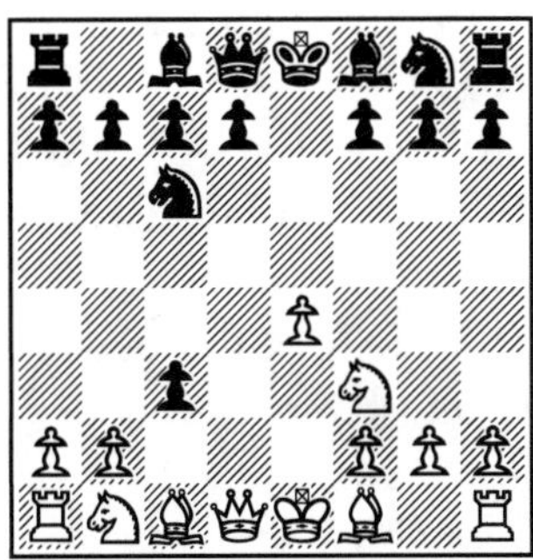

Diagram 91-White to move

White has sacrificed two pawns **(1. e4 e5 2. Nf3 Nc6 3. d4 exd4 4. c3 dxc3)**. Instead of regaining a pawn with 5. *Nxc3* or 5. *bxc3*, White developed a new piece with **5. Bc4.** After **5... cxb2 6. Bxb2** White is two pawns behind in material, but has a strong initiative and a commanding lead in development. The long-term outcome of White's early, speculative pawn sacrifices is uncertain; but White's aggressive Bishops rake Black's undeveloped position, and Black must pursue his lagging development quickly and defend carefully to survive. If Black can reach an endgame, his extra pawns may win.

Open Lines for Attack

Sacrifices to open lines for attack are usually directed toward the enemy King's position to permit attacking pieces to penetrate (Diagram 92):

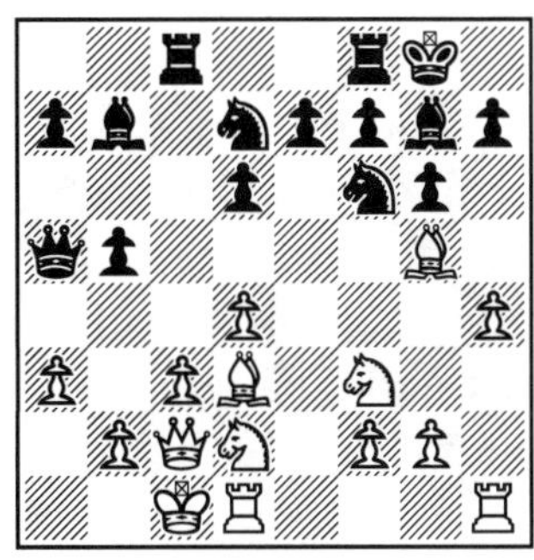

Diagram 92-White to move

White hopes to attack the black King along the h-file, and began with **1. h5,** sacrificing a pawn to open the h-file. Rather than allow *2. hxg6* opening the sensitive h-file, Black responded **1... Nxh5.** White next speculatively sacrificed the Exchange with **2. Rxh5!?** to disrupt the black King's pawn protection. The success of White's speculative sacrifices for a Kingside attack was uncertain, but the game continued **2... gxh5 3. Bxh7†** (regains a pawn and forces the black King to the vulnerable h-file) **Kh8 4. Rh1 f6** (attacks the white B/g5 and creates a flight square at f7) **5. Rxh5!** (sacrificing the B/g5 to attack the black King) **fxg5 6. Bf5† Kg8 7. Be6+ Rf7 8. Qg6!** (threatens *9. Qxf7 mate)* **Rcf8 9. Qh7 checkmate.**

Such spectacular sacrifices require exceptional foresight or intuition, but can produce winning attacks.

Improve Pawn Structure

For an even more farsighted example of a sacrifice, in this instance to establish a central pawn majority and a passed pawn early in the middlegame, consider Diagram 93:

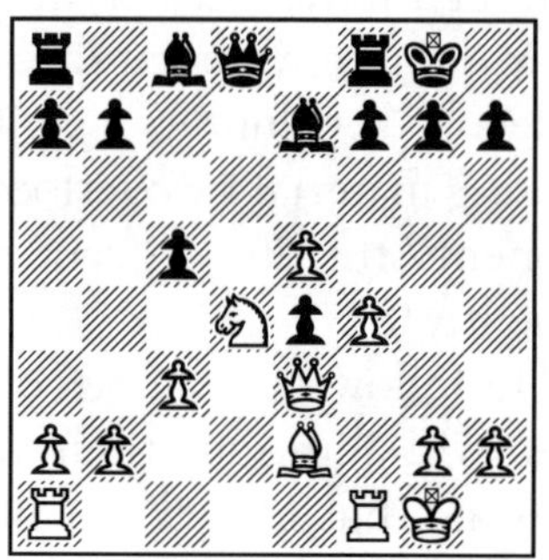

Diagram 93-White to move

Material is even, and Black has just played **1... c5,** attacking the white N/d4. Rather than retreat his threatened Knight, White speculatively sacrificed it for two pawns with **2. Qxe4!? cxd4 3. cxd4,** yielding a strong central pawn majority and a passed d-pawn. White's imposing central pawns proved decisive in just 11 moves: **3... Be6 4. Bf3!** (If *4. Rad1, ...Bd5!)* **Rb8 5. d5 Bc5† 6. Kh1 Bd7 7. f5 Qg5 8. e6 Bb5 9. Rfd1 Rbc8 10. a4! Ba6 11. d6 Rfd8 12. d7 Rc7 13. Qe5! Bb6 14. e7 Resigns.**

White will gain a new Queen or win decisive material.

Establish an Outpost

Diagram 94 illustrates a long-range sacrifice to establish an outpost:

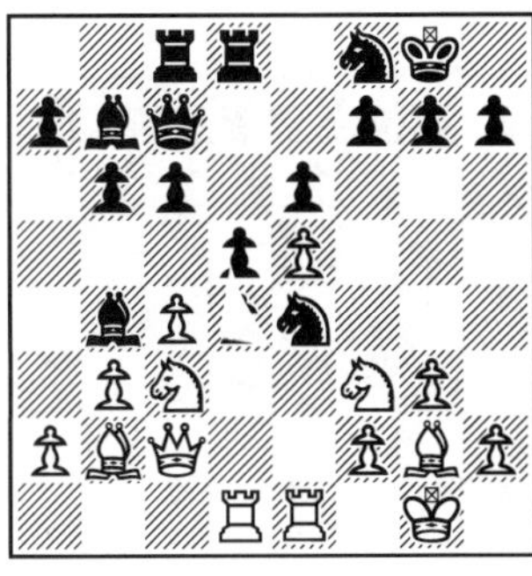

Diagram 94-White to move

In this early middlegame position with all material still on the board and no immediate tactical or attacking opportunities, White sacrificed the Exchange with **1. Nxe4!?** to gain a strong central outpost. After **1... Bxe1 2. Nd6** White obtained as compensation for his Exchange sacrifice a formidable Knight outpost on d6, a significant positional advantage. White reasoned that his secure N/d6 was more valuable than a black Rook in this semi-closed position. The consequences of such a daring, early, speculative Exchange sacrifice are difficult or impossible to foresee; but White's judgment was vindicated in this instance, as he eventually won the game 34 moves later, assisted by his strong Knight outpost.

Sacrifices embody merits and perils. Sound sacrifices can win chess games, and unsound sacrifices can lose chess games. Sacrifices yield no clear, immediate advantages, and, although they are often sound and promising, their risky nature discourages many chessplayers from playing them. Sacrifices represent an advanced level of play, and require sound judgment and extensive experience to succeed.

Unsound Combinations and Sacrifices

Not all combinations and sacrifices succeed — some backfire and lose material with scant, if any, compensation. Usually, the basic flaw in a misguided combination or sacrifice is failure to analyze *all* variations accurately and completely. Relying on an opponent's cooperation, rather than resistance, and overlooking or ignoring the opponent's best defense is also a common self-destructive trait. Two examples of an unsound combination and sacrifice will clearly demonstrate these common faults.

Diagram 95 illustrates a faulty combination involving incomplete analysis and wishful thinking:

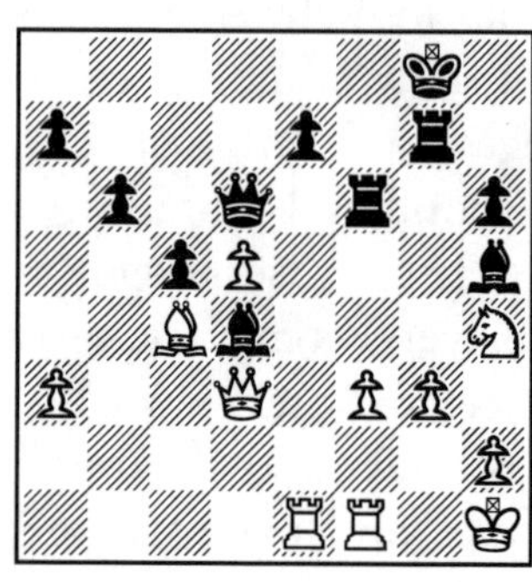

Diagram 95-Black to move

Material is even, and Black saw the possibility of a checkmating combination: *1... Rxg3 2. hxg3 Qxg3 3. Ng2 Qh3 mate*. Accordingly, Black initiated his intended mating attack with the Rook sacrifice **1... Rxg3?** White responded **2. hxg3,** and Black continued **2... Qxg3** as planned, threatening *3... Qh3 mate*. Instead of moving his threatened Knight (or playing *3. Re2*, so if *3... Qh3†* or *3... Qxh4†*, *4. Rh2*), White alertly countered with a mini-combination of his own: **3. Rg1!,** pinning the black Queen to the black King. After *3... Bxg1 4. Rxg1*, impetuous Black will lose his Queen for a Rook, plus a Bishop for two pawns — a net loss of five points.

Black's incomplete analysis and anticipation of cooperation, rather than resistance, from White led him into an unsound and losing combination.

An unsound sacrifice occurred in Diagram 96:

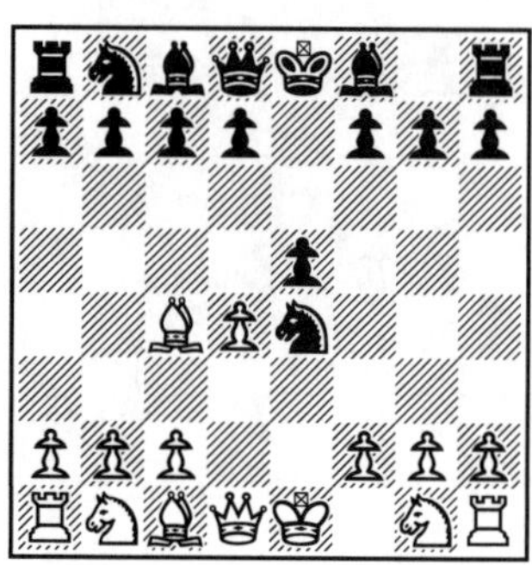

Diagram 96-White

In this opening position (after **1. e4 e5 2. Bc4 Nf6 3. d4 Nxe4),** White saw an opportunity to expose the black King and follow up with tactical threats. So White boldly played **4. Bxf7†?,** and after **4... Kxf7 5. Qf3†** threatened the black N/e4. Black retreated **5... Nf6** to save his Knight and interpose against check, and White continued **6. dxe5,** threatening the pinned N/f6. White's sacrifice appears to be paying off, as he threatens to regain his piece in a favorable position. However, this position is as far as White had calculated, and Black resourcefully responded **6... Qe8!,** counterpinning the white e5-pawn. Play continued **7. Bf4 d6 8. Ne2 dxe5 9. Bg5 Nbd7 10. 0–0 Be7** *(10... Qe6* was more accurate, to prevent *11. Qb3†)* **11. Nbc3 Rf8!** (Black will castle by hand) **12. Bxf6 Nxf6 13. Ne4 Kg8! 14. Nxf6† Bxf6 15. Qb3+**

Qe6 16. c4 b6 17. Rad1 Bb7.

The initial tactical flurry following White's sacrifice has subsided, and Black is a Bishop ahead with a solid position. White has no compensation for his lost piece, and Black won in 27 moves.

White's shortsighted and unsound sacrifice was refuted by accurate defense. When analyzing a contemplated combination or sacrifice, do not draw the curtain too soon!

Inaccurate or incomplete analysis and wishful thinking are the hobgoblins of combinations and sacrifices in chess. Because of the material being risked (and the more material, the greater the risk), it is essential to accurately analyze and carefully evaluate *all* possible responsive sequences of moves when planning a combination or sacrifice. Expect your opponent to find the *best* defense, and you find it first! Play only combinations and sacrifices which are sound in *all* foreseeable variations.

Summary

Combinations involving temporary sacrifices often play an important role on the board. Timely and effective combinations — both offensive and defensive — decide many chess games. All combinations should have a logical foundation and a *specific purpose*, and the key to any combination is *immediate and effective follow-up* with accurate, forcing tactical moves.

Sacrifices, for which the return is speculative and long-term, involve more risk than combinations do, and require greater insight and foresight to justify. The future gains from a sacrifice may be tangible; but expert play is often required to realize any advantage, and if the sacrifice fails, the game may be lost. The best advice is to master safer combinations first, then progress to pure sacrifices after gaining more experience.

Knowing how and when to play combinations and sacrifices is one hallmark of a strong chessplayer. You will learn to play combinations and sacrifices when necessary or expedient through study, practice, and experience. When considering any combination, a helpful technique is to try to refute your own combination. Ask yourself, **"If I were my opponent, how would I respond to these contemplated moves?"** If your proposed combination leads to a clear tactical or positional advantage — and you cannot find any refutation — play the combination with confidence!

Remember, a sacrifice can be accepted or declined. Always analyze both possibilities, whether the sacrifice offered is yours or your opponent's. If accepting an opponent's sacrifice would be dangerous or disadvantageous, decline the sacrifice.

Always remain alert to the opportunity of a winning combination or sacrifice throughout *all* phases of a chess game — opening, middlegame, and endgame. Opportunities for winning combinations and sacrifices are ubiquitous.

Combinations Exercises

Here are four challenging positions involving combinations, with solutions. Good luck with these instructive exercises, and good fortune with winning combinations and sacrifices in your games!

WHITE TO MOVE

Exercise 1-White to move

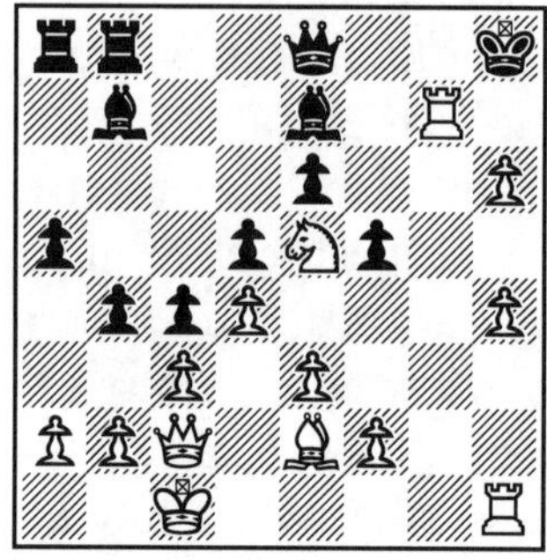

Exercise 2-White to move

BLACK TO MOVE

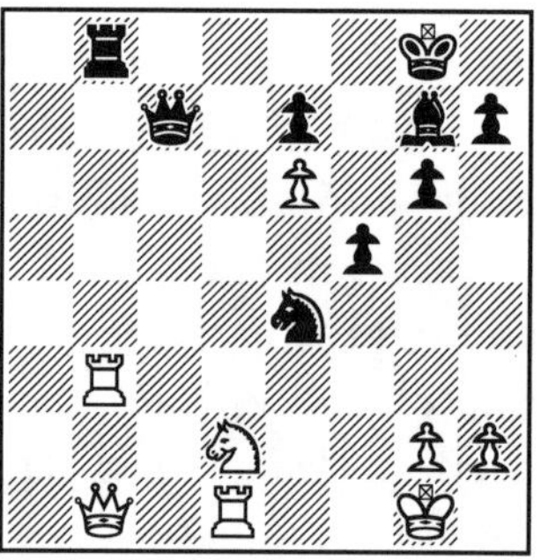

Exercise 3-Black to move

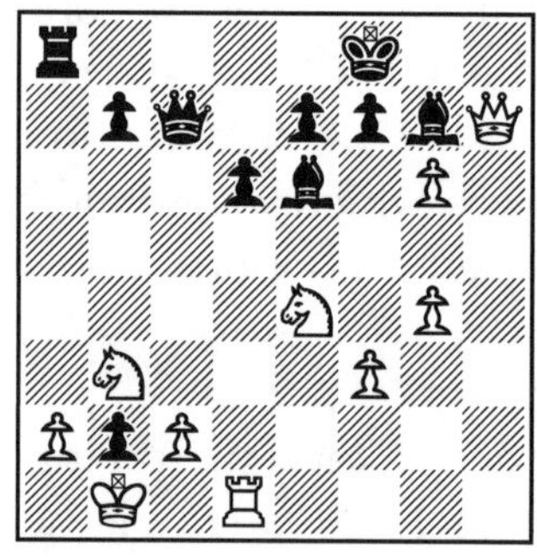

Exercise 4-Black to move

Solutions:

#1. **1. Rxh7†! Kxh7 2. Rh1† Bh6 3. Qf7† Kh8 4. Rxh6 mate.**

#2. **1. Qa4!!** (stronger than *1. Nf7†!* or *1. Ng6†!)* **Qxa4** (otherwise *2. Qxe8† Rxe8 3. Ng6* or *Nf7 mate)* **2. Ng6** (or *Nf7)* **mate.**

#3. **1... Qc5† 2. Kh1** (if *2. Kf1, ...Qf2 mate)* **Nf2† 3. Kg1 Nh3‡! 4. Kh1 Qg1†!! 5. Rxg1 Nf2 mate.**

#4. **1... Rxa2!! 2. Kxa2 Qa5† 3. Kb1 Qa1†! 4. Nxa1 bxa1=Q** (or *...=R)* **mate.**

Chapter 8

ATTACKING THE KING

The King is the primary target!

In chess, as in any conflict, success lies in attack. Checkmating attacks are a frequent and critical feature of middlegames.

Generally, your King must be safe and your position secure before embarking on an attack. Attacks against the enemy King are justified only by existing or potential weaknesses in the opponent's position. Be prepared to attack your opponent's King under these conditions:

- Enemy King is exposed or restricted
- Several of your pieces are near, or aimed at, the opposing King
- Few effective defenders are available near the enemy King

Any two or more of these conditions are a signal to attack.

The usual sequence in a successful checkmating attack is:

1. Open lines toward the enemy King (with pawn exchanges or sacrifices)
2. Penetrate with pieces (to squares near the enemy King)
3. Restrict the enemy King's flight squares
4. Remove key defenders (eliminate, deflect, immobilize)
5. Deliver winning checks

These five steps, in some sequence, are required to checkmate. The King is exposed by opening lines toward it with exchanges or sacrifices. Attacking pieces then penetrate to restrict the opposing King. Vital defenders are eliminated or deflected by exchanges, or sacrifices if necessary. Finally, decisive checks are played to force checkmate. For an attack against a King to succeed, the attacking pieces must expose the King to checks and eliminate safe flight squares.

This normal attacking sequence is illustrated in Diagram 97:

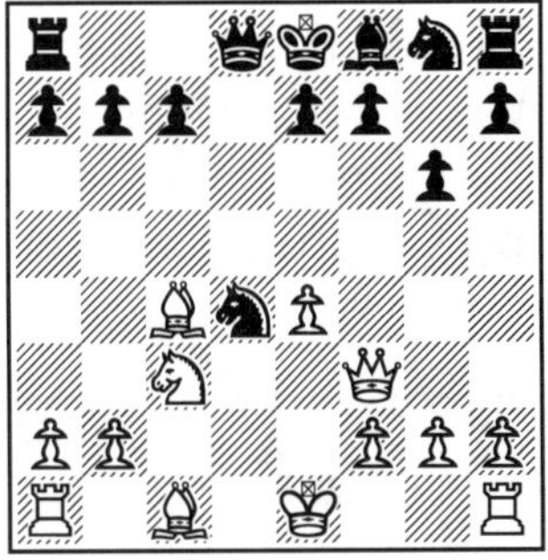

Diagram 97-White to move

Black, lagging in development because of moving pieces twice, has just unwisely won a pawn by capturing **1... Nxd4** with threats: ...*Nxf3* and ...*Nc2†*. But White's lead in development and concerted attack on Black's weak f7-square gave White a winning attack, beginning with **2. Bxf7†,** regaining the pawn and forcing Black to forfeit castling privileges. After the forced **2... Kd7, 3. Qd3** saved the white Queen and pinned the black N/d4 to the black King. Black defended his pinned Knight with **3... c5** (3... Bg7 might be better), and, now that the black King has been exposed, White played **4. Bf4!** to restrict the enemy King's dark flight squares (d6, c7, b8).

Black tried to improve his development with **4... Nf6,** and White continued **5. 0-0-0!** The subtle point of White's Queenside castling is that the white R/d1 now also pins the black N/d4, so the white Queen is now free to attack. Unaware of the impending danger, Black developed his last minor piece with **5... Bg7,** and White continued his attack with **6. Qb5†** (the black N/d4 is pinned by the white R/d1).

After **6... Kc8** (the black King's only safe flight square), White continued the attack with **7. Qxc5†,** removing one defender. Since interposing *7... Qc7??* would allow *8. Qxc7 checkmate*, Black was forced to play **7... Kd7.** White then removed the black King's last defender with **8. Rxd4†.** After **8... Nd5** (a futile interposition), White concluded his attack with **9. Rxd5 checkmate.**

White's forceful winning attack was a clear and convincing example of a superior position — lead in development — and the usual attacking sequence against a King.

Ultimately, in chess there is only one strategy — attack! The general procedure is to select a sector — Kingside, Queenside, or center — *in which you have an advantage*, and attack in that sector, being prepared to defend the others.

The two general strategies for winning a chess game are: 1) checkmating attacks against the enemy King; and 2) attrition — winning material, then simplifying to achieve a won endgame. Attacks sometimes offer a double advantage: a checkmating attack can win the game outright, or force the defender to surrender significant material and enable a win by attrition. When both methods are available, the approach chosen depends on the chessplayer's style and features in the position, primarily relative King safety, piece placement, and material status. Consider Diagram 98:

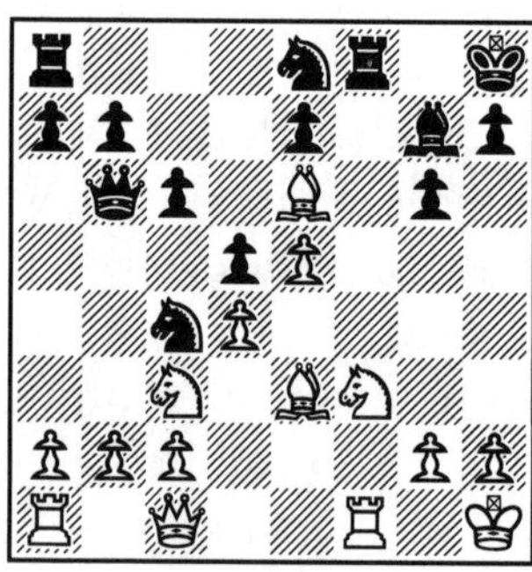

Diagram 98-White to move

White is a Bishop ahead and, with a sound position, can look forward to a nearly certain, if lengthy, win by attrition. However, White elected to return the extra material and attack: **1. Ng5! Rxf1† 2. Qxf1 Nxe3** (regaining the Bishop) **3. Nf7† Kg8 4. Nd8†! Kh8 5. Qf7 Nf6 6. Qg8†! Nxg8 7. Nf7 checkmate.**

A well-conceived attack should strike the weakest link in the defense. When executing an effective plan, your pieces and pawns should operate in concert. Diagrams 99 and 100 demonstrate the coordinated roles of pieces and pawns in attacking an enemy King:

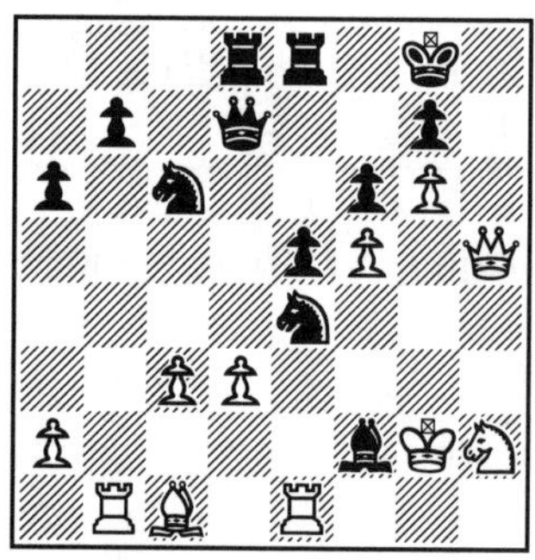

Diagram 99-White to move

The black King is restricted with few defenders nearby, and the white Queen is in the vicinity. Instead of restoring material equality with the safe *1. Rxe4*, White chose to play the imaginative attacking move **1. d4!** to cut off the black B/f2's retreat to c5 (and control of the a3-f8 diagonal). Black captured the white Rook with **1... Bxe1,** winning more material, and White tightened the noose around the black King with **2. Qh7† Kf8 3. Ba3† Nd6** (*...Nc5* leads to the same result; *...Ne7* or *...Qe7* allows *4. Qh8 checkmate*; and *...Qd6* succumbs to *4. Qh8† Ke7 5. Qxg7 mate)*. White culminated his attack against the black King with **4. Qh8† Ke7 5. Qxg7 mate.**

White alertly recognized the conditions for an attack against the black King and swiftly launched a successful attack. The loss of the white Rook was of no consequence, since checkmate leaves no weaknesses in its wake.

Timing can be critical in a mating attack (Diagram 100):

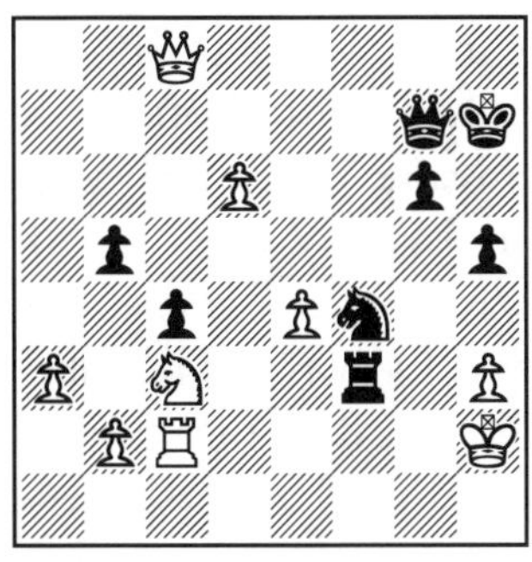

Diagram 100-Black to move

In this tense position, White has just advanced his central passed pawn to d6 and threatens to queen the pawn. But the white King is exposed and restricted with few effective defenders nearby, and Black has pieces near the white King — conditions for a mating attack.

Black continued **1... Rxh3† 2. Kg1 Qd4† 3. Rf2** (if *Kf1??, ...Rh1 checkmate!)*, and now Black can capture the dangerous white passed d6-pawn. Instead, Black chose to continue his attack against the white King with **3... Rh1†** (however truly forcing but prolonging is: 3... Rg3† 4. Kh1 Qxf2 5. Q† Kh6 6. Qh7† Kxh7 and mate in 1 or 4. Kf1 Qd3† 5. Re2 Qf3† 6. Ke1 Rg1† 7. Kd2 Qd3 *checkmate)* forcing **4. Kxh1,** then Black's **4... Qxf2** next threatened *5... Qg2 checkmate*.

White defended resourcefully with **5. Qb7† Kh6 6. e5!,** allowing the white Q/b7 to guard against the threatened mate on g2. Black persevered with the deep attacking move **6... g5!!,** and White advanced his passed pawn **7. d7,** threatening to gain a second Queen on the next move. Black then concluded his attack against the white King with **7... Qh4† 8. Kg1** (forced) **Nh3† 9. Kg2** (better is 9. Kh2 so that the Q/b7 can interpose on g2) **Qf2†!** (sacrificing the black Knight) **10. Kxh3** (if *Kh1, ...Qg1 mate)* **g4 checkmate!** In the final position, Black is a Knight behind in material and White has an advanced passed pawn poised to queen; but again, checkmate leaves no weaknesses.

These two preceding examples clearly illustrate the coordinated role pieces and pawns play in attacks against a King.

A useful technique when attacking a King is to *visualize* your pieces and pawns in an *IDEAL MATE* position, then define the *tasks* and play the moves necessary to reach it. To visualize the IDEAL MATE position, ask yourself, "If I could place any of my pieces and pawns safely on any squares (and remove any enemy pawns and pieces, if necessary), what would I put where, and which enemy pieces and pawns would I eliminate?" As the attack progresses, successive new IDEAL MATES may need to be developed to reflect changes in the position. This approach will enable you to recognize checkmating possibilities earlier, and to plan and play more purposeful mating attacks. Let us explore this technique further as we examine the three general situations which exist for attacking a King: an uncastled enemy King in the center, Kings castled on the same side, and Kings castled on opposite sides.

Uncastled Enemy King

A vulnerable uncastled King in the center can be attacked by opening lines with exchanges or sacrifices to expose it, followed by restricting it with attacking pieces, then delivering winning checks (Diagram 101):

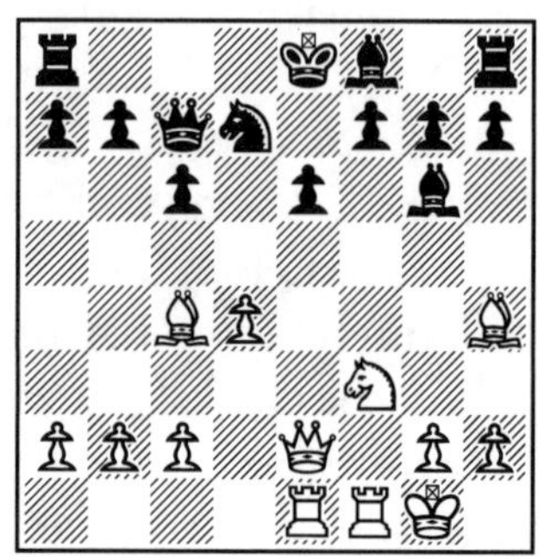

Diagram 101-White to move

White has the requisite superior position for an attack against the black King: all white pieces are developed and poised for attack, while several black pieces are still undeveloped, and the black King is precariously situated in the center of the board. Note especially the pressure of the white Queen and Rook on the e-file toward the black King, and the important white B/h4 which restricts the black King's dark flight squares e7 and d8 and prevents ...*0-0-0*. White sacrificed a pawn to achieve this position, and now needs only to open one or more lines quickly for a virulent attack.

White's initial IDEAL MATE is: white Q/e7, with the black e6-pawn and B/f8 eliminated.

White forcefully initiated his attack with **1. Bxe6!,** offering to sacrifice the Bishop for a pawn (to expose the black King to the power of the white major pieces on the e-file). Accepting the Bishop sacrifice would result in a quick forced mate (*1... fxe6?? 2. Qxe6† Be7 3. Qxe7 checkmate* — the IDEAL MATE), so Black tried **1... Nf6** to interfere with the white B/h4's attack on e7 and allow the black Q/c7 to defend the sensitive e7-square in front of the black King.

But White's attack was too strong. The second IDEAL MATE is: white Q/e6, black K/f7. Accordingly, White continued **2. Bxf7‡,** exposing the black King further. Since *2... Kxf7??* would succumb immediately to *3. Qe6 mate* — the second IDEAL MATE — Black played **2... Kd7** (*2... Kd8* allows mate one move sooner). The revised IDEAL MATE is now: white Q/e8, black K/d8. White concluded his mating attack on the exposed and restricted black King in the center with **3. Qe6† Kd8** (forced) **4. Qe8 checkmate** (the black N/f6 is pinned). A key to White's successful mating attack was visualizing successive IDEAL MATES.

Another example of a winning attack on a vulnerable King in the center is illustrated in Diagram 102:

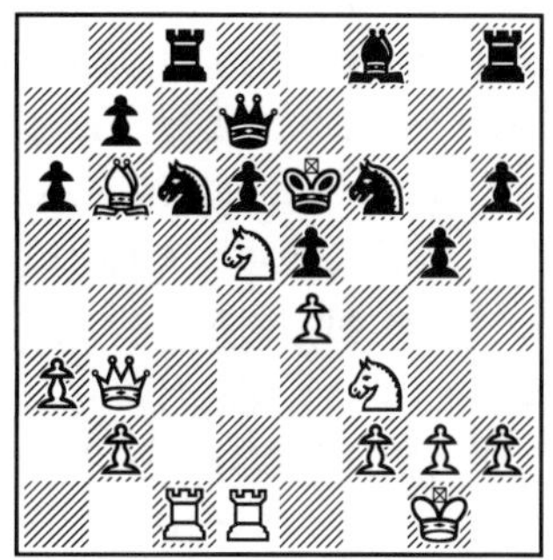

Diagram 102-White to move

In this more complex position, the uncastled black King is exposed and restricted in the center of the board, and all white pieces are poised to attack. The initial IDEAL MATE is: white N/c7, white Q/e8, black K/d8. But first, some key Black defenders, especially the Queen, must be eliminated. White began his assault with the double-check **1. Nc7‡** to open an attacking line for the white Queen and restrict the black King's flight squares, especially e8. (*Note: 1. Nf4‡ Ke7 2. Ng6†* would have won a Rook, but White was intent on checkmate.) After Black's forced **1... Ke7,** White went after the black Queen, a vital defender, by taking advantage of the pinned black d6-pawn with the preparatory Exchange sacrifice **2. Rxc6!,** removing a defender of the black e5-pawn. Black recaptured **2... bxc6** (*2... Qxc6?* allows the white Queen to penetrate decisively with

3. Qe6†, followed by a swift mate). White then continued **3. Nxe5!,** attacking the black Queen.

Since the black Queen's only safe move, *3... Qd8??* (although *3... d5* does prolong the game), allows the immediate *4. Qf7 checkmate!*, Black, material ahead as the result of White's recent Exchange sacrifice, surrendered his Queen for a Rook and Knight with **3... dxe5.** White continued **4. Rxd7†,** and Black responded **4... Kxd7** (if *4... Nxd7?, 5. Qe6+ Kd8 6. Qe8 checkmate* — the IDEAL MATE).

Now that White's preliminary exchanges have opened attacking lines toward the black King, eliminated key defenders, and severely restricted the black monarch, White concluded his well-conceived mating attack in strong style with **5. Qe6† Kd8** (forced) **6. Nd5† Rc7** (another forced move) **7. Bxc7 checkmate** — a modified version of the IDEAL MATE.

Kings Castled on the Same Side

With Kings castled on the same side — either Kingside or Queenside — the primary attack on the enemy King is usually conducted with pieces rather than pawns, since advancing pawns toward the opposing King to open lines with pawn exchanges would normally expose your own King to attack.

For an attack against a castled King to succeed, the enemy King's protective pawn shelter must usually be weakened or partially removed, usually by forcing or inducing one or more of these pawns to move or capture. Attacking pieces can then penetrate to the squares weakened by the pawn moves to restrict and check the King, rendering mating attacks possible. To illustrate, let us begin with Diagram 103:

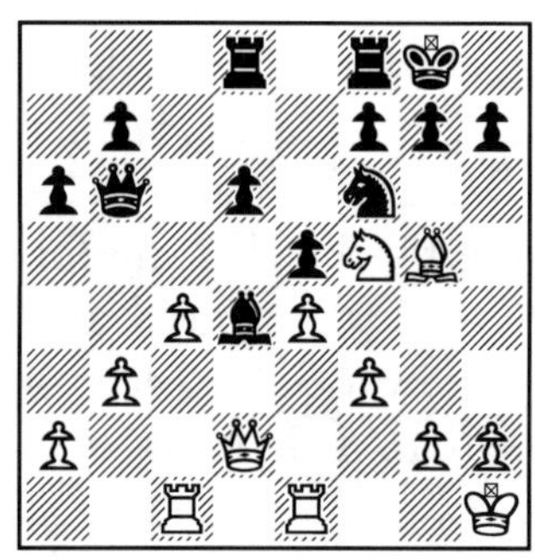

Diagram 103-White to move

The initial IDEAL MATE is: white Q/g7 supported by the white N/f5. The white Queen's path to g7 is via g5 or h6, so one of these squares must be made available. The interfering white B/g5 attacks the black N/f6 defended by the black g7-pawn, which also guards h6. Therefore, White began his attack by clearing the diagonal for his Queen with **1. Bxf6!** Black realized that recapturing the Bishop with *1... gxf6* would permit the white Queen to penetrate immediately and decisively with *2. Qh6* and *3. Qg7 checkmate* — White's IDEAL MATE — so Black let the captured Knight go and saved his threatened Rook with **1... Rc8** (*1... d5* prevents the mate although Black would lose a lot of material), leaving the g7-pawn to guard the h6-square. White relentlessly pursued his attack with **2. Qg5,** threatening *3. Qxg7 mate* — the IDEAL MATE. To prevent this, Black was forced to respond **2... g6** (finally, the pawn moves), but to no avail. White could have achieved his IDEAL MATE with *3. Qh6* and *4. Qg7 mate*, but instead simply played **3. Nh6 checkmate.**

Visualizing the IDEAL MATE in the initial position was the key to White's swift and successful mating attack.

A more sophisticated example of attacking a castled King by weakening its protective pawn shelter is shown in Diagram 104:

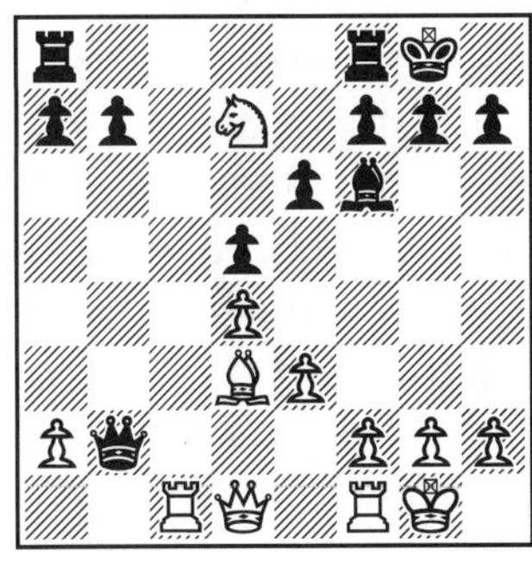

Diagram 104-White to move

The initial IDEAL MATE: white Q/h7 supported by the white B/d3. White, already a Knight ahead for a pawn, can win the Exchange with *1. Nxf8* or disrupt the castled black King's protective pawn shelter with *1. Nxf6†*. Instead, White chose **1. Qh5!,** threatening *2. Qxh7 checkmate* — the IDEAL MATE. Black realized that preventing immediate mate by *1... g6?* would lose the Bishop to *2. Nxf6†* with no abatement in White's attack, so Black moved **1... h6** — the weakening pawn advance White was seeking — whereupon White captured **2. Nxf6†** to further weaken the black King's pawn shelter. After **2... gxf6 3. Qxh6,** the black King's pawn protection has been stripped away and White has renewed the threat of *4. Qh7 checkmate* — White's IDEAL MATE. Black defended against immediate mate with **3... f5** to block the line of the supporting white B/d3.

With the black King's protective pawn shelter in shambles, the new IDEAL MATE is: white Q/h6, white R/g3, black K/g8. Therefore, White continued his attack with **4. f4!,** preparing the Rook "lift" *Rf3-g3 mate*. Black counterattacked with **4... Qd2** (again, a move like *4... Rfc8* will prolong the game), threatening to capture the white B/d3, the white e3-pawn with check, or the white R/c1 with check if White continued 5. *Rf3*. Undeterred, White boldly played **5. Rf3!,** sacrificing his R/c1. After **5... Qxc1† 6. Bf1** Black, faced with *7. Rg3 mate*, advanced **6... f6** to provide his threatened King a flight square at f7. With the black King's weakened pawn shelter nearly nonexistent, White neatly concluded his mating attack with **7. Qg6†!** (depriving the black King of the f7 flight square) **Kh8** (forced) **8. Rh3 checkmate** — a variation of White's second IDEAL MATE.

To expose and checkmate a castled King, its protective pawn shelter can often effectively be partially *removed* by sacrificing one or more *pieces*, especially if the enemy monarch has few defending pieces available. Pawns protecting the castled King become targets for demolition, particularly if they have advanced (Diagram 105):

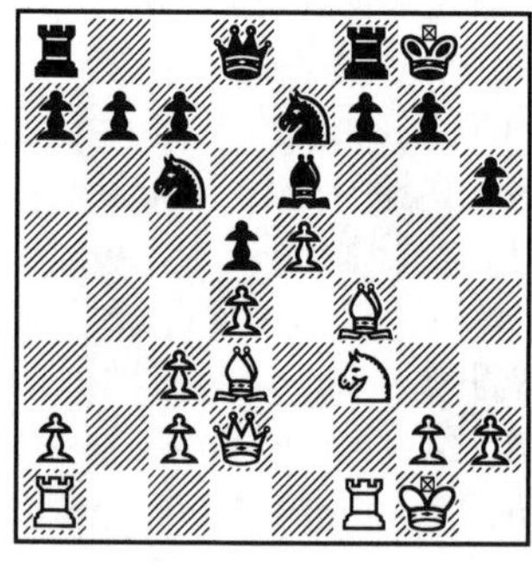

Diagram 105-White to move

The IDEAL MATE is: white Q/h7 supported by the white B/d3 (or N/g5), black K/g8, and black R/f8. Having just castled on the previous move, Black had earlier unwisely advanced his h-pawn (*...h6)* to prevent a possible pin of his N/e7 by a white Bishop on g5. This hapless black h-pawn near the black King is now a ripe target. White promptly sacrificed a Bishop with **1. Bxh6!** to remove the protective pawn. Black recaptured **1... gxh6** (*1... Nf5* would have been wiser), and after **2. Qxh6** the black King's protective pawn shelter has been all but removed. White now threatened *3. Qh7 checkmate* — the IDEAL MATE.

Black defended with **2... Ng6** (*2... Nf5* makes it tougher for White), blocking the line of the supporting white B/d3. White continued the attack against the exposed and restricted black King with **3. Ng5!,** renewing the threat of *4. Qh7 checkmate* — the IDEAL MATE. Black moved **3... Re8** (*3... Qxg5* should have been considered) to provide his beleaguered King a flight square at f8. White then concluded his mating attack in convincing fashion with **4. Qh7† Kf8 5. Rxf7†!** (the last protective black pawn is removed) **Bxf7** (forced) **6. Qxf7 mate.**

White's final mate was based on pursuit of the initial IDEAL MATE.

When there are few defending pieces nearby to protect an opposing castled King, a piece can often be effectively sacrificed to remove a vital — although unmoved — pawn, thus exposing the enemy King to a mating attack (Diagram 106):

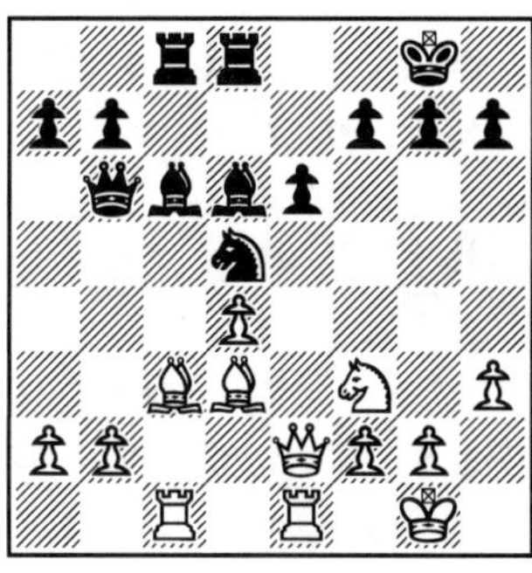

Diagram 106-White to move

Although perhaps obscure at first, the IDEAL MATE is: white Q/h8, black K/f8, and black e6- and h7-pawns removed. The pawn shelter protecting the castled black King is intact; but no black pieces are nearby to assist in protecting the King, and several white pieces are aimed at the black King's vulnerable position. White exploited this tactically volatile situation by sacrificing a Bishop with **1. Bxh7†!** to expose the black King. There followed **1... Kxh7** (*1... Kf8*, giving up the pawn but keeping the black King sheltered, would have been more prudent) **2. Ng5†** (to allow *Qh5*) **Kg8** (the apparently risky *2... Kg6* would have offered more resistance). White pursued the attack with **3. Qh5,** threatening a forced checkmate in six moves (*4. Qxf7† Kh8 5. Qh5† Kg8 6. Qh7† Kf8 7. Qh8† Ke7 8. Qxg7† Ke8 9. Qf7 mate*).

Black defended against White's threatened mate with **3... Be8** (*3... Rd7* is tougher), protecting the f7-pawn against the mate-initiating *4. Qxf7†*. But White followed with a second startling sacrifice, **4. Rxe6!!,** attacking the black King's flight square at e7 and threatening mate in two (*5. Qh7† Kf8 6. Qh8 checkmate* — the IDEAL MATE). Black was thus "forced" to accept White's stunning Rook sacrifice with **4... fxe6,** and White neatly concluded his mating attack against the exposed and restricted black King with a forced mate in four moves: **5. Qh7† Kf8 6. Qh8† Ke7 7. Qxg7† Bf7 8. Qxf7 mate.**

Visualizing an IDEAL MATE in the initial position enabled White to plan and execute a sophisticated and successful sacrificial mating attack.

As illustrated, the lack of nearby defending pieces (in *addition* to a protective pawn shelter) can be devastating to an enemy castled King.

Kings Castled on Opposite Sides

With Kings castled on opposite wings, pawnstorms — advancing pawns toward the opposing King to open lines with pawn exchanges — are the usual method of attack. After lines are opened and the King exposed, attacking pieces can penetrate to restrict the enemy King and deliver winning checks. The side succeeding in opening lines first usually wins. This attacking sequence is illustrated in Diagram 107:

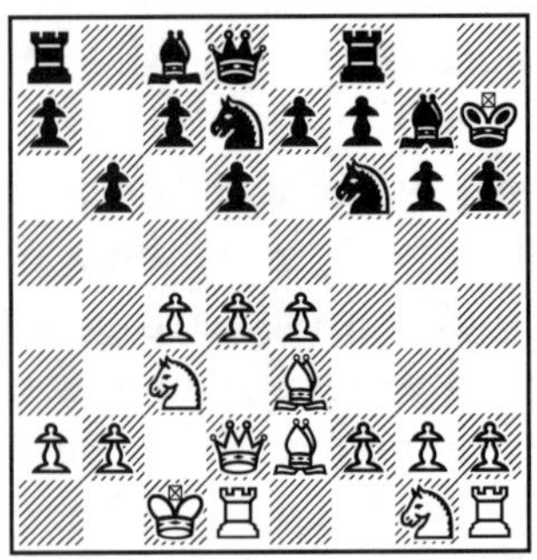

Diagram 107-White to move

With no precise IDEAL MATE in mind, but with the general plan of exposing and attacking the black King, White decided to launch an early Kingside pawnstorm with **1. g4!,** threatening *2. g5!* to force open the h-file. To avoid any immediate Kingside line-opening, Black retreated **1... Ne8.** The rest of White's successful attack is thematic (note how White opens attacking lines toward the black King with pawn exchanges and penetrates to the resulting weak squares with his pieces), and White's moves are clear and instructive: **2. h4 Bb7 3. f4 f6 4. Nf3 Rc8 5. h5! g5 6. e5! Bxf3 7. Bxf3 fxe5 8. Be4†! Kh8 9. fxg5 exd4 10. gxh6! dxe3 11. hxg7† Nxg7 12. Qxe3 Nf6 13. Qh6† Kg8 14. Bg6! e5 15. g5! Nge8 16. gxf6 Nxf6 17. Rhg1 Qe7 18. Be8† Resigns.** Mate is forced.

After initial line-opening pawn exchanges during a pawnstorm, a castled King can sometimes be driven from a safe or semi-safe pawn shelter into a mating net of hostile pieces and pawns (Diagram 108):

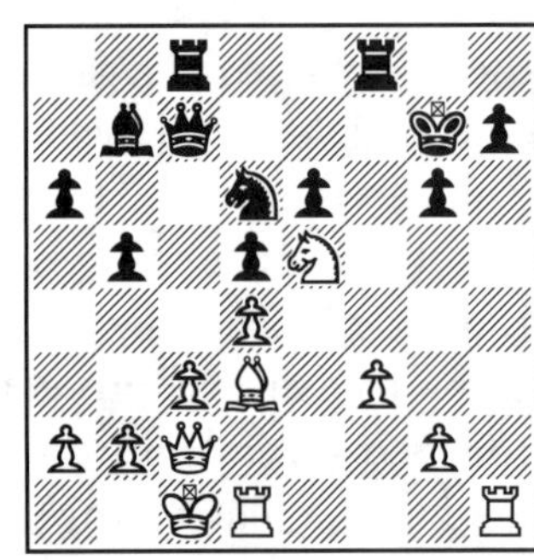

Diagram 108-White to move

White has half-opened the h-file with a partial pawnstorm by advancing his h-pawn and exchanging it on g6. White's initial IDEAL MATE is: white Q/g6 supported by the white N/e5, black K/

g7 with the black h7-pawn eliminated. Accordingly, White sacrificed his interfering Bishop with **1. Bxg6!** Since *1... hxg6??* would allow *2. Qxg6 checkmate!* — the IDEAL MATE — and White also threatened *2. Rxh7†* winning the black Queen with a skewer, Black moved his King with **1... Kf6.** White envisioned forcing the black King forward into a mating net of white Kingside pawns and pieces, and followed with **2. Rxh7** to restrict the black King's retreat; *2. Rxh7* also wins a pawn and attacks the black Q/c7, gaining a tempo in the attack.

After **2... Qa5, 3. Ng4†!** took the black King on a fatal stroll in which each lethal step was forced: **3... Kg5 4. Rh5+ Kf4 5. Qd2† Kg3** (one last step) **6. Rh3 checkmate.**

For a final example of a well-conceived attack against a King castled on the opposite wing, examine Diagram 109:

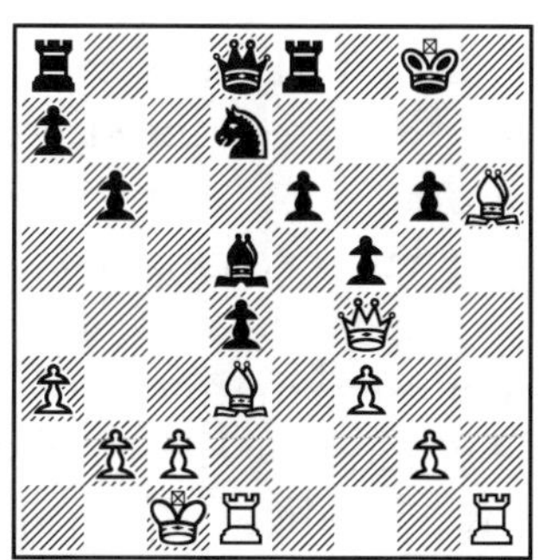

Diagram 109-White to move

The first obvious IDEAL MATE is: white Q/g7 supported by the white B/h6, black K/g8. However, if *1. Qxd4* (threatening *2. Qg7 mate*), *...Qf6!* thwarts White's attack. Therefore, another IDEAL MATE must be developed.

White visualized a second IDEAL MATE: white Q/h8, white R/h7, black K/f7 (forced there by a white Queen-check on h8). White defined his tasks to reach the IDEAL MATE as:

- Move the white Bishop off the h-file
- Move the white Queen to the h-file
- Prevent *...Nf8* from defending h7, the white Rook's mating square

White began his attack with **1. Bb5!,** attacking and pinning the black N/d7, a potential vital guard against checkmate. Black responded **1... e5,** protecting his extra pawn on d4, and attacking the white Queen. After **2. Qg3** (threatening *3. Qxg6†*), Black defended with **2... Bf7** (though *2... Re6* offers more flexibility).

Rather than capture the black Knight immediately, White saved a tempo in his attack with the finesse **3. Bg5!** — after **3... Qc8 4. Bxd7 Qxd7** the black Queen has been forced to move twice. White then zeroed in on the black King with **5. Qh4,** threatening 6. *Qh8 mate*. To give his King flight squares along the a2-g8 light diagonal, Black defended with **5... Bc4.** The black King now has a safe flight square at e6, so that flight square must be removed and the IDEAL MATE revised.

White envisioned a third IDEAL MATE: white Q/f6, white R/h8, black K/g8. White accomplished this IDEAL MATE with the forcing continuation **6. Qh8† Kf7 7. Qf6†! Kg8 8. Rh8 checkmate.**

By visualizing successive IDEAL MATES and defining the tasks and moves necessary to achieve checkmate, White developed and executed a well-planned and convincing mating attack.

Note: Although White was the attacker in the preceding examples, Black often has similar opportunities to attack the white King. The methods and techniques of attacking a King are identical for both sides.

Attack Guidelines

The following tips may be of help in your attacking plans:

- Attacks on a wing are usually best met by a counterthrust in the center, so control or close (i.e., "block") the center before launching a wing attack on the enemy King.
- Disguise your plans by playing the least committal moves first when preparing an attack.
- Look for ineffective or awkwardly placed defenders of the enemy King — they will facilitate your attack.
- Fortune favors the bold in chess, and the attacker has the advantage — slight mistakes by the attacker often lose only the initiative, whereas errors by the defender are apt to be more serious, and can prove fatal.
- Avoid premature, unjustified, and insufficiently prepared attacks — they can boomerang and leave your pieces scattered and vulnerable to a vigorous counterattack.

Summary

For an attack on a castled *or* uncastled King to succeed, attacking lines must be opened toward the King with exchanges or sacrifices to expose it, and attacking pieces must penetrate to weak squares around the King to restrict it (deny safe flight squares) and deliver winning checks. A castled King's protective pawn shelter must usually be weakened or partially removed, and key defenders must often be eliminated or deflected by exchanges or sacrifices.

Visualizing a possible IDEAL MATE position early can be extremely effective when attacking a King. Even if modified several times, an IDEAL MATE provides a useful map to checkmate.

Exercises on Attacking the King

Attacking the King is the most important aspect of chess, with checkmate the ultimate goal. For your practice in attacking a King, following are four instructive exercises. For maximum benefit, play *slowly*, and apply what you have learned.

BLACK TO MOVE

Set up this position, cover the moves, and find the best attacking moves for Black. Tally your correct moves to determine your strength in this game.

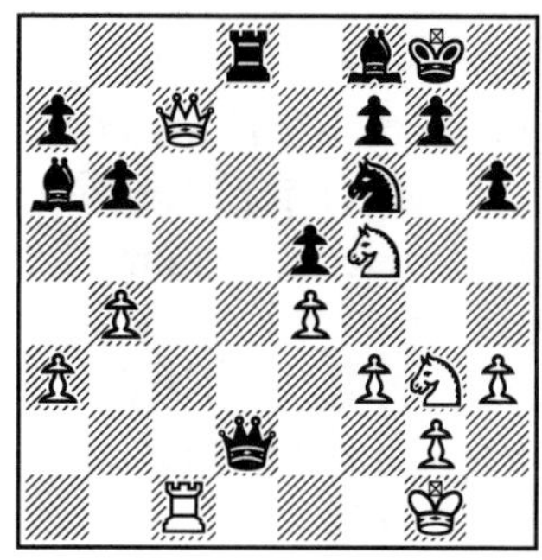

Diagram 110-Black to move

COVER UP:

1. ... Bc5†!

Wins the Exchange — the Bishop-check interferes with the white Queen's protection of the R/c1. *1... Rc8* also has its interesting points.

2. Rxc5

If *2. bxc5, ...Qxc1†*; or *2. Kh2 Rc8 3. Qxa7 Qxc1 (4. Qxa6?? Qg1 mate!)*.

2. ... bxc5

Gains the Exchange before continuing the attack.

3. Qxa7

Wins the pawn, threatens *Qxa6*.

3. ... Qe1†

Confines the white King to h2, allows the R/d8 to enter the attack.

4. Kh2

If *4. Nf1?, ...Qxf1† 5. Kh2 Rd2! (6. Nh4 g5!)*.

4. ... Rd1!

Threatens *...Qg1 mate*.

5. Ne7†

Vacates the f5-square with tempo (check) for the N/g3 (to free the g3 flight square for the white King).

5. ... Kh7

Avoids further checks.

6. Ngf5

Provides the g3 flight square for the white King.

6. ... Qg1†

Forces the white King toward the black Knight and pawns; seals off the f2 flight square.

7. Kg3

The white King's only flight square.

7. ... Nh5†

Forces the white King to abandon defense of the g2-pawn.

8. Kh4

If 8. *Kg4?, ...Qxg2†* and 9. *Kxh5* (or *Kh4*) *Qg5 mate*; or 9. *Ng3 Qxg3† 10. Kxh5* (or *Kf5*) *Qg5 mate*.

8. ... Qxg2

Threatens *...Qg5 mate*.

9. f4

Defends against *...Qg5 mate* (if 9. *Kxh5, ...Qg5 mate)*.

9. ... g5†!

Traps the white King.

10. Kxh5

On *10. fxg5, ...Qxg5 mate*.

10. ... Be2 mate

Correct Moves:	*Your Strength*
9-10	Outstanding
7-8	Superior
5-6	Excellent
3-4	Good
1-2	Fair

WHITE TO MOVE

Set up this position, cover the moves, and find the best attack for White. Tally your correct moves.

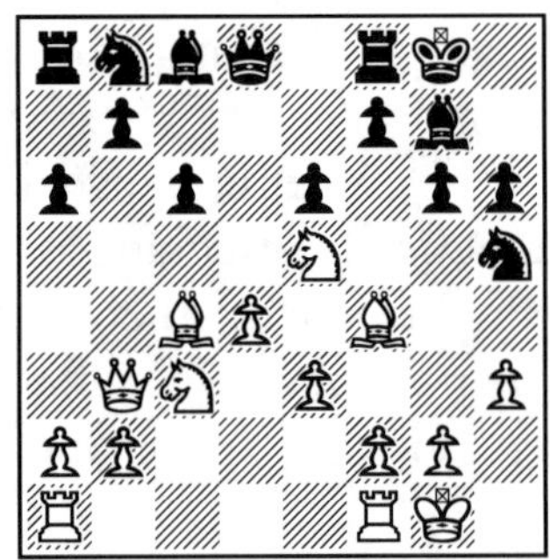

Diagram 111-White to move

COVER UP:

1. Bh2

Preserves the Bishop and avoids doubled pawns.

1. ... Nd7

Planning *...Nxe5* or *...Nb6*, but obstructs the B/c8.

2. Nxf7!

Disrupts Black's castled position, threatens *Nxd8*.

2. ... Kxf7

If *...Rxf7, 3. Bxe6* pins and wins the black R/f7.

3. Bxe6†

Exposes the black King, gains a second pawn for the sacrificed Knight.

3. ... Ke8

If *...Ke7, 4. Ne4* threatens *5. Bd6†* skewer.

4. Bd6

Restricts the black King, attacks the R/f8.

4. ... Rf6

The only "safe" square; if *...Rh8??, 5. Bf7 mate.*

5. Ne4

Wins the Exchange, at least.

5. ... Nc5

Counterattacks the white Queen; also threatens *...Rxe6*.

6. Nxf6†

Wins the Exchange (priority of check).

6. ... Nxf6

Returns the black Knight to play.

7. Bf7†

Vacates e6 for the white Queen after the forced *...Kd7*.

7. ... Kd7

The only choice.

8. dxc5

Wins more material and threatens *Qe6 mate*.

8. ... Qa5

Provides a flight square (d8) for the black King. The mate can be stopped by *8... Nd5*.

9. Qe6†

Closes in on the black King.

9. ... Kd8

The black King's only move.

10. Qe7 mate

Correct Moves:	*Your Strength*
9-10	Outstanding
7-8	Superior
5-6	Excellent
3-4	Good
1-2	Fair

BLACK TO MOVE

Cover the moves and find the best moves for Black. Tally your correct moves.

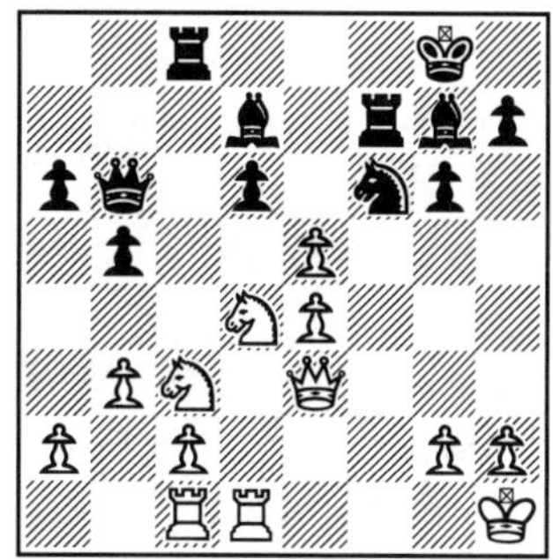

Diagram 112-Black to move

COVER UP:

1. ... dxe5

Recovers a pawn, saves the N/f6, threatens the N/d4.

2. Nce2

Defends the N/d4, but *Nf5!* saves the Knight because of the threat on the black Queen.

2. ... exd4

Wins Knight for pawn.

3. Nxd4

Gains a pawn for the Knight, centralizes the Knight.

3. ... Ng4

Attacks the white Queen and f2-square.

4. Qd2

Saves the Queen, protects the doubly attacked N/d4; if *4. Qd3?, ... Nf2†* wins the Queen.

4. ... Bh6

Sharp move wins the Exchange (also credit for *...Nf2†*).

5. Qb4

Saves the Queen, protects the N/d4.

5. ... Bxc1

Wins Rook for Bishop.

6. Rxc1

Recovers a Bishop for the lost Rook.

6. ... Rxc2!

Threatens *...Rxc1 mate*, deflects the N/d4 (opens g1-a7 diagonal for the black Queen).

7. Nxc2

If *...Rxc2??, Rf1 checkmate!*

7. ... Nf2†

Initiates mate.

8. Kg1

The white King has no choice.

8. ... Nh3‡!

Closes the mating net.

9. Kh1

The white King's only move.

9. ... Qg1†!!

This startling Queen sacrifice forces mate on the next move.

10. Rxg1

White's only legal move.

10. ... Nf2#

A classic smothered mate.

Correct Moves:	*Your Strength*
9-10	Outstanding
7-8	Superior
5-6	Excellent
3-4	Good
1-2	Fair

WHITE TO MOVE

Play a winning attack for *White*. Tally your correct moves.

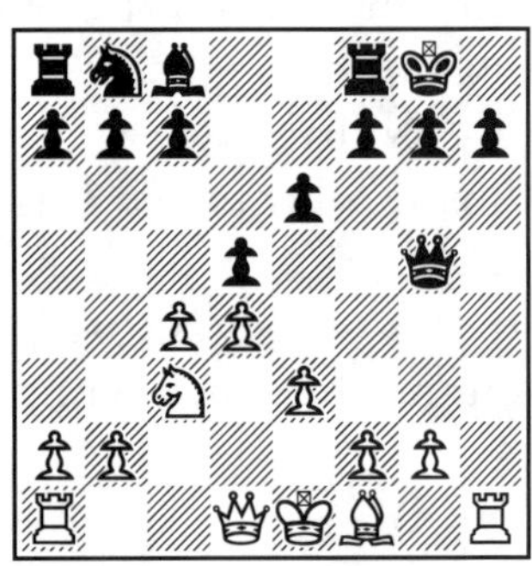

Diagram 113-White to move

COVER UP:

1. Qc2

Threatens *Qxh7 mate*.

1. ... Qg6

Defends against the mate threat, offers Queen trade.

2. Bd3!

Attacks the black Queen and h7-pawn.

2. ... f5

Interposes the attack on the black Queen.

3. cxd5

Prevents *...dxc4*, deflecting the well-placed B/d3.

3. ... Qxg2

Wins a pawn, threatens *...Qxh1†*.

4. 0-0-0

Saves the R/h1, connects Rooks, safeguards the King.

4. ... exd5

Regains the pawn; Black is plus-2 pawns.

5. Rdg1

Attacks the black Queen, aligns with the black King.

5. ... Qf3

The black Queen's only safe move.

6. Nxd5!

Regains one pawn, centralizes the Knight.

6. ... Nd7

Develops a piece, headed for f6 to reinforce the Kingside; if *6... Qxd5?, 7. Bc4!* pins and wins the black Queen.

7. Ne7†

The Knight encroaches on the black King.

7. ... Kh8

On *...Kf7, 8. Nxf5* restores material equality with a superior White position.

8. Qe2!

Forces the black Queen to abandon her attack on the h1-square.

8. ... Qxe2

The black Queen has no safe retreat square.

9. Rxh7†!!

Rook sacrifice forces quick mate.

9. ... Kxh7

The black King has no choice.

10. Rh1†

The confined black King is trapped.

10. ... Resigns

10... Qh5 11. Rxh5 mate.

Correct Moves: ..... Your Strength

9-10 .... Outstanding
7-8 .... Superior
5-6 .... Excellent
3-4 .... Good
1-2 .... Fair

Chapter 9

CHECKMATE PATTERNS

Checkmate is the goal of chess!

Checkmating attacks are a frequent feature of the middlegame. To play them successfully, a chessplayer must learn to coordinate the various pieces involved.

Numerous basic mating patterns are illustrated in this chapter. Only minimum material is shown, to highlight the essential features (most of these checkmating patterns actually arise with other chessmen on the board). Study these important skeleton patterns carefully, and learn to recognize the existence or possibility of similar patterns in your games.

Checkmate consists of two elements: the enemy King must 1) be in check, and 2) have no means of escaping check (capture attacker, interpose, or move to safe flight square). The mating pieces coordinate to achieve these elements.

The following checkmating patterns are organized according to the MATING and supporting pieces involved:

- QUEEN and King
- QUEEN and Rook
- QUEEN and Bishop
- QUEEN and Knight
- QUEEN and Pawn
- QUEEN
- ROOK and King
- ROOK and Queen
- ROOK and Rook
- ROOK and Bishop
- ROOK and Knight
- ROOK and Pawn
- ROOK
- TWO BISHOPS and King
- TWO BISHOPS and Knight
- BISHOP, KNIGHT, and King
- KNIGHT and Bishop

A diagram of each of these basic checkmates appears in each section, followed by other variations. Study the diagrams, and set up the variations on a board to become familiar with the mating possibilities of various combinations of pieces. The Queen is involved in the vast majority of checkmates, so pay particular attention to the role of the Queen.

Queen and King

Diagram 114

Variations:

	White	Black
#1	Q/b8 K/e6	K/e8
#2	Q/c8 K/f6	K/e8
#3	Q/g7 K/f6	K/h8
#4	Q/g8 or h6 K/f7	K/h8

Queen and Rook

Diagram 115

Variations:

	White	Black
#1	Q/g8 R/a7	K/e8
#2	Q/c8 R/a7	K/e8
#3	Q/g7 or h7 R/a7	K/h8
#4	Q/h8 R/h1	K/g8 P/f7, g7
#5	Q/h7 R/h1	K/g8 R/f8 P/f7, g7

Queen and Bishop

Diagram 116

Variations:

	White	Black
#1	Q/g8	K/h8
	B/c4	
#2	Q/h4	K/h8
	B/c4	P/g7
#3	Q/c7	K/c8
	B/g3	
#4	Q/h8 or g7	K/g8
	B/b2	P/f7, g6, h7
#5	Q/g7	K/g8
	B/h6	P/f7, g6, h7
#6	Q/d8	K/g8
	B/h6	P/f7, g6, h7

Queen and Knight

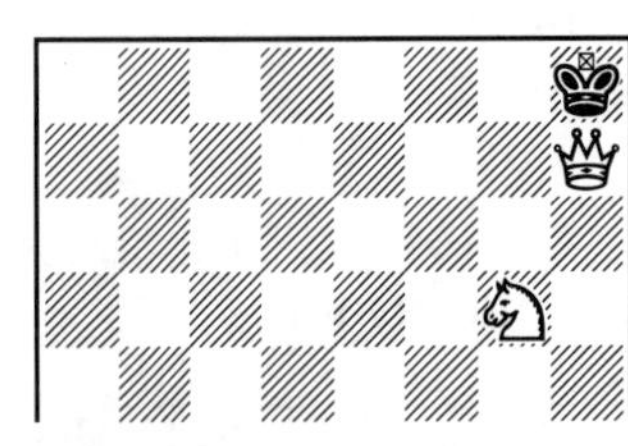

Diagram 117

Variations:

	White	Black
#1	Q/h7	K/g8
	N/g5	R/f8
		P/g7
#2	Q/g7	K/g8
	N/f5	
#3	Q/g8 or h7	K/h8
	N/f6	

Queen and Pawn

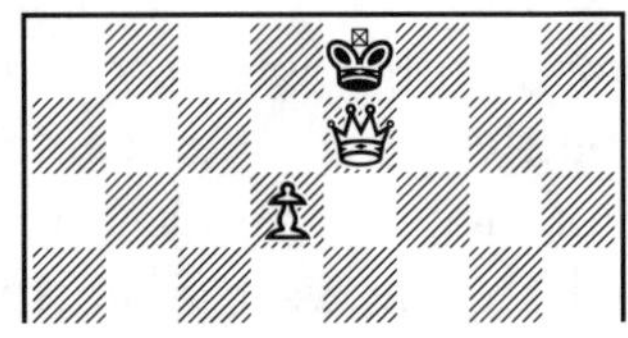

Diagram 118

Variations:

	White	Black
#1	Q/g7	K/h8
	P/f6 or h6	
#2	Q/g7	K/g8
	P/f6 or h6	P/f7, g6, h7
#3	Q/h7	K/g8
	P/g6	R/f8
		P/g7

Queen

To checkmate alone, a Queen requires the cooperation of opposing pawns or pieces:

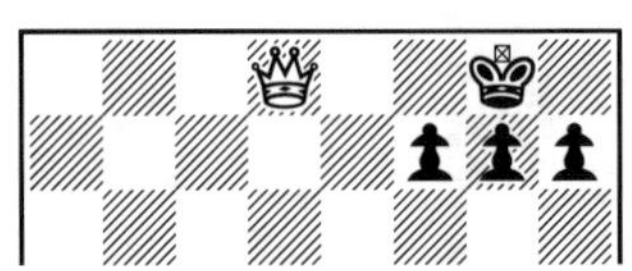

Diagram 119

Variations:

	White	Black
#1	Q/f8	K/h8
		P/h7

#2	Q/h6	K/h8
		R/g8
#3	Q/e6	K/e8
		R/d8, f8

Rook and King

Diagram 120

Variations:

	White	Black
#1	R/b8	K/h8
	K/g6	
#2	R/h1	K/h8
	K/f7	

Rook and Queen

Diagram 121

Variations:

	White	Black
#1	R/a8	K/f8
	Q/c7	
#2	R/h1	K/h8
	Q/e7	R/g8
#3	R/h8	K/g8
	Q/h3	P/f7, g7
#4	R/h8	K/g8
	Q/d4	P/f7, g6
#5	R/d8	K/g8
	Q/h6	P/f7, g6, h7
#6	R/g1	K/g8
	Q/d4	R/f8
		P/f7, h7
#7	R/h1	K/h8
	Q/c4	P/g7

Rook and Rook

Diagram 122

Variations:

	White	Black
#1	R/h7	K/g8
	R/g7	R/f8
#2	R/h8	K/g8
	R/h1	P/f7, g7

Rook and Bishop

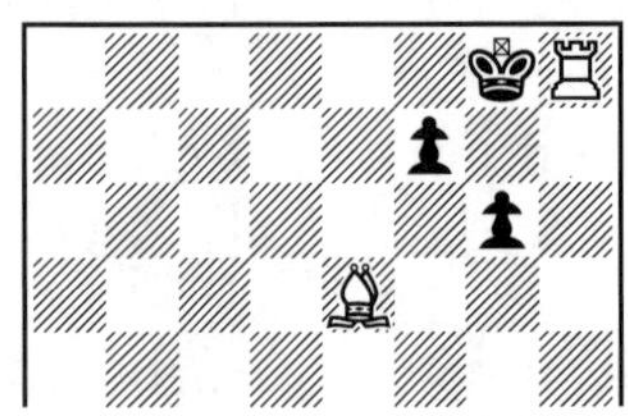

Diagram 123

Variations:

	White	Black
#1	R/d8	K/g8
	B/h6	P/f7, g6, h7
#2	R/g1	K/g8
	B/b2	R/f8
		P/f7, h7
#3	R/h1	K/h8
	B/c4	P/g7
#4	R/h7	K/h8
	B/d3	R/g8

Rook and Knight

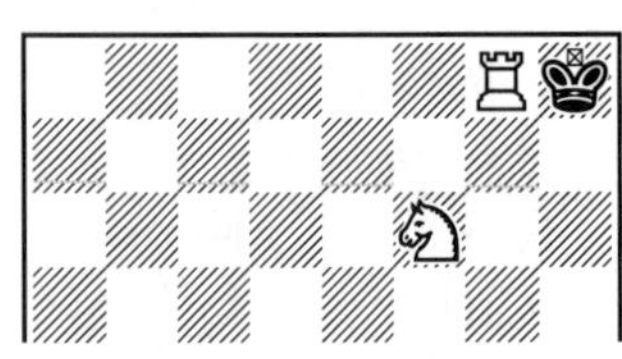

Diagram 124

Variations:

	White	Black
#1	R/h7	K/h8
	N/f6	
#2	R/h1	K/h7 or h8
	N/e7	P/g7
#3	R/e6	K/e8
	N/e5	R/d8, f8

Rook and Pawn

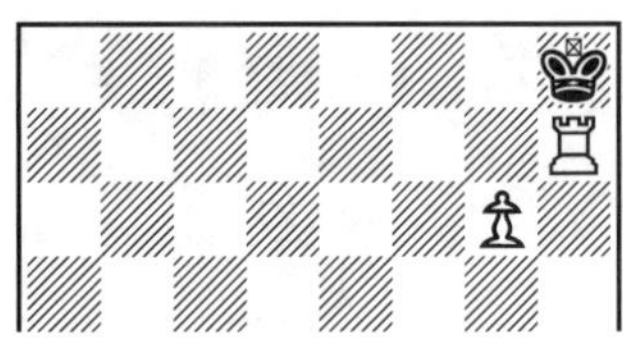

Diagram 125

Variation:

	White	Black
#1	R/h1	K/h8
	P/f6	R/g8

Rook

To checkmate alone, a Rook requires the cooperation of opposing pawns or pieces:

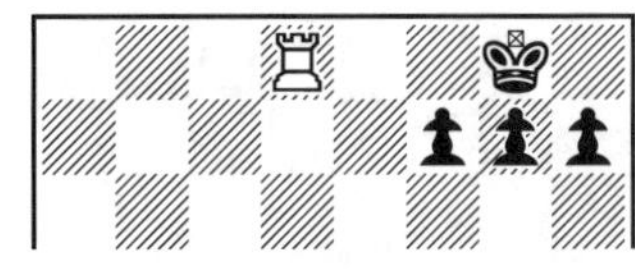

Diagram 126

Variations:

	White	Black
#1	R/e8	K/g8
		B/h7
		P/f7, g7, h6
#2	R/f8	K/h8
		N/g7
		P/h7

Two Bishops and King

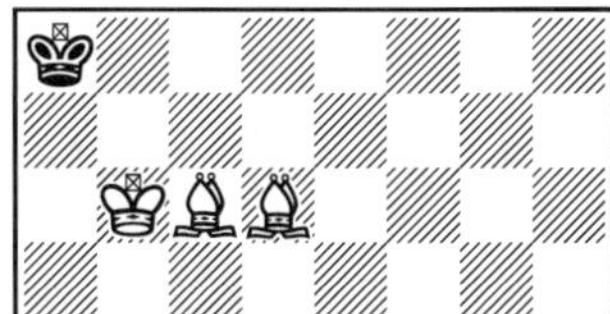

Diagram 127

Two Bishops and Knight

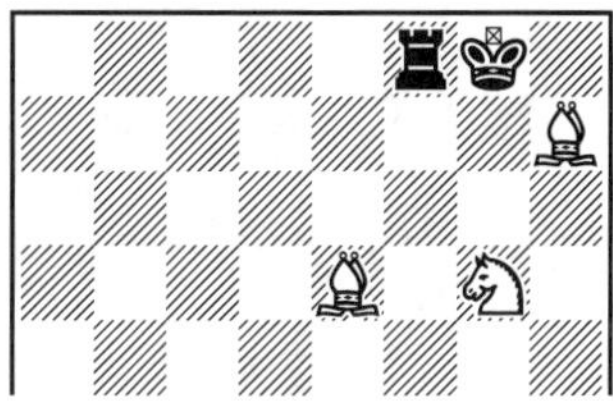

Diagram 128

Bishop, Knight, and King

Diagram 129

Variation:

	White	Black
#1	N/c6	K/a7
	B/b7	
	K/c7	

Knight and Bishop

Diagram 130

Variation:

	White	Black
#1	N/h6	K/g8
	B/b2	R/f8
		P/f7, h7

Summary

The preceding checkmate patterns are essential weapons of a strong chessplayer. A working knowledge of these patterns enables a chessplayer to recognize mating possibilities early and to plan and conduct more effective attacks. For checkmate, the enemy King must be in check, be unable to capture or interpose against the checking piece, and have no safe flight squares; hence, along with the checking piece, additional coordinated supporting pieces are usually necessary.

Study these basic checkmating patterns carefully, then be alert for opportunities to develop them in your games.

Part III

THE ENDGAME

Chapter 10

THE ENDGAME

Play the opening like a book, the middle game like a magician, and the endgame like a machine.

— Spielmann

The middlegame evolves into the endgame when the number of pieces on the board has been greatly reduced and pawn play and King activity become primary factors. Many intermediate chessplayers dislike, even fear, the endgame, primarily because of lack of confidence and skill. Some basic endgame knowledge will dispel fear, strengthen endgame play, and boost confidence.

Goals in the Endgame

In priority, endgame goals are:

- Checkmate
- Pawn promotion

while preventing your opponent from accomplishing these same objectives.

Let us now examine the material and techniques necessary to accomplish the primary endgame goal, checkmating the enemy King.

Checkmate

Concluding a chess game efficiently is one hallmark of a strong chessplayer.

The minimum material necessary to force checkmate against a lone King is:

- King and Queen
- King and Rook
- King and two Bishops
- King, Bishop, and Knight

These four basic scenarios are covered in this section. Endgame mates with a King and Queen (or Rook) are frequent, and should be mastered—faced with such a mate, an opponent will usually resign; nevertheless, a chessplayer should be able to checkmate efficiently with these minimum pieces if necessary. Checkmates with the King and minor pieces (Bishops and Knights) rarely occur, but should be practiced to gain skill.

Note: The best way for a defending lone King to prolong mate is to stay near the center of the board for as long as possible — especially avoiding corners — to maintain safe flight squares.

King + Queen vs. King

To checkmate with a King and Queen, you must first drive the lone enemy King to any edge (or corner) of the board. The simplest and most reliable method is to progressively maneuver the Queen a *Knight's move away* from the defending King until it is forced into a corner, then advance the attacking King to support checkmate. If it is impossible initially to move the Queen a Knight's move away, first move the Queen so as to most restrict the lone King.

(*Note:* To avoid stalemate, the attacking King must be advanced *immediately* after the defending King reaches a corner.)

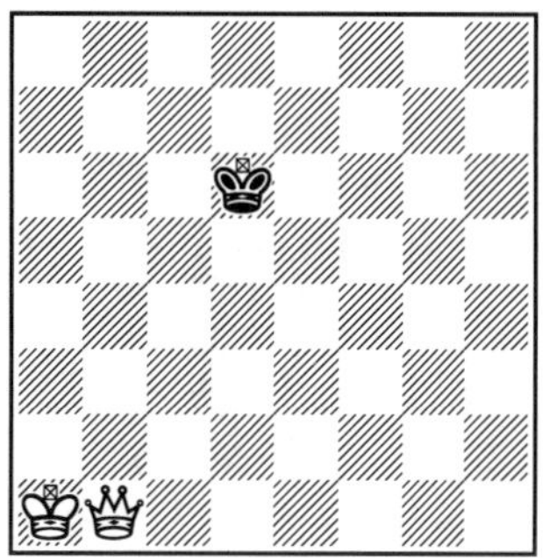

Diagram 131-White to move

A simple checkmating procedure with a King and Queen against a lone King from the position in Diagram 131 is: **1. Qf5 Kc6 2. Qe5 Kd7 3. Qf6 Kc7 4. Qe6 Kb7 5. Qd6 Kc8 6. Qe7 Kb8 7. Qd7 Ka8 8. Ka2!** (not 8. *Qc7?? stalemate!)* **Kb8 9. Ka3 Ka8 10. Ka4 Kb8 11. Ka5 Ka8 12. Ka6 Kb8 13. Qb7** (or *Qd8*) **checkmate.**

A faster technique involves using the attacking King more actively earlier. Again from the position in Diagram 131, play might proceed: **1. Kb2 Kd5 2. Kc3 Ke5 3. Qb6 Kf4 4. Kd4 Kf5 5. Qd6 Kg4 6. Qf6 Kg3 7. Ke4 Kg4 8. Qg6† Kh4 9. Kf3 Kh3 10. Qg3** (or *Qh5* or *Qh6* or *Qh7)* **checkmate.**

This faster method requires more careful thought (taxing, in an endgame) and increases the defender's chances for a stalemate, while the first method (moving the Queen a Knight's move away) is usually not appreciably longer, and is virtually foolproof.

King + Rook vs. King

The lone King must be driven to any edge of the board to be checkmated. One method is to successively align the Kings in *near* opposition (facing each other one square apart) on a rank or file, then force the defending King to retreat with Rook checks (the first Rook move should restrict the lone King as much as possible). When approaching the defending King with the attacking King, it is important to *lag* the enemy King by one file (or rank), to force it to move into opposition.

The lone King can delay, but not prevent, mate by moving to harass the Rook. When attacked, the Rook moves to the opposite wing on the same rank (or file). The Rook can also make waiting (tempo) moves to establish a favorable position to force opposition.

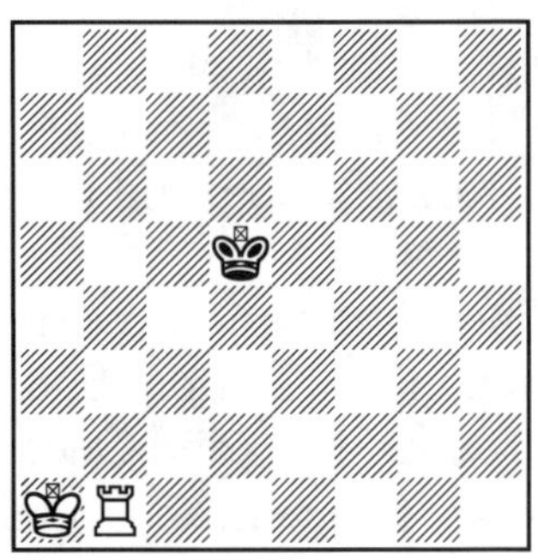

Diagram 132-White to move

Checkmating from the position in Diagram 132 could proceed: **1. Rb4 Kc5 2. Rh4 Kd5 3. Kb2 Ke5 4. Kc3 Kd5 5. Ra4 Kc5 6. Ra5+ Kd6 7. Kc4 Ke6 8. Kd4 Kd6 9. Ra6+ Ke7 10. Kd5 Kd7 11. Ra7+ Kc8 12. Kd6 Kb8 13. Rh7 Kc8 14. Rg7 Kb8 15. Kc6 Ka8 16. Kb6 Kb8 17. Rg8#.**

A faster method also exists, again by using the attacking King more actively. Using this method, from the position in Diagram 132 play might continue: **1. Kb2 Kd4 2. Kc2 Ke4 3. Kc3 Ke5 4. Kc4 Ke4 5. Re1+ Kf5 6. Kd4 Kf4 7. Rf1+ Kg5 8. Ke4 Kg6 9. Ke5 Kg5 10. Rg1+ Kh4 11. Kf5 Kh3 12. Kf4 Kh2 13. Rg3 Kh1 14. Kf3 Kh2 15. Kf2 Kh1 16. Rh3#.**

This latter method requires more thought and care, while the former method, although usually longer, is simpler and easier to execute.

King + Two Rooks vs. King

The checkmate with a King and two Rooks against a lone King is simple and swift, and does not require the assistance of the attacking King. The two Rooks progressively "scissor" the lone King to any edge of the board to mate. In the process, the Rooks stay on separate files (or ranks) to allow scissoring, while alternately *restraining* (to prevent escape) and *checking* (to force retreat) the lone King. If attacked by the opposing King, a Rook moves to the opposite side of the board. The first Rook move should restrict the lone King as much as possible.

(*Note:* A Queen and Rook can mate in similar fashion.)

Diagram 133-White to move

A fast checkmating procedure from Diagram 133 is: **1. Rh4 Ke5 2. Ra5† Kf6 3. Rh6† Kg7 4. Rb6 Kf7 5. Ra7† Ke8 6. Rb8#.**

King + Two Bishops vs. King

To checkmate, you must drive the lone King into any corner by the coordinated efforts of the attacking King and two Bishops. The Bishops "scissor" the defending King into a corner, with the aid of the King.

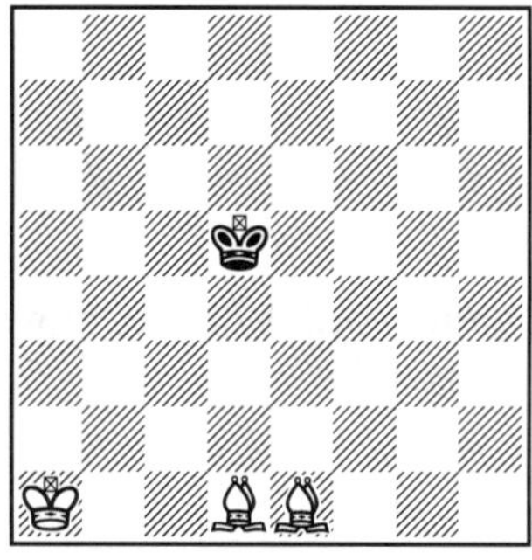

Diagram 134-White to move

A checkmating procedure from the position in Diagram 134 is: **1. Kb2 Ke4 2. Kc3 Kd5 3. Bf3† Ke5 4. Bg3† Ke6 5. Kd4 Kf5 6. Kd5 Kf6 7. Bg4 Kg5 8. Bd7 Kf6 9. Bh4+ Kg6 10. Ke5 Kf7 11. Kf5 Kg7 12. Be8 Kf8 13. Bg6 Kg7 14. Be7 Kg8 15. Kf6 Kh8 16. Bf5 Kg8 17. Kg6 Kh8 18. Bd6 Kg8 19. Be6† Kh8 20. Be5#.**

King + Bishop + Knight vs. King

This checkmate is the most difficult, and may require as many as 34 moves. The lone King must first be driven to any edge of the board, then into a corner *of the same color as the Bishop*. The lone

King will attempt to stay in the center or near a safe corner (opposite color of the Bishop).

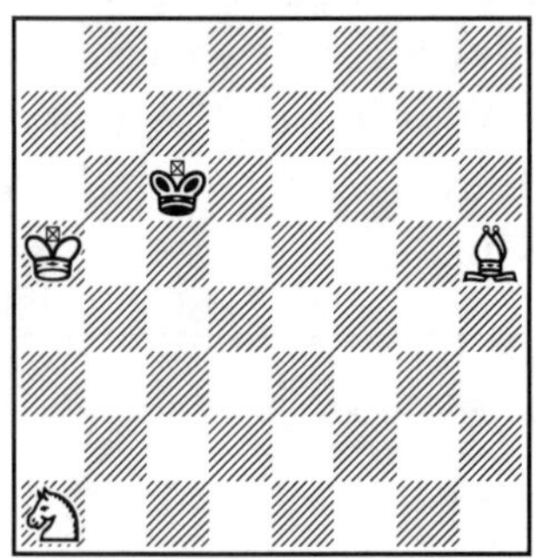

Diagram 135-White to move

From the scattered position in Diagram 135, the procedure is: **1. Nb3 Kd6 2. Kb5 Kd5 3. Bf7† Ke5 4. Kc5 Kf6 5. Bc4 Ke5 6. Nd2 Kf4 7. Kd6 Kf5 8. Bd3† Kf6 9. Nf3 Kf7 10. Ke5 Kg7 11. Ng5 Kg8 12. Kf6 Kf8 13. Nf7 Kg8 14. Bf5 Kf8 15. Bh7 Ke8 16. Ne5 Kf8 17. Nd7† Ke8 18. Ke6 Kd8 19. Kd6 Ke8 20. Bg6+ Kd8 21. Nc5 Kc8 22. Bd3 Kd8 23. Bb5 Kc8 24. Bd7† Kb8** (if *24... Kd8, 25. Ne6#*) **25. Kc6 Ka7 26. Kc7 Ka8 27. Kb6 Kb8 28. Na6† Ka8 29. Bc6#.**

Each basic endgame mate illustrated above requires one or more *pieces*, in addition to the King. As the middlegame evolves into the endgame, however, the number of pieces on the board is usually drastically reduced, if not entirely eliminated. The resulting lack of fire-power is remedied by attention to the second major goal of the endgame, *pawn promotion*.

Pawn Promotion

With diminished material, endgames are characterized by increased *King activity* and *pawn play*; the primary thrust becomes the promotion of one or more pawns. The King, which should be quickly mobilized to the center of action, becomes a *fighting piece* in the endgame, to attack, capture, block, and restrain enemy pawns, hinder the opposing King, protect pawns, and escort pawns to promotion. After a brief discussion of four basic concepts involved in pawn promotion, we will explore their application in the various tactics available to you for this critical endgame activity.

Principles

The following four basic endgame principles contribute to promoting pawns, and you should become thoroughly familiar with them:

- Queening square
- Opposition
- *Zugzwang*
- Triangulation

Queening Square

The *queening square* of a passed pawn is the square, geometric space on the chessboard within which an enemy King can catch and capture a passed pawn before or immediately after it promotes. The queening square is constructed by drawing an imaginary diagonal line from the passed pawn to the eighth rank (or first rank, for a black pawn), then completing the square thus defined (Diagram 136):

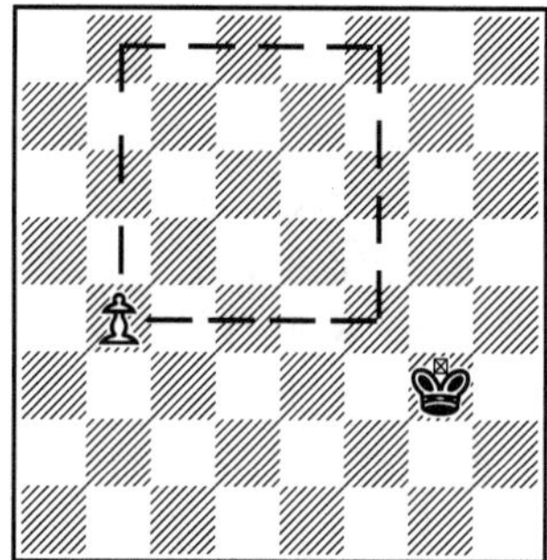

Diagram 136

To capture an enemy passed pawn, a King must be within, or be able to move within, the queening square of the pawn, and the King must be able to *stay* within the queening square, which diminishes as the pawn advances.

If Black moves first in the position in Diagram 136, the black King can enter the queening square of the white passed pawn and capture it immediately after it promotes: **1... Kf4 2. b5 Ke5 3. b6 Kd6 4. b7 Kc7 5. b8=Q† Kxb8.**

If White moves first, however, the black King cannot enter the queening square of the pawn, and the white passed pawn becomes a standing new Queen: **1. b5 Kf4 2. b6 Ke5 3. b7 Kd6 4. b8=Q†.**

Note also that the queening square for a passed pawn on the second rank must be constructed as though the pawn were on the *third* rank, since the pawn can advance two squares (to the fourth rank) in one move.

Blockaders can prevent a King from staying within the queening square of a passed pawn (Diagram 137):

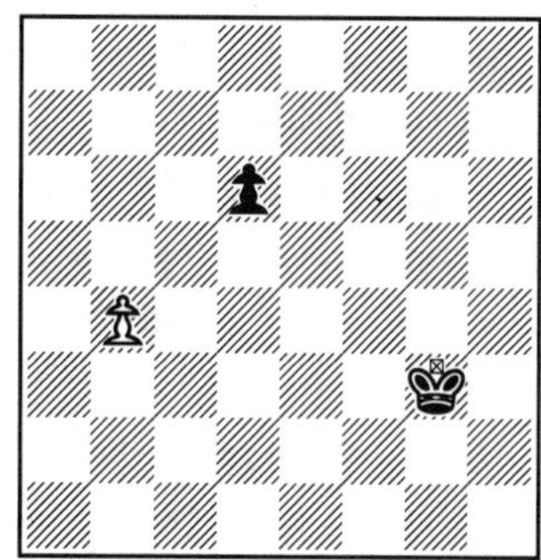

Diagram 137-Black to move

This is the same position as in the previous diagram, except for the black d6-pawn — but the black pawn makes a big difference! Unlike the previous position, the black King, even with the move, cannot stay within the queening square as the white passed pawn advances, because of the blockading black d6-pawn: **1... Kf4 2. b5 Ke5 3. b6 Kd5 4. b7 Kc6 5. b8=Q.**

For safety in the endgame, a King should always stay inside the queening square of enemy passed pawns or, at most, one square outside the queening square with the move.

Opposition

Opposition occurs when the two Kings are aligned on a file, rank, or diagonal an *odd* number of squares apart. A distance between Kings of five squares is called the *distant* opposition, three squares, the *medium* opposition, and one square, the *near*, or direct, opposition. The side which does NOT have to move has the opposition.

The significance of the opposition in a King-and-pawn endgame is that the King *without* the opposition must yield while the opposing King penetrates, ultimately to the seventh rank, to escort a pawn to promotion. With the opposition, the King and pawn win; without the opposition, the game is drawn with best play.

The importance of the opposition is illustrated in Diagram 138, a fundamental endgame position:

Diagram 138

The two Kings are in opposition; if Black must move first, White has the opposition and wins; if White moves first, Black has the opposition and draws.

Black moves first: **1... Kd8 2. d7 Kc7 3. Ke7 Kc6 4. d8=Q wins.**

White moves first: **1. d7† Kd8 2. Kd6 Draw (stalemate)** (or 2. *Kf7 Kxd7 drawn*).

The key to winning is to advance the passed pawn to the seventh rank *without check*. To win, the attacking King must usually have (or be able to gain) the opposition, and must stay *ahead* of the passed pawn until the pawn reaches the sixth rank.

The winning opposition can sometimes be forced by a sacrifice to deflect the enemy King (Diagram 139):

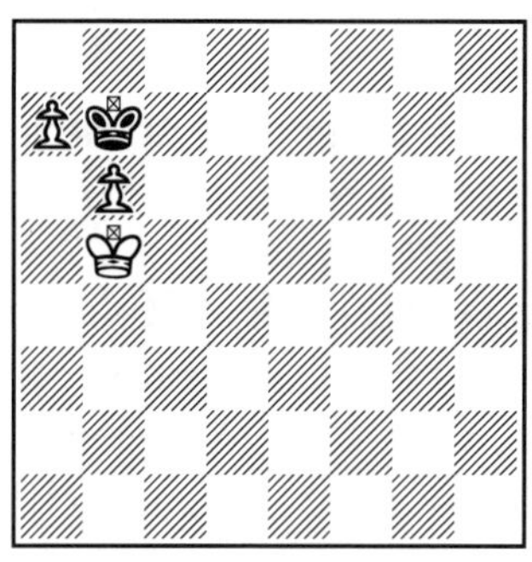

Diagram 139-White

Despite being two pawns behind, Black is threatening to draw by shuttling his King back and forth between b7 and a8; encroachment by the white King (*Kc6)* with the black King on a8 is stalemate.

However, White wins by sacrificing one pawn to deflect the black King and seize the opposition, then promoting the remaining pawn. Play continued **1. a8=Q†!,** forcing **1... Kxa8.** Then **2. Kc6** seized the diagonal near-opposition, and the white b-pawn queened: **2... Kb8 3. b7 Ka7 4. Kc7 Ka6 5. b8=Q.** A swift mate ensued: **5... Ka5** (forced) **6. Qb3! Ka6 7. Qb6#.**

Seizing the opposition with a deflection sacrifice was the key to White's pawn promotion and swift win.

Having the opposition is normally required to win a King + P endgame. The two exceptions are: 1) when the defending King is outside the queening square of an advancing passed pawn, and cannot move (and stay) inside it; and 2) when the attacking King is on the *sixth rank* ahead of a safe passed pawn on the same file — *then the side with the pawn always wins, regardless of who moves first*. Diagram 140 illustrates this important latter exception:

Diagram 140

White wins, regardless of which side has the opposition and who moves first:

Black moves first: **1... Kd8 2. Kf7 Kd7 3. e6+ Kd8 4. e7† Kc7 5. e8=Q wins.**

White moves first: **1. Kd6 Kd8 2. e6 Ke8 3. e7 Kf7 4. Kd7 Kf6 5. e8=Q wins.**

Had the white pawn been on the second, third, or fourth rank instead, White still wins by keeping his King in place and simply advancing the passed pawn to the fifth rank, reaching the position in the diagram.

Note: Once the Kings are aligned an odd number of squares apart, the opposition is determined by which King has to move. A tempo move, by a pawn for example, reverses the opposition. Saving pawn tempo moves to insure the opposition in the endgame is a wise precaution.

Drawing with a lone King against a King and pawn is simple, provided the King with the pawn cannot gain the opposition. The defending King makes three types of moves: 1) block the passed pawn; 2) seize the opposition; and 3) retreat *straight back* when retreat is necessary (Diagram 141):

Diagram 141-Black to move

1... Ke7! (Retreats *straight back. 1... Kd7??* allows *2. Kd5!*, and White gains the opposition and wins.) **2. Kd5 Kd7** (seizes the opposition) **3. e6† Ke7** (blocks the passed pawn) **4. Ke5 Ke8!** (Retreats straight back again! *4... Kd8??* [or *4... Kf8??]* allows *5. Kd6!* [or *5. Kf6!]* and White gains the opposition and wins.) **5. Kd6 Kd8** (seizes the opposition again) **6. e7† Ke8** (blocks the pawn) **7. Ke6 *Drawn*** (stalemate).

EXCEPTION: Rook-pawns are a notable exception in King-and-pawn endgames. A King and a Rook-pawn against a lone King is *always* a draw if the defending King can reach the corner promotion square. Even if the side with the pawn has a Bishop, the game is drawn *if* the Bishop is of *opposite color* than the pawn's promotion square — on reaching the promotion square, the defending King simply shuttles back and forth on adjacent squares in the corner, and the pawn cannot be promoted. Sooner or later, attempts to promote the pawn result in stalemate.

A Rook-pawn with a Bishop of the *same* color as the promotion square is a win, however, since the defending King can be driven out of the corner. Practice some examples to convince yourself.

The preceding examples illustrate the importance of the *opposition* in determining whether the outcome of a King-and-pawn endgame is a win or a draw. Whether attacking or defending in a King + P endgame, **seize and maintain the opposition!**

Zugzwang

Zugzwang is a German chess term meaning "having to move, and any move loses" (Diagram 142):

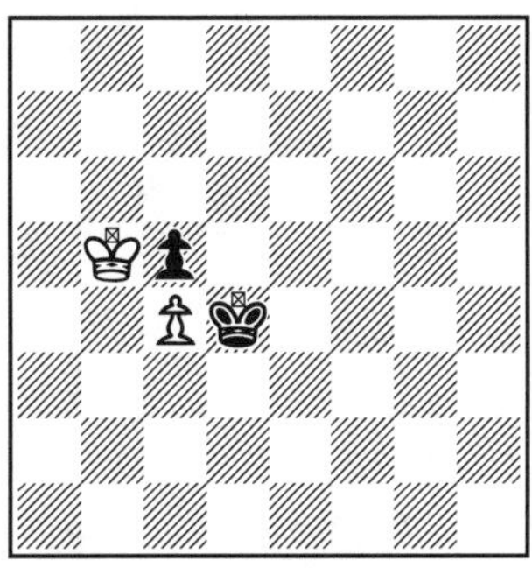

Diagram 142

Whichever side moves first is in *zugzwang*, and loses — the King must abandon its threatened pawn (say, *1. Ka4* or *1... Ke5*) and lose the pawn and the game. The attacking King will capture the enemy pawn, then reach the sixth rank ahead of its safe extra pawn; the pawn will soon queen.

Triangulation

Triangulation refers to a triangular King maneuver which uses two moves (instead of one) to reach an adjacent square. The purpose of triangulation is to force the enemy King into *zugzwang* (Diagram 143):

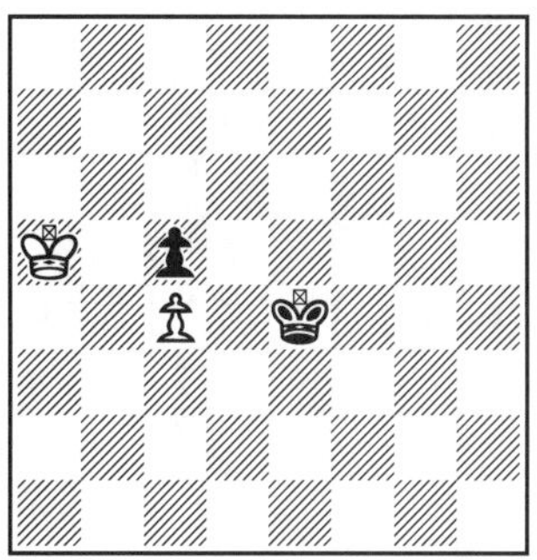

Diagram 143-White to move

White wins by triangulating to b5, starting with **1. Kb6!,** attacking the black c5-pawn (not *1. Kb5?? Kd4!*, and it is White who is in *zugzwang* and loses — see the previous diagram). After **1... Kd4** (to protect the threatened black pawn) White triangulates with **2. Kb5** (see Diagram 142), and Black is in *zugzwang* — the black King must abandon its pawn and lose the game, as the white King will capture *3. Kxc5*, reach the sixth rank ahead of the safe white c-pawn, and promote the pawn.

Now that you have a working knowledge of the four basic principles of queening square, opposition, *zugzwang*, and triangulation, we can move on to explore how they influence pawn promotion in the endgame.

Pawn-Promotion Tactics

Every pawn is a potential Queen.
— Mason

Endgame tactics which can effect or assist the pawn-promotion process are:

- Passed pawns
- Sacrifices
- Multiple queening threats
- Offside pawn majority
- Superior King position
- Restricting the enemy King

We will next examine these important, advanced endgame tools. Several practical examples are included for your instruction and practice.

Passed Pawns

A *passed* pawn is a pawn which faces no hostile pawns on the same or adjacent files to block or impede its progress to its promotion square. If it also is protected by one or more pawns, it is a *connected* passed pawn. An *outside* passed pawn is one which is removed from the remaining pawn structure by one or more files (Diagram 144):

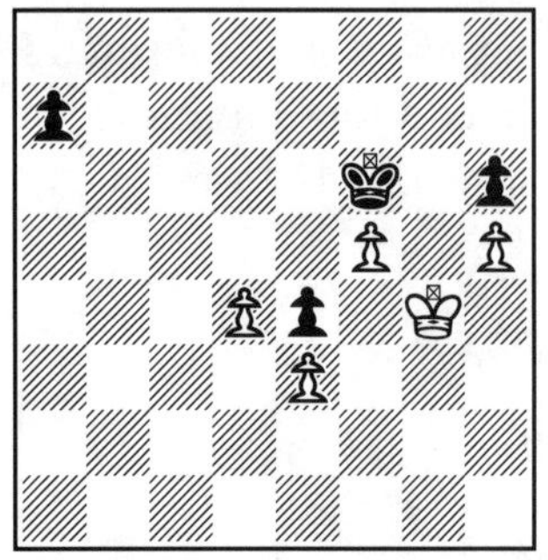

Diagram 144

The white f5-pawn is a passed pawn (even though blocked by the black King), the white d4-pawn is a connected passed pawn, and the black a7-pawn is an outside passed pawn.

All new Queens were once passed pawns, so it is essential to create and advance passed pawns at every safe opportunity. *Connected* passed pawns and *outside* passed pawns distant from the enemy King are strongest.

Passed pawns are created by pawn advances and exchanges (Diagram 145):

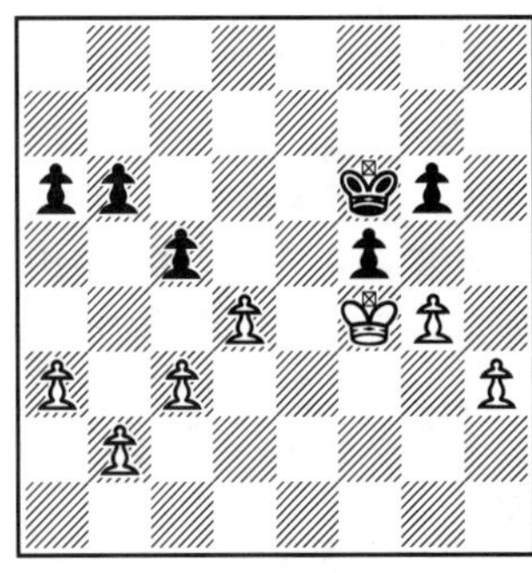

Diagram 145-White to move

White can create a passed pawn on the d-file by advancing *1. d5*, or create an outside passed pawn on the h-file by exchanging *1. gxf5 gxf5*. In the game, White first played **1. gxf5 gxf5,** then **2. d5!,** to achieve two passed pawns. White quickly won, as the black King was unable to prevent one of the passed pawns, assisted by the white King, from queening.

A passed pawn can be a powerful tactical weapon (Diagram 146). How should Black continue?

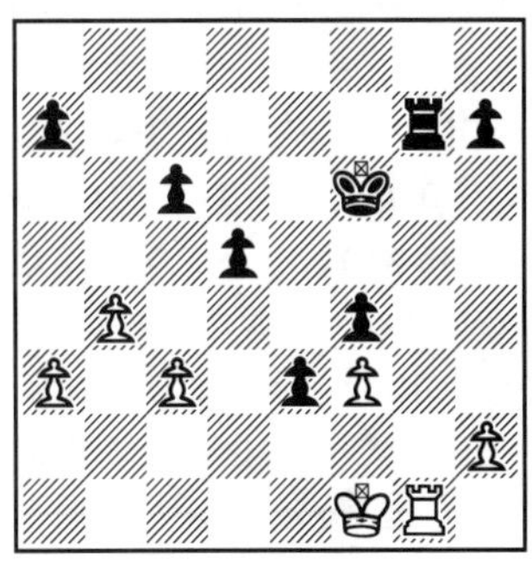

Diagram 146-Black to move

Black has an advanced connected passed e3-pawn. The white King is overworked, guarding the attacked white R/g1 and defending against *...e2* and *...e1=Q*. The immediate *1... Rxg1?* fails to win because of *2. Kxg1 e2 3. Kf2* and the black passed e-pawn is lost. Instead, Black first played the sharp **1... e2†!** If *2. Kxe2, ...Rxg1* wins, so White responded **2. Kf2.** Black continued **2... Rxg1!,** and the overworked white King is in *zugzwang:* White must lose his Rook (if *3. Kxe2)* or allow the black pawn to queen *(3. Kxg1 e1=Q†)*. White resigned. A clear example of the power of a passed pawn.

Let us next examine some specific endgame situations which involve passed pawns:

In an endgame queening race with advancing solo passed pawns on both sides, one side will promote a pawn one or more tempi ahead of the other. If only a one-tempo difference in queening is involved, the game is usually a draw, unless the second new Queen can be won by a skewer of the enemy King and new Queen. If two or more tempi differences exist, the side obtaining the first new Queen wins, unless the enemy pawn is a protected Bishop- or Rook-pawn, which draws. The following examples will illustrate.

The simplest winning strategy

of the side queening first is to block and attack the advanced enemy passed pawn with the new Queen, then approach the enemy pawn with the King to support the Queen's capture of the pawn (Diagram 147):

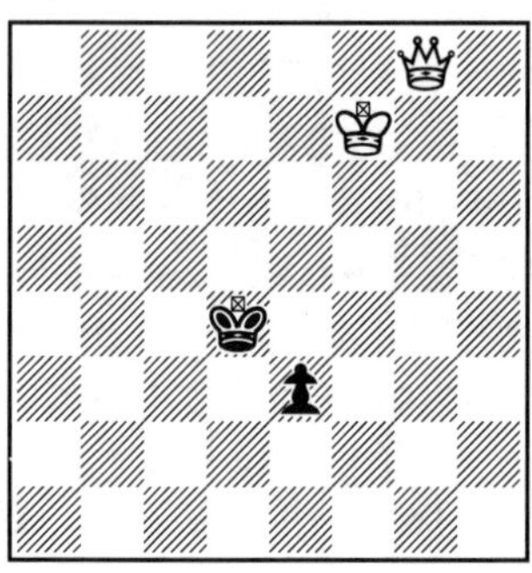

Diagram 147-White to move

On the previous move, White played **g8=Q** and Black advanced **...e3.** White's correct first move now is **1. Qg1!,** to gain access to e1 (the black pawn's promotion square) and block the advanced enemy passed pawn. Play might continue: **1... Kd3 2. Qe1! e2 3. Ke6 Ke3 4. Ke5 Kf3 5. Kd4 Kg3 6. Qxe2** and wins.

If the advanced enemy pawn is on the *seventh rank*, protected by the enemy King, the winning strategy with a distant King and Queen is to advance the Queen to force the defending King in *front* of the passed pawn (onto the pawn's promotion square), which prevents the pawn from queening. The attacking King is then progressively advanced until the enemy pawn can be captured. The King defending the pawn on the seventh rank will attempt to avoid blocking the pawn's promotion (Diagram 148):

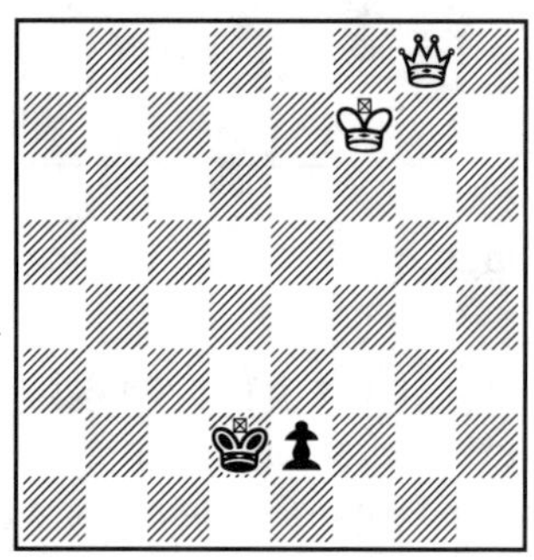

Diagram 148-White to move

From Diagram 148 play might proceed: **1. Qd8† Kc1 2. Qe7 Kd1 3. Qd6† Kc1 4. Qe5 Kd1 5. Qd4† Kc1 6. Qe3† Kd1 7. Qd3† Ke1 8. Kf6 Kf1 9. Qf3† Ke1 10. Ke5 Kd2 11. Qf2 Kd1 12. Qd4† Kc1 13. Qe3+ Kd1 14. Qd3† Ke1 15. Ke4 Kf2 16. Qf3† Ke1 17. Kd3 Kd1 18. Qxe2† Kc1 19. Qc2#.**

Bishop- and Rook-pawns on the seventh rank require special consideration: a distant King and Queen against a protected advanced *Bishop-pawn* on the seventh rank is a draw, since the attacking King cannot gain tempi to advance because of stalemate (Diagram 149):

Diagram 149-White to move

If White plays the prescribed **1. Qg3†,** instead of blocking the passed pawn (*...Kf1)* Black responds **1... Kh1!** Now if *2. Qxf2, ...draw!* (stalemate). A white King move (e.g., *2. Kf6)* allows *2... f1†=Q* also with a draw, and white Queen moves (say, *2. Qf3† Kg1)* lead to a repetition of the position.

The dilemma of a *Rook-pawn* on the seventh rank is similar, as the distant King cannot advance without allowing a draw by stalemate (Diagram 150):

Diagram 150-White to move

Black is threatening *1... h1=Q* drawing, and if White tries *1. Qg3†* Black plays *1... Kh1*, and any move by the white King forces immediate stalemate. White Queen moves also cause stalemate (*2. Qf2)* or lead to a repetition of the position (*2. Qf3† Kg1)*. Other white Queen moves do not win (*2. Qe1† Kg2*, and the black passed pawn again threatens to queen). The position is a draw.

Endgame queening races are fairly frequent, and these winning techniques and drawing resources should be learned.

Sacrifices

To promote a pawn to a game-winning Queen, other pawns — or sometimes even pieces — can be sacrificed.

Winning *pawn* sacrifices to promote another pawn usually occur when the enemy King is outside the queening square of a potential passed pawn (Diagram 151):

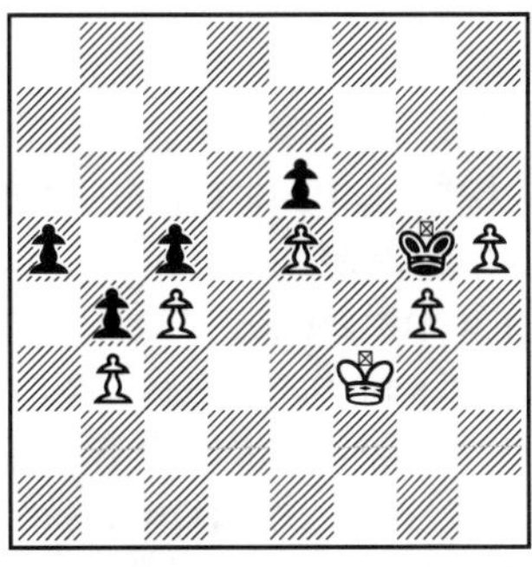

Diagram 151-Black to move

Although White has an extra pawn and two passed pawns (g4 and h5), Black, with no passed pawns, has a simple endgame win based on a timely pawn sacrifice. Black played the forcing **1... a4!,** threatening to advance *...a3-a2-a1=Q* winning, since the white King is outside the queening square of the black a-pawn. After **2. bxa4 b3!** the white King is outside the queening square of the black passed b3-pawn, which queened and won the game.

A similar pawn sacrificial idea in slightly more complex form arose in the position in Diagram 152. What is Black's best move?

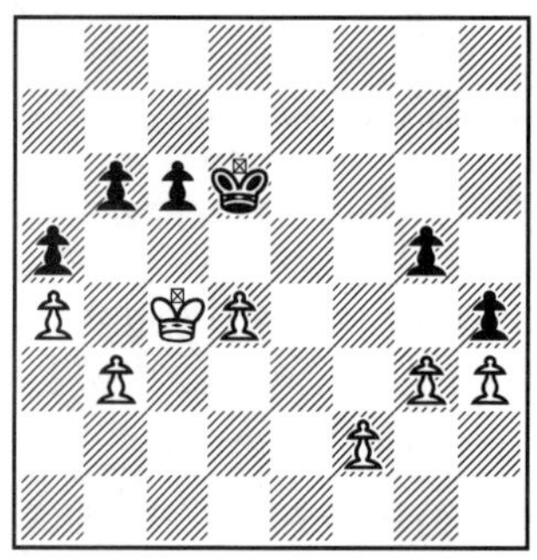

Diagram 152-Black to move

White enjoys an extra Kingside f2-pawn, and has just played **1. g3?,** intending to initiate pawn exchanges to force a passed pawn on the Kingside. Black alertly responded with the pawn sacrifice **1... g4!,** sacrificing either the black g4- or h4-pawn to queen the other: if *2. hxg4, ...h3!*, and the black passed h-pawn will queen before White's passed g-pawn; if *2. gxh4* (or *2. Kd3), ...gxh3!*, and again the black h-pawn will queen first. The white King is outside the queening square of the resulting black passed h-pawn after either sequence, and Black will queen first and win the game. (White overestimated the strength of his kingside pawn majority.)

Piece sacrifices to promote a pawn usually involve removing enemy blockaders or defenders, thus opening lines for the pawn to safely advance to promotion (Diagram 153). How should White continue?

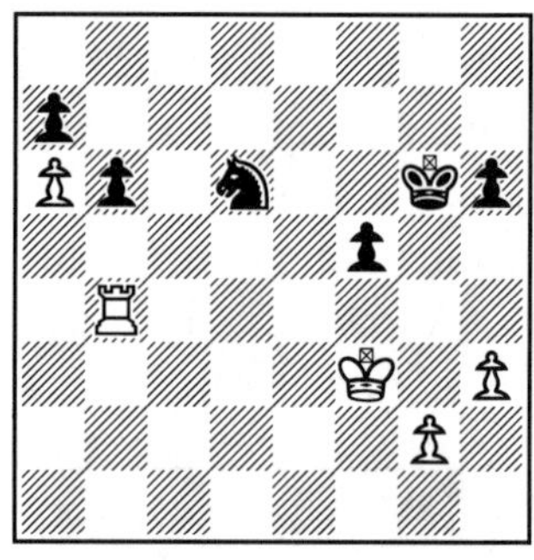

Diagram 153-White to move

White is the Exchange ahead for a pawn, but has no passed pawns. The advanced white a6-pawn is near queening, but is blocked by the black a7-pawn. White removed this blockader by sacrificing his Rook with **1. Rxb6!,** threatening to capture the pinned black N/d6 next. After Black's reluctant **1... axb6, 2. a7** guaranteed the promotion of White's passed a-pawn.

A winning piece sacrifice to promote a pawn in the endgame must usually be carefully planned and accurately timed. Diagram 154 illustrates a brief winning sequence featuring the sacrifice of a Queen to promote a pawn.

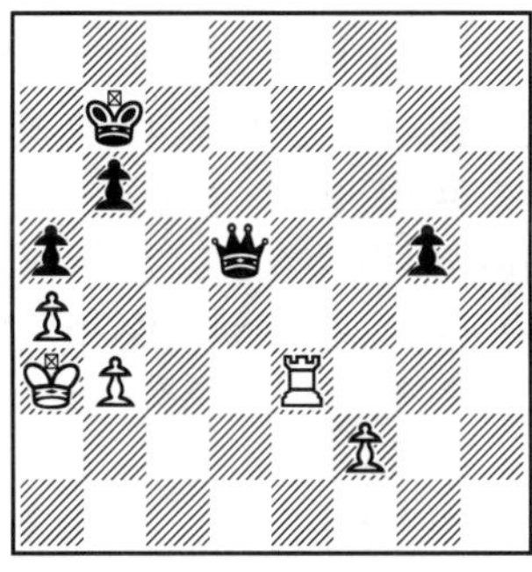

Diagram 154-Black to move

Black is the major Exchange (Queen for Rook) ahead and has a queening candidate g5-pawn, provided the white f2-pawn can be eliminated or deflected to the e-file. Black began with the forcing **1... Qc5†,** checking the white King and attacking the white R/e3. After **2. Kb2,** Black sacrificed his Queen with **2... Qxe3!,** and after **3. fxe3 g4!** the black g-pawn will queen by one tempo (*4. Kc2 g3 5. Kd2 g2 6. Ke2 g1=Q)*.

Multiple Queening Threats

A fundamental principle of winning advanced endgame play is to create multiple queening threats, preferably on opposite wings. Multiple queening threats can stretch an enemy King beyond its defensive limits and force the promotion of a pawn. The defending King is not elastic, and cannot parry queening threats on both sides of the board (Diagram 155):

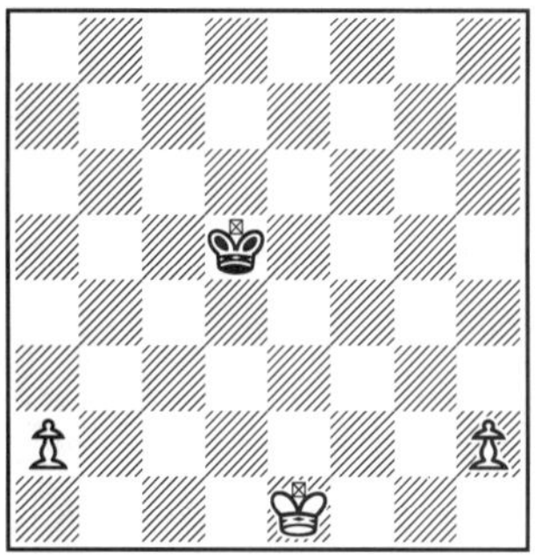

Diagram 155

In this position, the black King is well within the queening squares of both white outside passed pawns. Nevertheless, even without the white King moving, the black King cannot prevent a white pawn from queening. If it is Black's move, the black King can only temporize in the center. If it is White's move, *1. h4 Ke5 2. a4* and the black King faces an early dilemma — chasing either white pawn allows the other to queen. As the white pawns advance, their respective queening squares diminish, and soon the black King will be forced outside the reduced queening square of one pawn. The black King cannot successfully defend against White's multiple queening threats on opposite sides of the board.

This important principle can win endgames even if material is even, as discussed next.

Offside Pawn Majority

An *offside pawn majority* is a majority of pawns on the wing opposite the enemy King. Since Kings usually castle Kingside, offside pawn majorities are often on the Queenside.

The significance of an offside pawn majority is that, if *healthy* (no doubled, isolated, or backward pawns), it can forcibly produce a winning outside passed pawn which creates dangerous queening threats on both sides of the board, either directly (by promoting to a new Queen) or indirectly (by serving as a decoy to lure the enemy King away from defense of its pawns on the opposite wing — the attacking King can then capture them and assist the promotion of its own pawn, on the side opposite the outside passed pawn).

Diagram 156 illustrates the benefits of an offside pawn majority:

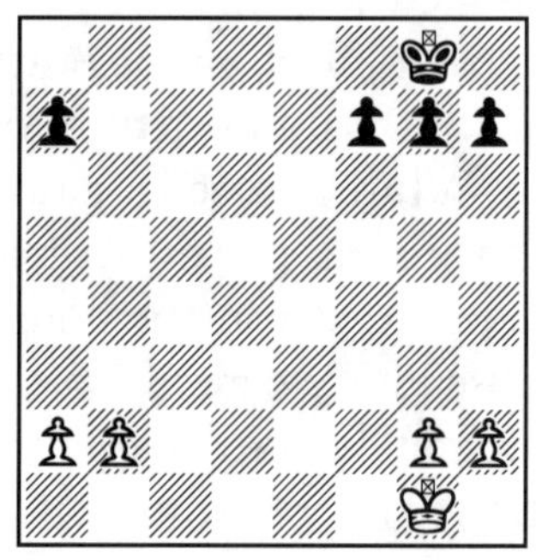

Diagram 156-White to move

Material is even, but White's 2:1 Queenside pawn majority and the distant black King are significant advantages for White. The winning plan for White consists of three phases:

1. Centralize the white King
2. Advance Kingside pawns
3. Create Queenside passed pawn

After accomplishing these three tasks, White will win, either by promoting his Queenside passed pawn or, if the black King defends the Queenside, by capturing the remaining black Kingside pawns with his King, then promoting a Kingside pawn.

From the position in Diagram 156 with White to move, play might continue: **1. Kf2 Kf8 2. Kf3 Ke7 3. Ke4 Ke6** (Phase 1 is complete) **4. g4 h6 5. h4 g5 6. h5** (Phase 2 is complete) **f6 7. b4**

(The "break square" on which the pawn exchange will occur with the pawn majority to create a passed pawn is always the square in front of the *unopposed* pawn — *7. a4? a5!*, for example, would hold both white pawns) **a6 8. a4 Kd6 9. Kf5 Ke7 10. b5 axb5 11. axb5** (Phase 3 is complete).

White wins, for if the black King continues to defend his attacked f6-pawn with *11... Kf7*, then *12. b6!*, and the white outside passed b-pawn queens; if the black King chases the white outside passed b-pawn with *11... Kd7*, then the white King will capture the black Kingside pawns, and a white Kingside pawn will queen: *12. Kxf6 Kd6 13. Kg6 Kc5 14. Kxh6 Kxb5 15. Kxg5 Kc5 16. h6* and the white passed h-pawn will queen. White will queen a pawn on either the Queenside or Kingside because of the outside passed pawn resulting from his earlier offside (Queenside) pawn majority.

The dilemma faced by the black King in the previous position is typical of the problems associated with defending against an offside pawn majority in the endgame. For an example of excellent defense in such a situation, consider Diagram 157:

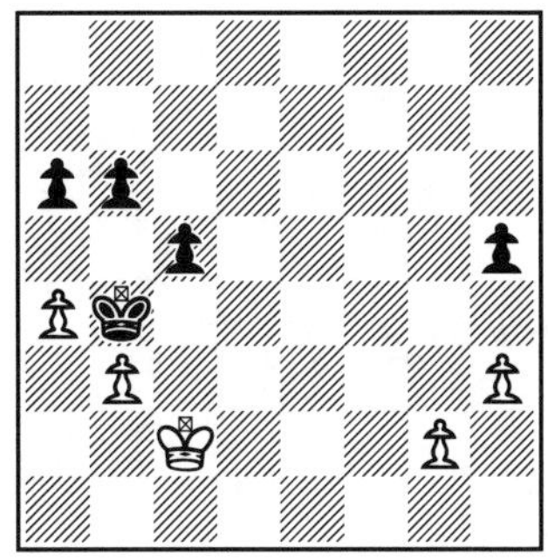

Diagram 157-Black to move

Material is even, but White has an offside pawn majority on the Kingside, and threatens *g4!* creating a dangerous and potentially winning outside passed pawn. Black stopped this White threat with **1... h4!** Now if *2. g4??, ...hxg3 e.p.!* and the black passed g-pawn will queen first and win the game.

White's Kingside majority is not healthy — his g2-pawn is backward — and the single black pawn restrains the two white Kingside pawns. Black is now free to develop an advantageous Queenside passed pawn with his healthy pawn majority there. (**Note:** If the white Kingside pawns were farther advanced, White could sacrifice his g-pawn and queen his h-pawn first.)

Endgame themes are often combined. For a cogent example of an endgame win combining a sacrifice, outside passed pawn, and multiple queening threats, consider Diagram 158:

Diagram 158-White to move

Black, a Knight behind for a pawn, has two advanced connected central passed pawns (on d3 and e4). Black is threatening *1... e3†!* advancing a dangerous passed pawn and winning the white Knight (*2. Kd1 Kxc3*). But White has the advantage of an outside passed a4-pawn, which the black King must prevent from queening. White therefore played to eliminate Black's dangerous central passed pawns and to create queening threats on both wings with the sacrifice **1. Nxe4!** Play continued: **1... Kxe4 2. a5 Kd5 3. Kxd3 g6 4. a6 Kc6 5. Ke4 Kb6 6. Ke5 Kxa6 7. Kf6 g5 8. g4 Kb6 9. Kg6 Resigns.** The white King will mop up Black's remaining Kingside pawns, and a white pawn will promote. A likely finish would have been *9... Kc6 10. Kxh6 Kd6 11. Kxg5 Ke6 12. Kg6 Ke7 13. g5 Kf8 14. Kh7*, and the white g-pawn will queen.

The two most important endgame factors are *pawn structure* (number and formation) and *King position*. The previous examples have demonstrated the significant role of pawn structure (e.g., passed pawns, outside passed pawns, offside pawn majority). Now we examine the often critical role of King position.

Superior King Position

A superior, aggressive King position is an advantage in an endgame and, even with no material disparity, can be decisive (Diagram 159):

Diagram 159-White to move

Material is even, but White has a more aggressive King position. To promote a pawn and win, White must capture at least the black d6-pawn. White utilized his superior King position to triangulate and out-tempo the defending black King: **1. Kb6 Kd8** (if *1... Ke7?*, *2. Kc7* wins the black d6-

pawn immediately) **2. Kc6 Ke7 3. Kc7 Kf7 4. Kxd6 Kf6 5. Kc7** followed by *6. d6, 7. d7, 8. d8=Q* wins.

White wins in Diagram 159 even if Black moves first, again by triangulation: **1... Kc7 2. Ka6 Kc8 3. Kb6 Kd7 4. Kb7 Kd8 5. Kc6 Ke7 6. Kc7 Kf7 7. Kxd6 Kf6 8. Kc7** and wins (*9. d6, 10. d7, 11. d8=Q*).

This example clearly illustrates the importance of a superior King position, as does Diagram 160:

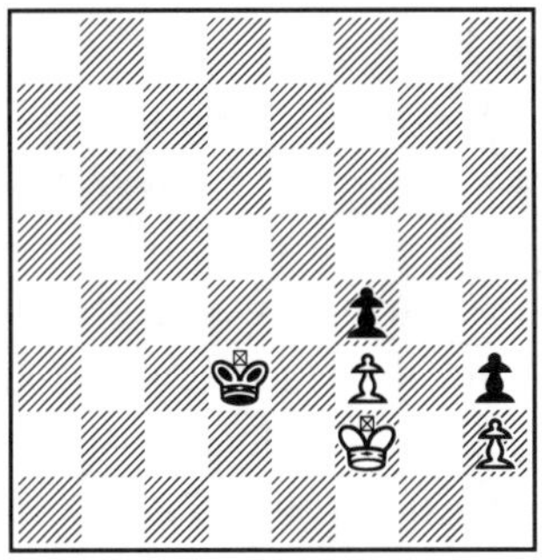

Diagram 160-Black to move

Both sides have two pawns, but Black has the superior, aggressive King position. To win, Black must capture the white f3-pawn, promote his f4-pawn, and avoid stalemate. Black continued: **1... Kd2 2. Kf1 Ke3 3. Kg1 Ke2!** (To seize the opposition on the next move. *3... Kxf3?* only draws, since after *4. Kf1* the white King has the opposition and leaves no escape via g2.) **4. Kh1 Kxf3 5. Kg1 Ke2 6. Kh1 f3 7. Kg1 f2† 8. Kh1 f1=Q#.**

For a final, dramatic example of superior King position, consider the following endgame position from a United States Amateur Championship tournament game (Diagram 161):

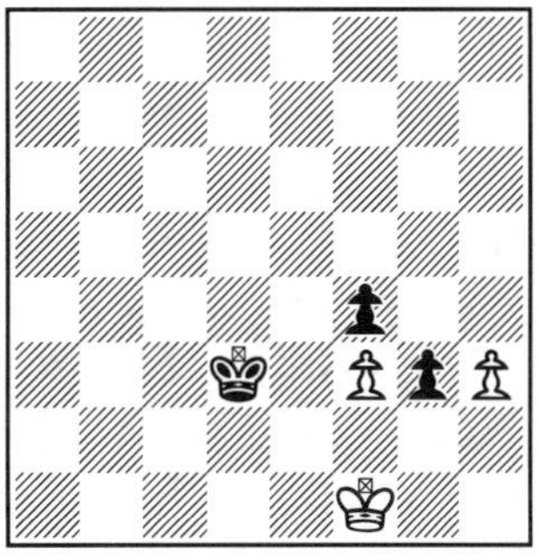

Diagram 161-Black to move

Material is even and the game appears to be a draw (in fact, White has just offered a draw), since both Kings are tethered to the defense of an enemy passed pawn: the white King to the black g3-pawn, and the black King to the white h3-pawn. Triangulation with the black King to win the white f3-pawn loses: *1... Ke3 2. Kg2 Ke2?? 3. h4!* and the white passed h-pawn will queen and win the game.

Black spurned White's offer of a draw, however, and, exploiting his superior King position, played the startling **1... Kd2!!** (Moving *outside* the queening square of the white passed h3-pawn!) **2. h4** ("I think you have just lost the game," White remarked.) **Ke3 3. h5** (If *3. Kg2* instead to defend the white f3-pawn, *3... Kd4!* and the black King reenters the queening square of the passed white h-pawn, which will be lost. After capturing the white h-pawn, the black King would return to win the white f3-pawn by triangulating as in the two previous examples, then promote a black pawn and win.) **Kxf3** (the white passed h5-pawn cannot be caught) **4. h6 g2† 5. Kg1 Kg3 6. h7 f3 7. h8=Q f2#!**

A stunning example of superior King position in the endgame! Black's win, which required extraordinary foresight and exact calculation, was forced in all variations.

The preceding examples clearly demonstrate the critical importance of a superior King position in the endgame, where the King becomes a formidable fighting piece (equivalent to about 2½ points). Centralize the King early in the endgame, and use it aggressively!

Restrict the Enemy King

To prevent an enemy passed pawn from queening, a defending King must be able to approach the pawn. Sometimes, the passed pawn can be shielded from the defending King by the opposing King (Diagram 162):

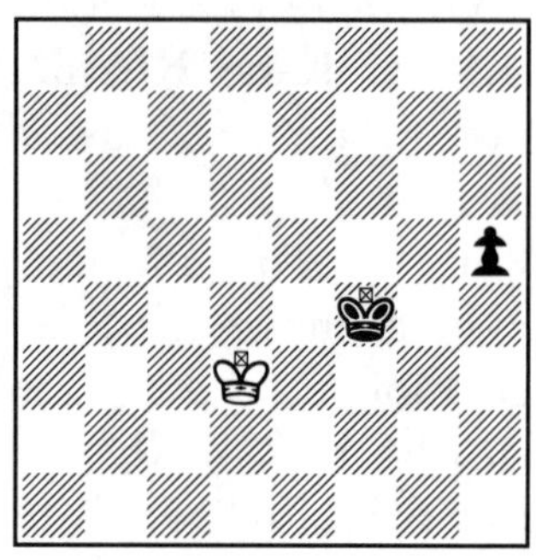

Diagram 162-Black to move

The white K/d3 is within the queening square of the black passed h5-pawn. Nevertheless, Black can use his King to restrict the white King and shield the pawn: **1... Kf3! 2. Kd2 Kg2 3. Ke2 h4,** and the black passed pawn will queen.

Rook-and-pawn endings are frequent; if only one side has a Rook, it can often be used to restrict the defending King, permitting a passed pawn to queen (Diagram 163):

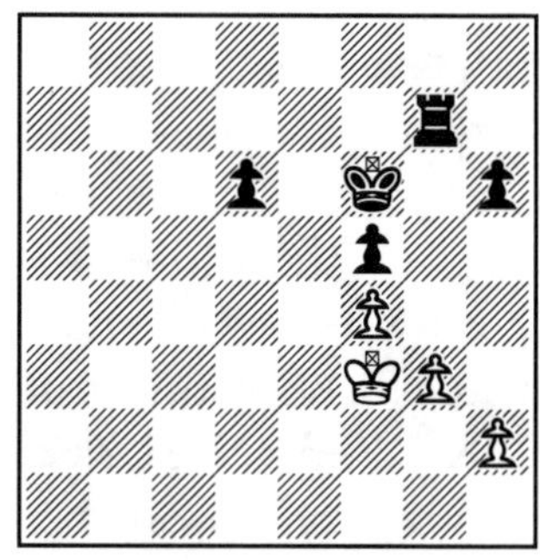

Diagram 163-Black to move

Black's fastest win is to promote his passed d6-pawn to a queen to enable checkmate. Accordingly, Black played **1... Re7!** to restrict the white King. The black R/e7 erects a "brick wall" along the e-file which cuts off the white King so that the black passed d6-pawn can advance directly to queen.

Even in an ending when both sides have Rooks, a defending King can sometimes be restricted to enable or facilitate the promotion of a pawn (Diagram 164):

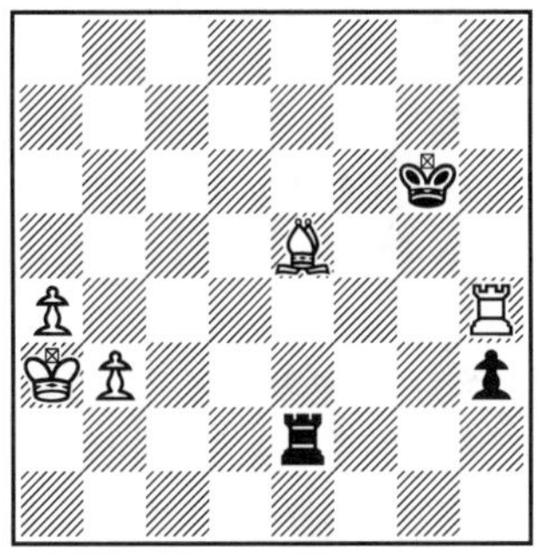

Diagram 164-White to move

White is a Bishop and pawn ahead, but Black has an advanced passed h3-pawn currently under surveillance by the white R/h4 and B/e5 (which is attacked by the black R/e2). White has two Queenside passed pawns (a4 and b3), and these queening candidates can prove decisive if the black King can be restricted to the Kingside. Therefore, White began by sacrificing his Bishop for Black's advanced passed pawn with **1. Rxh3!** to eliminate Black's only queening threat. Following **1... Rxe5, 2. Rf3!** barricades the black King from crossing the f-file.

Black's Rook proved no match for the white King and two passed Queenside pawns. The black Rook can only defend against the white passed pawns from the rear, laterally, or in front (Black tried all three methods), and all attempts fail. Play continued: **2... Re1 3. a5 Ra1† 4. Kb4 Ra2 5. Kb5 Rb2 6. b4 Rd2 7. a6 Rd5† 8. Ka4 Rd7 9. b5 Rd4+ 10. Ka5 Rd8 11. a7 Ra8 12. b6 Rd8 13. Rb3! Rd5† 14. Ka6 Rd8 15. b7 Rd6† 16. Rb6 Resigns.**

Restricting the enemy King in endgames removes one defender and facilitates the promotion of a pawn.

Endgame Guidelines

To round out your expertise, keep the following important additional guidelines for playing winning endgames in mind:

- *Keep Rooks active*. In the endgame, Rooks protect passed pawns, attack and block enemy passed pawns, and restrict the opposing King. Passive Rooks are a liability in the endgame — keep your Rooks active!
- *Place Rooks behind passed pawns*.

Protecting passed pawns from *behind*, Rooks do not obstruct the queening paths; Rooks also gain mobility (access to new ranks) as the passed pawns advance.

- *Blockade enemy passed pawns.* Enemy passed pawns pose a dangerous threat of queening in the endgame, and should be "kept under lock and key" — blockaded with pieces — once they reach the fifth rank. Knights are excellent blockaders, since they attack the pawn support squares of a passed pawn; but use the King, Bishops, Rooks, even the Queen if necessary, to blockade dangerous enemy passed pawns.
- *Bishops are usually more valuable than Knights.* Long-range Bishops, which can cover both sides of the board quickly, are usually more effective than Knights in the endgame, except in blocked positions or positions with pawns on only one side of the board. Bishops are especially advantageous if there are pawns on both sides of the board, a situation ill-suited for short-stepping Knights.
- *Keep your pawns off squares of your Bishop's color.* A Bishop requires open diagonals to be effective. Avoid blocking your Bishop with your own pawns. A "bad" Bishop, hemmed in by pawns of its own color, is a handicap in the endgame — keep your Bishop's lines open.
- *If one pawn ahead, exchange pieces, not pawns.* In the endgame, save your pawns for promotion. If endgame pawn exchanges leave you with only one pawn, an opponent can sacrifice a minor piece for your solo pawn to draw the game (insufficient checkmating force). Promoting a pawn grows easier as the number of opposing pieces on the board diminishes; so, with an extra pawn, exchange pieces — not pawns.

Six Common Mistakes

Mistakes to avoid in the endgame include:

1. Moving the King outside the queening squares of enemy passed pawns
2. Creating weak pawns
3. Allowing double attacks by your opponent
4. Moving too quickly
5. Allowing stalemate
6. Allowing drawing sacri-

fices by your opponent

Summary

The primary objectives of an endgame are to: 1) checkmate the enemy King; and 2) promote one or more pawns to enable checkmate. Several fundamental endgame principles and techniques—queening square, opposition, *zugzwang*, and triangulation—can decisively assist this winning process. Develop skill with these principles and the guidelines offered, and you will be a threat in every endgame.

Remember, the King is a fighting piece in the endgame!

Combine endgame knowledge and expertise with your opening and middlegame skills to improve your chessplaying strength and become a more balanced, complete chessplayer.

Chapter 11

ENDGAME TACTICS

An opponent surprised is half-beaten.

— Proverb

Tactics, as you now know, are not confined to the opening and middlegame. In the endgame, pieces and pawns participate in a coordinated, gradual advance with the objective of promoting one or more pawns. During this advance, winning tactical opportunities can arise.

The following compendium of endgame positions includes the principles covered in the preceding chapter, and is offered here to further exercise and expand your new endgame skills. Study each diagram and form your own opinion before reading the explanations which follow. You will be surprised by how much you know!

Offensive Tactics

Let us begin with Diagram 165:

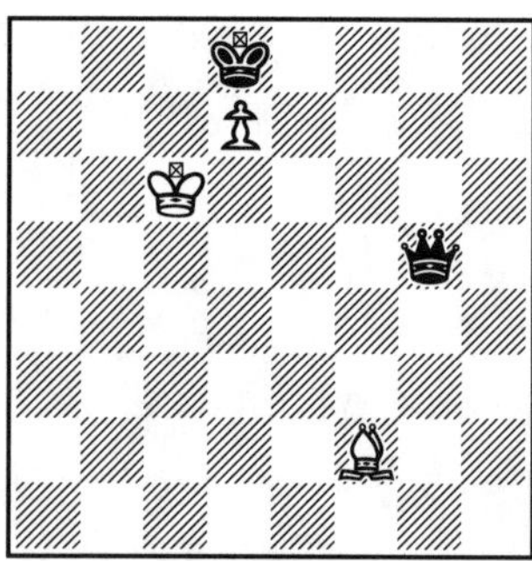

Diagram 165-White to move

Black has the advantage of a Queen against a Bishop and pawn —

an apparent win, since the advanced white passed d7-pawn is blockaded by the black King, and can be immediately attacked and captured by the black Queen (the dark-squared white B/f2 cannot defend the lone white pawn). However, the black King and Queen are in line (a weakness), and White removed the critical blockader of his passed d7-pawn and won the game with **1. Bb6†! Ke7** (forced) **2. d8=Q†,** promoting his pawn and winning the black Queen with a skewer. Simple and forcing, White's endgame tactic was immediately decisive.

A more subtle example of a similar idea arose in Diagram 166:

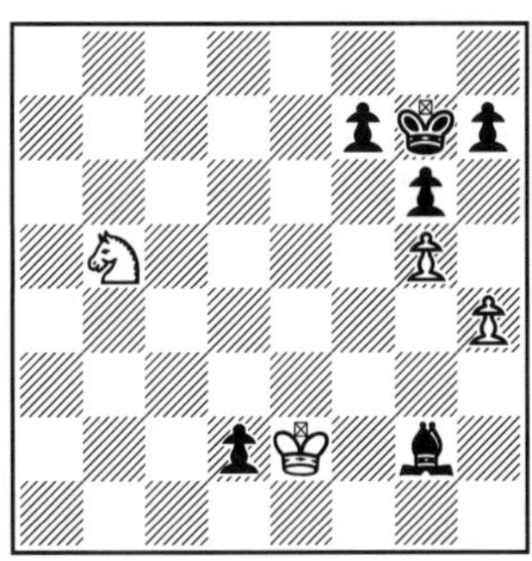

Diagram 166-Black to move

Black, faced with immediate loss of his valuable advanced passed d2-pawn and a likely drawn endgame, alertly played the sacrificial skewer **1... Bf1†!,** to either deflect the white King and queen the black pawn (if *2. Kxf1, ...d1=Q†)* or win the white N/b5 (if *2. Kxd2, ...Bxb5)*, with an easy win in either instance. Black's timely endgame skewer decided the game.

Checkmate is even possible in certain endgame positions in which the enemy King is confined or cramped (Diagram 167):

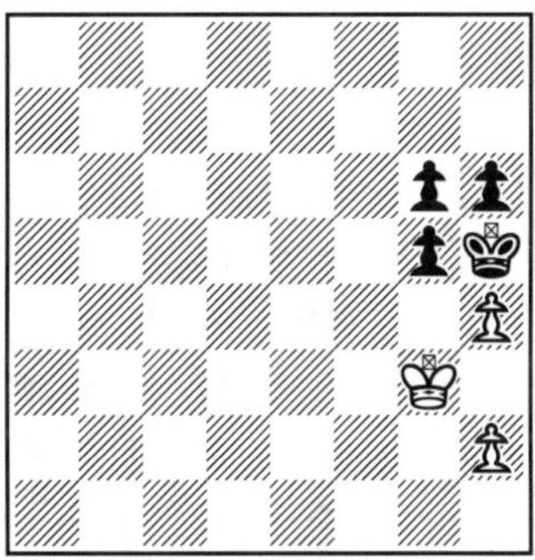

Diagram 167-White to move

With only Kings and pawns remaining, Black is a pawn ahead; but his extra pawn is doubled, and the black King is confined. White began with **1. h3!,** and Black responded **1... gxh4†** (if *1... g4??, 2. hxg4#)*. Play continued: **2. Kf4 g5+** (forced) **3. Kf5 g4** (forced) **4. hxg4#.**

While instances of checkmate with only Kings and pawns on the board are infrequent, the presence of pieces (or the promotion of a pawn) and a restricted King often makes checkmate a realistic possibility (Diagram 168):

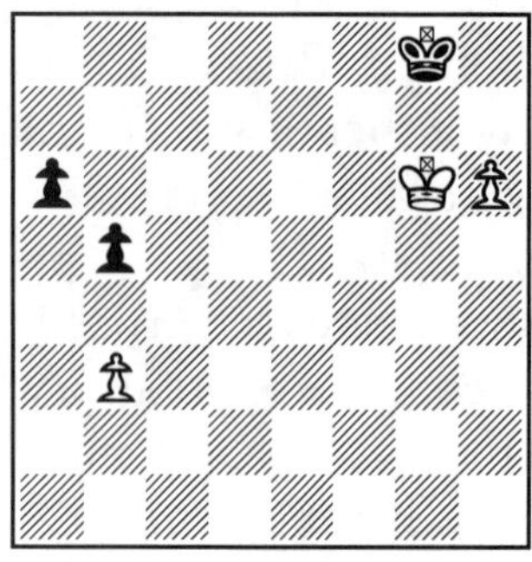

Diagram 168-White to move

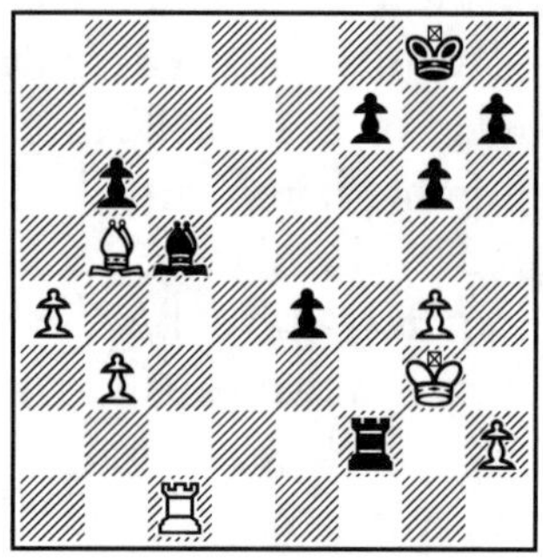

Diagram 169-Black to move

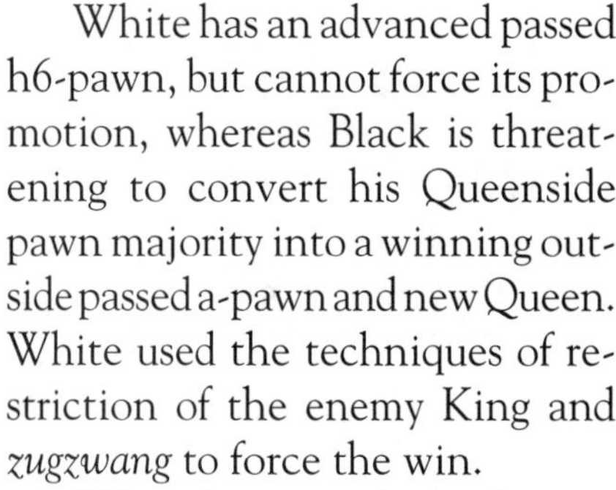

White has an advanced passed h6-pawn, but cannot force its promotion, whereas Black is threatening to convert his Queenside pawn majority into a winning outside passed a-pawn and new Queen. White used the techniques of restriction of the enemy King and *zugzwang* to force the win.

White began with the forcing **1. h7†.** After **1... Kh8** (*...Kf8??* allows *2. h8=Q†* winning) **2. b4!** Black is in *zugzwang:* he has only one move, and it loses by one tempo. After **2... a5** the game — all Black moves forced — concluded: **3. bxa5 b4 4. a6 b3 5. a7 b2 6. a8=Q#.**

Pieces always pose the threat of checkmate, even in the endgame, especially if the enemy King is restricted (Diagram 169):

Black is a pawn ahead, and both sides have a Rook and Bishop. White is threatening *2. Rxc5! bxc5 3. Kxf2* winning a Bishop, eliminating Rooks, and establishing an outside passed a-pawn which would quickly queen and win the game. What should Black do?

Black advanced his central passed pawn with **1... e3!** to secure his R/f2. White responded **2. Re1** to block Black's passed e-pawn. Now that the black R/f2 is defended, Black played **2... Bd6†!** After **3. Kh4** (if *3. Kh3, ...Rxh2#)* Black continued **3... Rxh2†.** White was forced to play **4. Kg5,** and Black quietly responded **4... Kg7!,** threatening the unstoppable *5...h6#* against the restricted white King. White resigned. Endgame checkmates during the pawn promotion process are relatively uncommon, but checkmate is always highest priority; so be alert for opportunities to force checkmate at all times! For example, *4... h6†! 5. Kf6 Rf2* is also checkmate!

Endgame tactics are often played to force the promotion of a pawn (Diagram 170):

Diagram 170-Black to play

Each side has a light-squared Bishop and passed pawn, but Black's passed g3-pawn is one square farther advanced. Exploiting this one-tempo advantage, Black began with the tactical interference move **1... Be4,** shielding the black passed g3-pawn's advance to g2 from the white B/d5, and also threatening the white Bishop (*2... Bxd5*). Play continued **2. Bxe4** (otherwise, the black passed g3-pawn queens, and the black B/e4 attacks b7 — a square the white passed b-pawn must cross to queen) **Kxe4 3. b6 g2 4. b7 g1=Q 5. b8=Q Qb1†!,** and the stinger skewer at the end won the new white Queen and the game.

Endgame tactics to force the promotion of a pawn often involve sacrifices (Diagram 171):

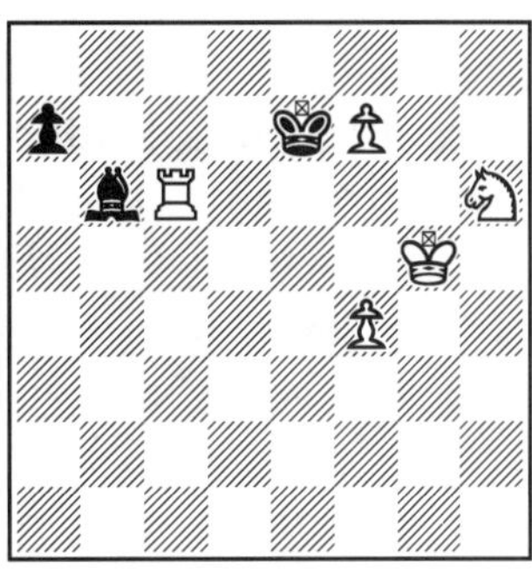

Diagram 171-White to move

With an advanced f7-pawn queening candidate, White boldly played the surprising Rook deflection sacrifice **1. Re6†!** Black faced a dilemma: if *1... Kxe6, 2. f8=Q* wins for White; or if *1... Kf8, 2. Re8† Kg7 3. Rg8* (or *f8=Q*) will checkmate. White's timely and energetic endgame tactic, a Rook sacrifice, won the game.

Surprise endgame tactics to force the promotion of a pawn often catch an opponent off guard (Diagram 172)

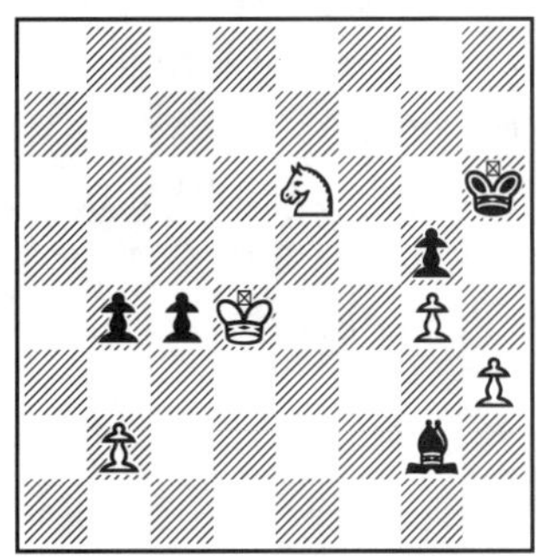

Diagram 172-Black to move

White expects a comfortable draw, or even a win, since the white King attacks the black c4-pawn, and the white Knight can assist in attacking the black Queenside pawns (if ...*Bf1*), so both black Queenside pawns appear lost. The white N/e6 also attacks Black's solo Kingside g5-pawn, and can sacrifice (*Nxg5*) if necessary to eliminate Black's only other chance for a new Queen (e.g., *1... Bxh3 2. Kxc4 Bxg4 3. Nxg5 Kxg5 4. Kxb4*, with a draw). To win, Black must be resourceful.

Black first played **1... c3,** threatening *2... cxb2* and *3... b1=Q*; so White captured **2. bxc3.** Black continued **2... b3!,** bypassing the white c3-pawn and threatening to queen his b-pawn. White responded **3. Kd3** to catch the black passed b-pawn, and Black shattered White's hopes for victory with a Bishop sacrifice **3... Be4†!!** White resigned, for if *4. Kxe4* (or *Kd2*), *...b2* and the advanced black passed b-pawn will queen. Resourceful tactics often win endgames!

Another example of resourceful sacrificial tactics in a tense endgame is illustrated in Diagram 173:

Diagram 173-White to move

Material is even, but Black is on the verge of capturing White's advanced passed b7-pawn, and has a potentially dangerous outside passed a6-pawn. Can White save this game?

Knight-and-pawn endgames are tricky, and White resourcefully began by sacrificing a pawn with **1. g5!,** threatening *2. g6-g7-g8=Q*. Black accepted White's pawn sacrifice with **1... fxg5.** Having removed the black e5-pawn's pawn defender (the purpose of *1. g5!*), White next offered the Knight sacrifice **2. Nxe5†!** Now if *2... Nxe5*, *3. b8=Q* wins; or if *2... Kxb7*, *3. Nxd7* wins the overworked black Knight and the endgame. Black resigned.

Successful sacrifices in general, and endgame sacrifices in particular, must be accurate and well-timed, and not all sacrifices work as planned. For an exemplary illustration of a misguided endgame sacrifice, examine Diagram 174:

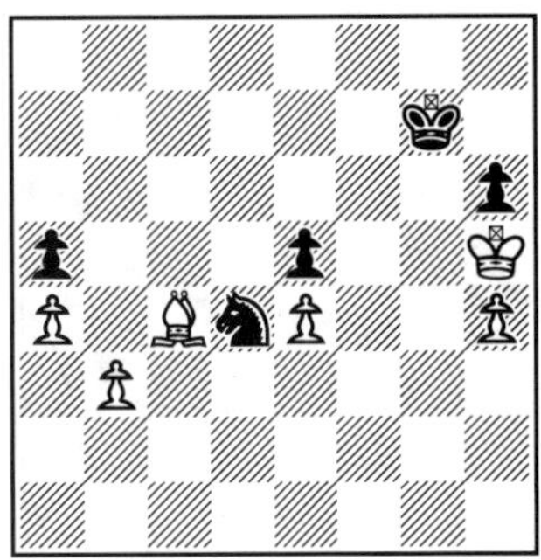

Diagram 174-White to move

White is a pawn ahead with a Queenside pawn majority, and developed the plan of sacrificing his b-pawn to create a passed a-pawn. Further (after *b4 axb4*), if the black b-pawn advances to b3 White can sacrifice his Bishop with *Bxb3*, since if *...Nxb3* the black Knight cannot return to stop the white passed a-pawn from queening.

White confidently began **1. b4?** as planned, and Black captured **1... axb4.** After **2. a5 b3 3. Bxb3 Nxb3 4. a6,** White thought his win was certain. Black played **4... Nc5,** and White advanced **5. a7.** Black responded **5... Nd7,** and, since *...Nb6* next would guard the white passed a-pawn's promotion square, White continued **6. a8=Q,** obtaining his new Queen as planned — whereupon Black played **6... Nf6#!** (Surprise!) White's confined King was the flaw in his sacrificial plan.

A final, sophisticated example of an endgame tactic to force the promotion of a pawn is illustrated in Diagram 175:

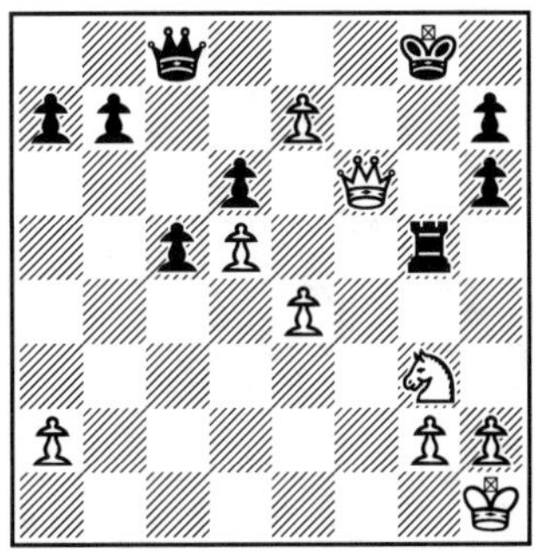

Diagram 175-White to move

White is the Exchange behind, but has an advanced passed e7-pawn. Black has his back rank adequately defended, and threatens *...Rg6* evicting the white Queen, followed by *...Qe8* blocking the white passed e7-pawn.

White cleverly forced the promotion of his passed e7-pawn with the double-attack **1. Qe6†!,** threatening *2. Qxc8* winning the black Queen. After **1... Qxe6 2. dxe6** the black King is denied access to f7, and the black King and Rook must stand idly by while the white e7-pawn safely queens, leaving White a winning Queen and Knight-versus-Rook endgame.

Defensive Tactics

Timely and effective defensive

tactics can frequently save otherwise lost games, as illustrated in the following interesting examples.

Consider White's dilemma in Diagram 176:

Diagram 176-White to move

White appears lost in this endgame: his distant King cannot protect his c5-pawn. After capturing it, the black King will be in front of his own d7-pawn and can gain the opposition (with a pawn tempo move if necessary), then promote the black d-pawn and win. Is White lost?

White relied on a defensive tactical resource and sacrificed his desperado c-pawn with **1. c6!** Following **1... dxc6** (if *1... Kd6, 2. cxd7 drawn)* **2. Ke3 Kd5 3. Kd3,** White seized the opposition and forced a draw (if *3... c5, 4. Kc3* draws, since the black King is not ahead of the pawn). A clever, accurately timed defensive tactic earned White the draw.

Consider Black's predicament in Diagram 177:

Diagram 177-Black to move

Black has insufficient mating material and can hope for only a draw at best, while White's two extra pawns confer an apparent winning endgame advantage. Relying on the fact that a lone King which can reach the promotion square can draw against a King, Rook-pawn, and Bishop — if the Bishop is of opposite color than the promotion square — Black forced a draw with the defensive sacrifice **1... Bxh4!** If *2. gxh4*, the drawing conditions are met immediately; if *2. g4* (to prevent *2... Bxg3*, drawing by insufficient mating material), the black Bishop simply shuttles safely along the h4-d8 diagonal and captures the white g-pawn when it eventually advances to g5. Black's timely Bishop sacrifice averted a loss.

In Diagram 178, Black faces an apparently overwhelming material deficit. Black is a Bishop and two pawns behind, and White has a protected advanced outside passed g6-pawn. Prospects of even a draw for Black seem dismal. Is he lost?

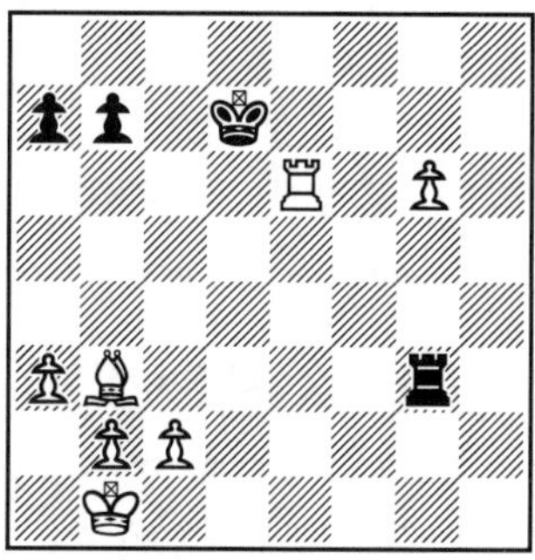

Diagram 178-Black to move

Black first played the tactical combination **1... Rxb3! 2. cxb3** (2. Rf6! is a better winning try) **Kxe6,** winning a Bishop and weakening (doubling) White's Queenside pawns. White advanced his King with **3. Kc2.** Still faced with a 4:2 White pawn majority, including an advanced white Kingside pawn, Black rushed to capture the white passed g6-pawn with **3... Kf6.** There followed **4. Kc3 Kxg6 5. Kc4.** Quickly returning to defend his Queenside pawn minority, Black continued **5... Kf6,** and the game concluded: **6. Kc5 Ke6 7. b4 Kd7 8. b5 Kc7 9. a4 Kd7 10. a5 Kc7 11. b4 Kc8 12. b6 a6 13. b5 axb5 14. Kxb5 Kb8 15. a6 bxa6† 16. Kxa6 Ka8** (seizing the opposition) **17. b7† Kb8 18. Kb6 Drawn** (stalemate).

With a timely endgame tactical combination and accurate defense, Black salvaged a draw from an otherwise certain loss.

For an example of *winning* endgame defensive tactics, examine the apparently disheartening position in Diagram 179:

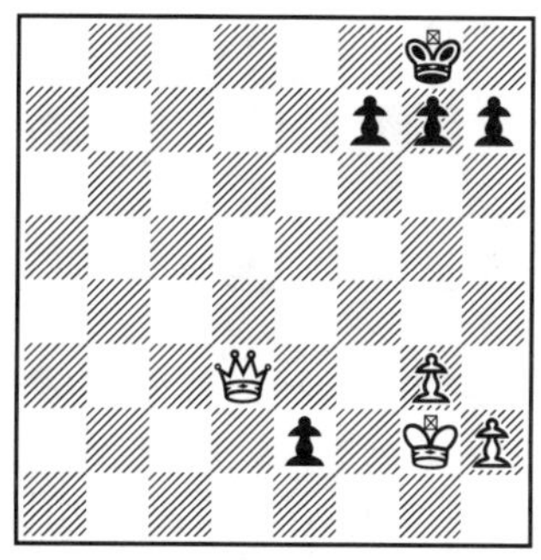

Diagram 179-Black to move

White threatens both *Qd8#* and *Qxe2* winning easily. Can Black save this game?

1... e1=Q fails to *2. Qd8† Qe8 3. Qxe8#*, so Black resourcefully played **1... e1=N†!,** underpromoting his pawn to a Knight with check and forking the white King and Queen. After **2. Kf1 Nxd3** Black enjoyed a winning endgame. Black's resourceful underpromotion tactic not only saved, but won, the game.

In our final position (Diagram 180), White is on the verge of promoting his advanced passed f7-pawn to a new Queen and entering a difficult, but winning, Queen-versus-Rook endgame. Black cannot prevent the white pawn from queening, and has no safe checks — can Black save this game?

Diagram 180-Black to move

Black played the clever defensive move **1... Rg4!!**, threatening *2... Rf4†* winning the advanced white passed f7-pawn by double-attack. After **2. f8=Q Rf4†!! 3. Qxf4** (forced, to avoid losing the Queen), the game is a draw (stalemate)! Black's resourceful defensive Rook sacrifice averted a certain loss.

Summary

Tactical opportunities frequently arise in the endgame, and an alert, resourceful chessplayer recognizes and exploits these opportunities to win games and force draws in inferior positions. Both offensive and defensive tactics may occur — stay alert for decisive tactics in the endgame!

Endgame Tactical Exercises

To challenge and expand your endgame tactical skills, following are eight exercises for your practice. Solutions to the exercises follow the problems. Good luck with these interesting exercises, and good fortune with winning tactics in your endgames!

WHITE TO MOVE

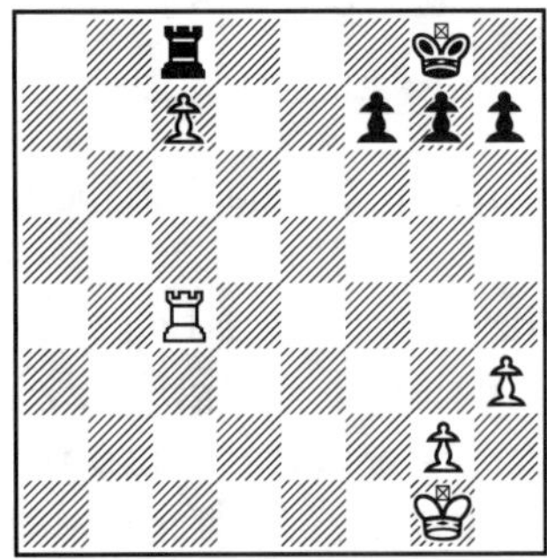

Exercise 1-White to move

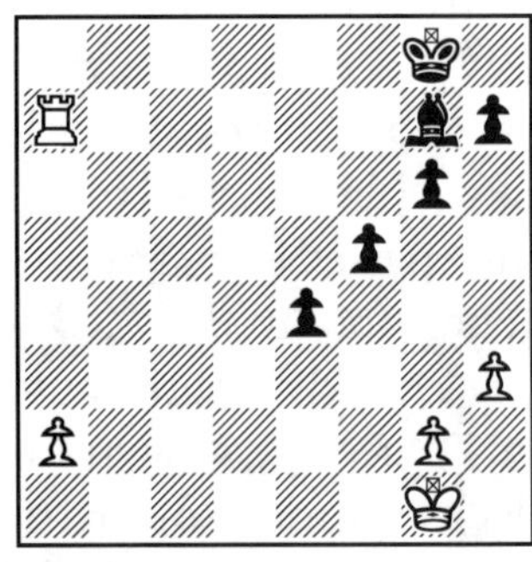

Exercise 2-White to move

Exercise 3-White to move

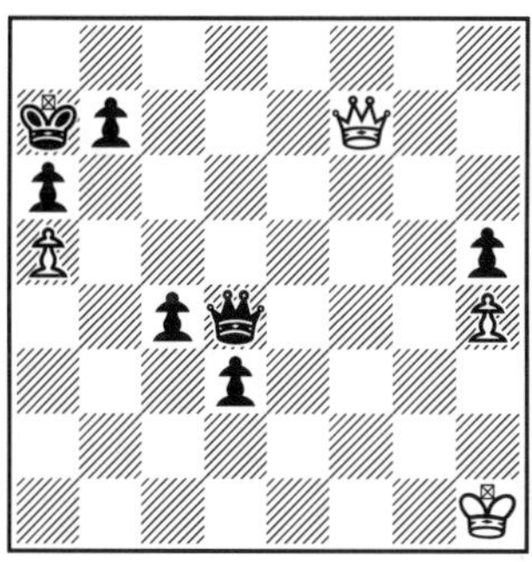

Exercise 4-White to move

Solutions:

1. **1. Rd4!** (any move) **2. Rd8†** wins.
2. **1. Rxg7†! Kxg7 2. a4** wins.
3. **1. Kg3! Resigns** (*zugzwang — if 1... black Rook leaves fifth rank, 2. Re5#; if 1... Re5, 2. Rxe5#; or 1... Rc5 2. bxc5 b4 3. Re5#).*
4. **1. Qf2! Qxf2** (forced, to avoid losing the black Queen) **Drawn** (stalemate).

BLACK TO MOVE

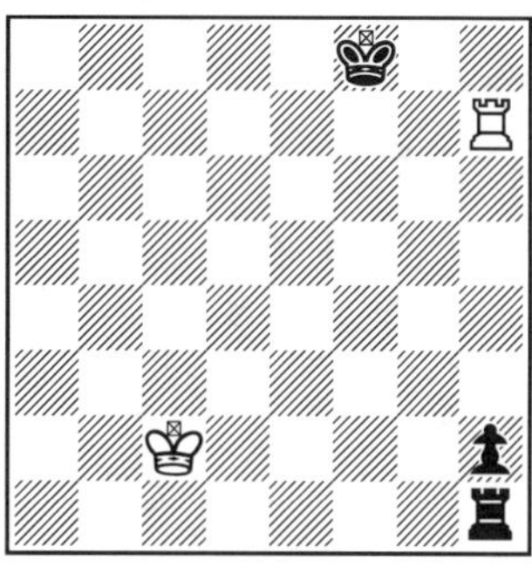

Exercise 5-Black to move

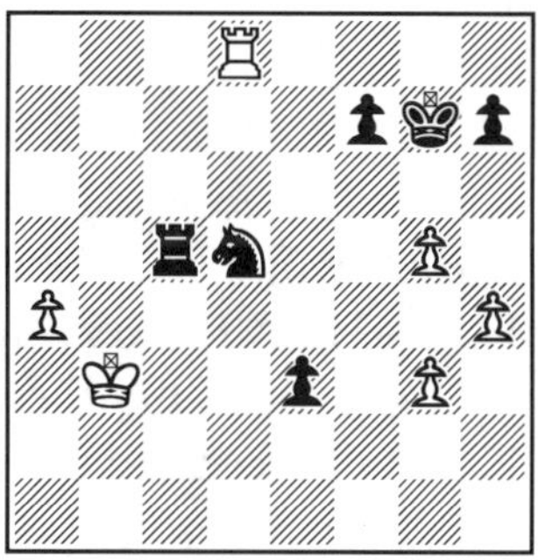

Exercise 6-Black to move

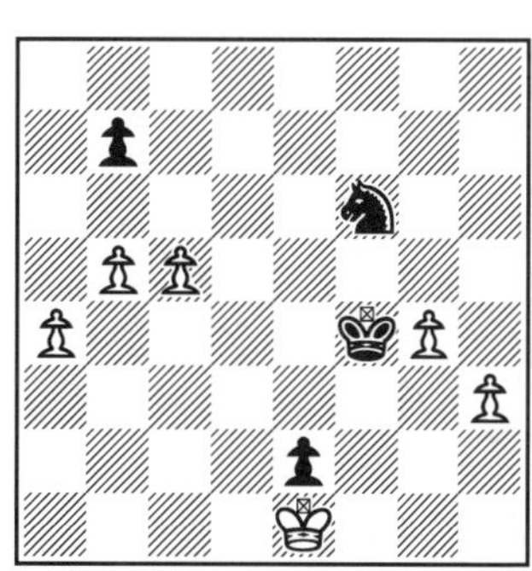

Exercise 7-Black to move

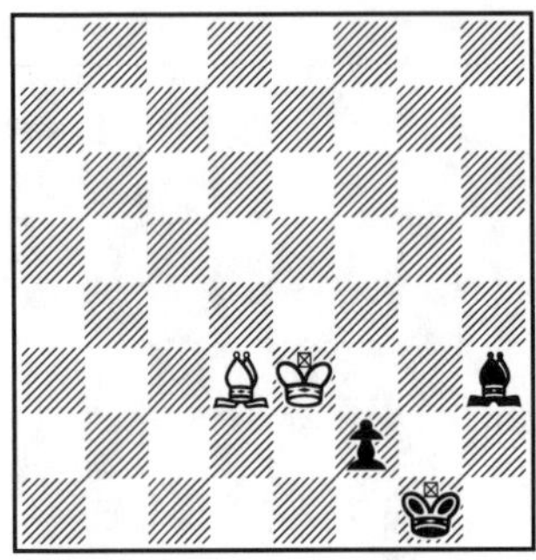

Exercise 8-Black

Solutions:

5. **1... Ra1! 2. Rxh2 Ra2†** wins.
6. **1... e2 2. Re8 Rc3† 3. Kb2 Re3!** wins.
7. **1... Ke3! 2. c6 Nd5 3. cxb7 Nf4 4. b8=Q Nd3#.**
8. **1... Bf1 2. Bf5 Bc4 3. Bh3 Be6!** wins.

Part IV

PRACTICE AND PROGRESS

Chapter 12

ENDGAME PRACTICE

In chess, knowing what *to do is half the battle; knowing* when *to do it is the other half.*

For practice in applying your new endgame skills, following are some examples of endgames emphasizing the important roles of recognizing advantages, planning, and applying sound endgame techniques.

For maximum benefit, set up each position, analyze carefully, try to form a winning plan (try to anticipate and act, rather than merely react), then cover the winner's moves and try to find the best moves for the winning side.

In the first example (Diagram 181), material is even and White has the only passed pawn (e3). What is Black's advantage, what should his winning plan be, and how should he continue?

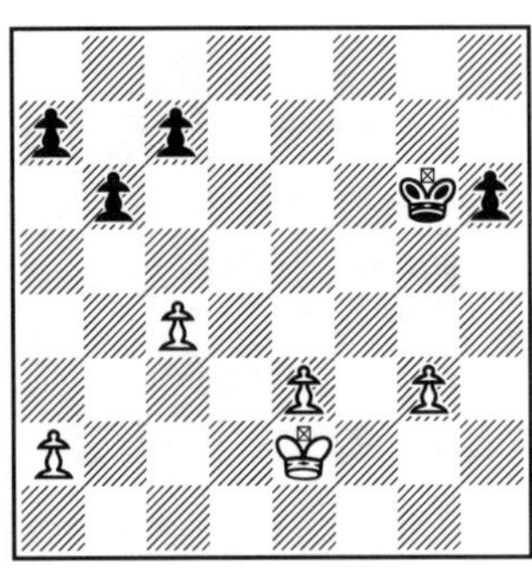

Diagram 181-Black to move

Although pawns are even, all the white pawns are isolated and weak;

Black's trump is his healthy 3:2 Queenside pawn majority, which can create an outside passed pawn. His winning plan is threefold:

1. Blockade the white passed e-pawn with the black King
2. Create an outside passed pawn on the Queenside
3. Promote a passed pawn on the Queenside; or, use the Queenside outside passed pawn as a decoy, capture the white Kingside pawns, then promote the black h-pawn to queen

With this direct plan in mind, Black's play is easy to understand:

1.	**...**	**Kf5**
2.	**Kf3**	**h5**
3.	**e4†**	**Ke5**
4.	**Ke3**	**c6**
5.	**a4**	**a6**
6.	**Kd3**	**b5**
7.	**cxb5**	**cxb5**
8.	**axb5**	**axb5**
9.	**Ke3**	**b4**
10.	**Kd3**	**b3**
11.	**Kc3**	**Kxe4**
12.	**Resigns**	

The black King will capture the white g3-pawn, then advance to g2 to shield the passed h-pawn; the black h-pawn will queen. Black's multiple queening threats on both wings prevailed.

In the next position (Diagram 182), White has an extra pawn, and both sides have two passed pawns: white d3- and e3-pawns and black a7- and b5-pawns. Given that a lone King can prevent two connected passed pawns from queening, but cannot safely capture either pawn, develop a winning plan for White.

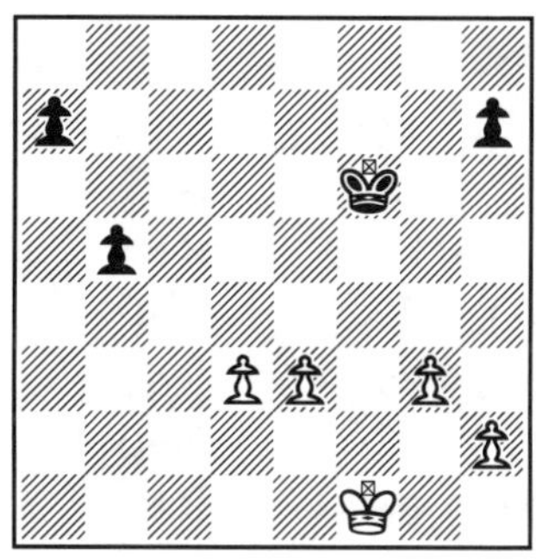

Diagram 182-White to move

With offsetting Queenside and center connected passed pawns, and a healthy 2:1 Kingside pawn majority, White developed the following winning plan:

1. Block the black Queenside connected passed pawns with the white King
2. Advance the white central passed pawns
3. Advance the white Kingside pawn majority to create a Kingside passed pawn
4. Promote a pawn in the center or on the Kingside

White's subsequent straightforward play followed this plan:

1.	Ke2	a5
2.	Kd2	b4
3.	Kc2	a4
4.	d4	Ke6
5.	e4	a3
6.	d5†	Ke5
7.	Kb3	Kd6

If *7... Kxe4??, 8. d6!* wins.

8.	g4!	

If *8. Kxb4??, 8... a2!* wins.

8.	...	Ke5
9.	h4	Kf6
10.	d6	Ke6
11.	e5	Kd7
12.	g5	Ke6
13.	h5	Kf7
14.	d7	Ke7
15.	e6	Kd8
16.	g6	hxg6
17.	hxg6	Ke7
18.	g7	**Resigns**

A white pawn will queen. Again, multiple queening threats are decisive.

In the next example (Diagram 183), a superior pawn structure is combined with a more active King. Find a winning plan for Black.

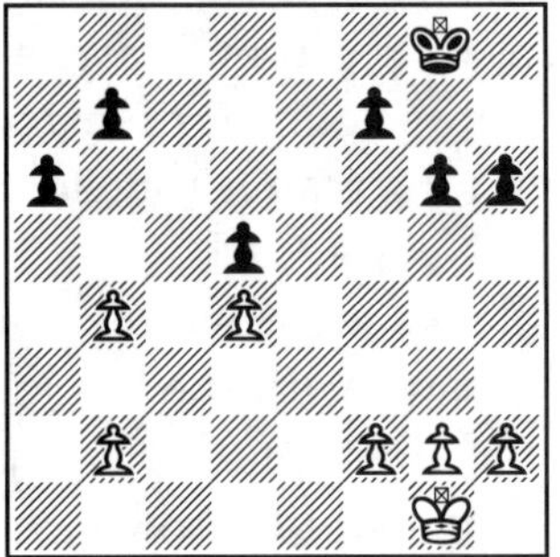

Diagram 183-Black to move

Material is even, but White has weak doubled and isolated Queenside pawns. Black forced a win in this position by combining the principles of *zugzwang*, offside pawn majority, and multiple queening threats. The winning plan Black developed was:

1. Attack the weak white b4-pawn with the black King (white King will defend)
2. Establish *zugzwang* for the defending white King by forcing White to exhaust his pawn moves
3. Capture the white b4-pawn with the black King
4. Utilize the resulting Black 2:1 Queenside pawn majority to create a Queenside outside passed pawn
5. Promote the Queenside passed pawn; or use it as a decoy, and win in the center or on the Kingside by

capturing white pawns with the black King, then promoting a black center or Kingside pawn

This lengthy and sophisticated, but eminently logical, multiphase plan succeeded for Black, as play continued:

1.	...	Kf8
2.	Kf1	Ke7
3.	Ke2	Kd6
4.	Kd3	Kc6
5.	Kc3	Kb5
6.	f4	Ka4!
7.	b3†	Kb5
8.	h4	h5
9.	g3	f5!
10.	Kc2	Kxb4
11.	Kb2	a5
12.	Kc2	b6!
13.	Kb2	b5
14.	Kc2	a4
15.	bxa4	bxa4
16.	Kb2	Kc4
17.	Ka3	Kxd4
18.	Kxa4	Kc3
19.	Ka3	d4
20.	Ka2	Kc2!
21.	Ka1	d3
22.	**Resigns**	

Black's King was more active, and Black's outside passed a-pawn served as an effective decoy to create multiple queening threats for Black.

A final, complex example from a tournament game (Diagram 184) illustrates simplifying, a more active King, and the possibility of winning pawn sacrifices by the defender. Can you find a winning plan for Black?

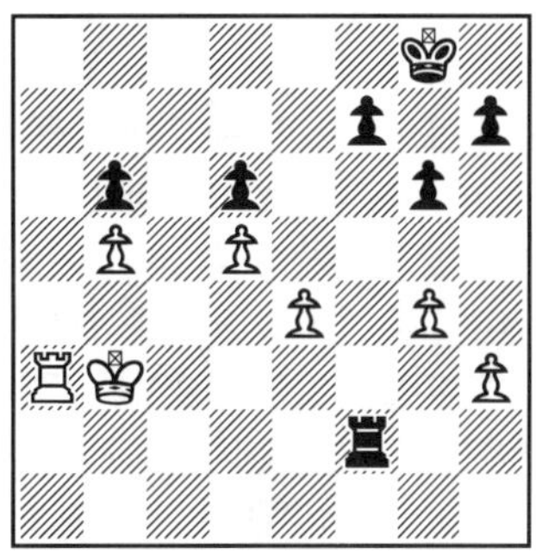

Diagram 184-Black to move

Material is even. White has a 2:1 central pawn majority, Black has a 3:2 Kingside pawn majority, and both sides have a Rook. The isolated black b6- and d6-pawns are vulnerable to the white Rook (*Ra6-Rxb6-Rxd6*), and if the black pawns were lost, White would have dangerous advanced outside passed b5- and d5-pawns. White has two backward pawns at e4 and h3, and Black will need to capture at least one of these weak white pawns to clear a path for a black Kingside pawn to queen.

Black visualized that if both Rooks were eliminated, Black would have the favorable King-and-pawn endgame because of White's weak pawns, and Black developed this winning plan:

1. Exchange Rooks (to protect the black b6- and d6-pawns)
2. Win the white h3- and g4-pawns with the black King
3. Promote a Kingside pawn

In the simplified endgame position following the forced exchange of Rooks, Black will use the principles of superior King position, triangulation, and *zugzwang* — carefully avoiding potential winning pawn sacrifices by White — to convert the Black 3:2 Kingside pawn majority into a win.

Black's initial target is the white h3-pawn; to keep White from advancing it to h4 and sealing the Kingside against entry by the black King, the black King must threaten to capture the white e4-pawn on his path to h3. This will keep the white King busy defending the vulnerable e4-pawn and not allow time for White's defensive *h3-h4* advance. Also, the black King must stay within the queening square of the white d5-pawn as long as the winning pawn sacrifice by White, *e5!*, is possible (*e5! dxe5*, *d6-d7-d8=Q*).

With all these considerations in mind, Black began:

1.	**...**	**Rf3†!**
2.	**Kb4**	**Rxa3**
3.	**Kxa3**	**Kg7**
4.	**Kb4**	

4. h4? allows the black King to reach and capture the backward white e4-pawn.

4.	**...**	**Kf6**
5.	**Kc4**	**Ke5**
6.	**Kd3**	**Kf4**

Heading for the weak white h3-pawn.

7. Kd4

Now the hasty *7... Kg3??* would lose to *8. e5!* (*8... dxe5† 9. Kxe5 Kxh3 10. d6!*).

7. ... f6!

To permit *...fxe5* if White plays *e5*.

8. Kd3

And now on the premature *8... Kg3??*, *9. g5!* wins for White, e.g., *9... fxg5* (else *10. gxf6* wins) *10. e5! dxe5 11. d6* and wins. These potential winning pawn sacrifices by White are worth careful study.

8. ... g5!

Now White's queening threats are over.

9. Kd4 Kg3

Finally.

10. Ke3 Kxh3

At last, the white h-pawn falls.

11. Kf3 Kh4!

Triangulating with the black King to win a second white pawn by *zugzwang*.

12.	**Ke3**	**Kxg4**
13.	**Ke2**	**Kf4**
14.	**Kd3**	**h5**
15.	**Resigns**	

Black has two extra pawns and

connected passed g- and h-pawns, and the black King threatens to win all the remaining white pawns if the white King defends against the advancing black Kingside passed pawns.

In this close endgame, one vital, early tempo made the difference. Black's more active King was one square closer to the center after the forced exchange of Rooks, which allowed the black King to penetrate White's vulnerable Kingside pawn formation. By threatening to capture the white e4-pawn with the black King, Black gave White no time to play the prophylactic *h3-h4* to prevent the black King's incursion.

These examples of practical endgame play should reinforce the knowledge and skills you will need to win close endgames. Effective endgame play begins with a sound plan based on advantages in pawn structure or King position, and all the preceding examples of practical endgame play featured sound, winning plans based on these features.

Chapter 13

STUDY LESSON GAMES

Learn one lesson from each game and you will soon become a strong chessplayer.

The successful chessplayer is a student of the game. An intermediate player desiring to improve has two primary needs. The first is to increase his practical chess *knowledge* by studying instructive positions and well-played games, to develop skill in recognizing mistakes and learn winning chess ideas and techniques. The second is to organize, summarize, remember, then *apply* in his own games the key lessons learned from the positions and games studied.

Both practical needs are addressed in this chapter. Seven annotated Study Games played by an Expert with opponents of various strengths are presented. Each Study Game offers an important lesson.

The primary lessons and openings in the seven Study Games are:

1.	Strong center	*Ruy Lopez*
2.	Premature attack	*Bishop's Opening*
3.	Sacrifices	*Curry's Opening*
4.	Weaknesses	*Tartakower's Defense*
5.	Pawnstorm	*King's Indian Defense*
6.	Counterattack	*Sicilian Defense*
7.	Positional play	*English Opening*

These Study Games feature key chess principles and reflect positions similar to those you will encounter. The losing mistakes are typical, and the winning refutations — tactical and positional — are highly instructive. For maximum benefit, cover the Expert's moves and try to find his best move before uncovering the move actually played. The ratings of the opponents are indicated (Class A, very strong; Class B, strong; Class C, average tournament chessplayer strength).

A strong chessplayer has more knowledge, evaluates positions more correctly, and analyzes positions more accurately. Studying these instructive games will help you develop these important skills.

1. Strong Center

(Ruy Lopez)

A strong pawn center yields more maneuvering space and cramps the opponent, dividing enemy pieces and restricting their coordination. The spatial advantage conferred by a strong center often serves as a basis for effective middlegame strategy and tactics, and can lead to early attacking opportunities.

Expert Class C

1. e4

The classic opening move.

1. ... e5

The classic reply.

2. Nf3

Develops a piece with an attack on Black's e5-pawn.

2. ... Nc6

Defends the threatened e-pawn by developing a piece.

3. Bb5

The venerable and powerful Ruy Lopez opening, with themes of central pressure and ultimately a Kingside attack.

3. ... a6

Paul Morphy's defense, still sound over a century later.

4. Ba4

White cannot win a pawn with *4. Bxc6 dxc6 5. Nxe5* because *5... Qd4* recovers the pawn favorably.

4. ... Nf6

5. 0–0 Be7

Opting for the safer Closed Variation. *5... Nxe4* is the tactical Open Variation, in which White soon recovers his pawn with complicated play.

6. Re1 b5

7. Bb3 0–0

8. c3

Prepares 9. *d4* for a STRONG CENTER, and provides a retreat square (c2) for the B/b3.

8. ... Bb7

Indirect pressure on White's e4-pawn.

9. d4 exd4?

A strategic mistake. After *10. cxd4* White will have a STRONG IDEAL CENTER (pawns abreast at d4 and e4) dominating the center.

Instead of surrendering the center with 9... *exd4*, Black should have reinforced his e-pawn with

9... *d6*. Then if *10. dxe5, ...dxe5* and Black retains his share of center control.

10. cxd4 Bb4

Attacks White's R/e1 and moves the Bishop outside the black pawn chain before playing *...d6*, which would otherwise hem in the Bishop at e7.

11. Nc3 Ne7

Attacks White's e4-pawn twice. *11... Bxc3 12. bxc3* instead would only strengthen White's already STRONG CENTER.

12. Bc2

Guards the e-pawn twice (White's N/c3 is pinned).

12. ... Re8

Adds indirect pressure on White's e-pawn.

13. Qd3

Threat: *14. e5!* followed by *15. Qxh7†*. Threats are beginning to arise from White's STRONG CENTER.

13. ... d6!

Good defense! Now on *14. e5 dxe5 15. dxe5, ...Qxd3* stops White's attack.

14. a3

Forces a decision from the black B/b4.

14. ... Bxc3

Strengthens White's imposing center. *14... Ba5* (if *15. b4, ...Bb6)* would have been preferable for Black.

15. bxc3 Nc6

15... Ng6, blocking the line of White's Queen-and-Bishop battery, was far more prudent.

16. Bg5

A delayed but effective pin.

16. ... h6

17. Bh4

Holds a strong pin.

17. ... Na5

The black Knight is headed for a Queenside outpost on c4, but the action is in the center and on the Kingside.

Black's pieces are not cooperating well, due to the cramping effect of White's STRONG CENTER.

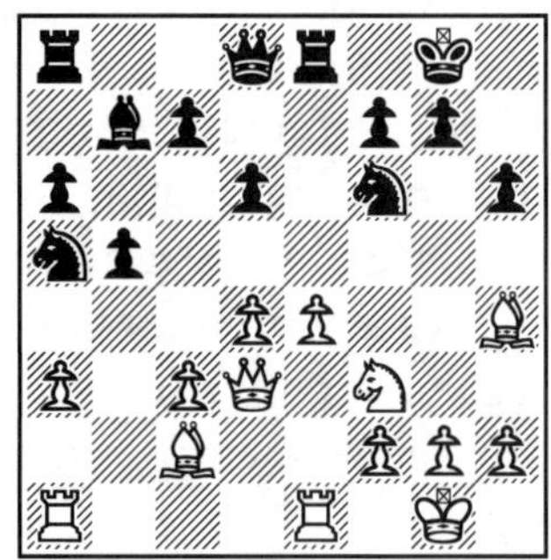

Diagram 185-White to move

18. e5!

The breakthrough—opens the b1-h7 diagonal for the white Queen.

18. ... dxe5

19. Nxe5

Occupies a strong central outpost. *19. dxe5* instead allows *...Qxd3!*, reducing White's attacking advantage.

Compare the present activity of the white and black pieces!

19. ... Qd5

Black desperately strikes back with the brutal threat *20... Qxg2#!*

20. f3 Re6

To answer *21. Bxf6* with *21... Rxf6*, placing the black Rook in an attacking position and avoiding doubled Kingside pawns; but *...g5* (to prevent *Bxf6)* was Black's last hope.

21. Bxf6! Rxf6

21... gxf6 succumbs to *22. Qh7† Kf8 23. Qxf7#*. White's secure, centralized N/e5 is decisive.

22. Qh7† Kf8

Forced. The stage is set for a decisive sacrifice.

23. Nd7†!!

A startling and winning line-clearing sacrifice with check that eliminates the black King's e-file flight squares and must be accepted. A Knight check cannot be interposed, and the black King has no flight squares.

23. ... Qxd7

A sad, forced choice.

24. Qh8#

White established a STRONG CENTER early, and used it effectively — first to cramp and split Black's forces, then to thrust in the center and achieve a powerful, centralized piece position which quickly developed into a winning attack.

Black's puny center offered little scope for his pieces and minimum chances for effective resistance.

2. Premature Attack (Bishop's Opening)

Premature attacks are early, unjustified attacks, often involving unsound sacrifices, without effective, immediate follow-up. They pose dangers for unwary or careless defenders, but accurate defense will repel or refute such unjustified attacks, often leaving the attacker in a vulnerable position with scattered and undeveloped pieces. The antidote to a premature attack is patient consolidation followed by vigorous counterattack.

Class C Expert

1. e4 e5
2. Bc4 Nf6
3. d4

The ancient (circa 1500) Bishop's Opening.

3. ... Nxe4

3... exd4 is "book." Then *4. e5* is met by *...d5!*; or if *4. Qxd4*, *...Nc6* gains a tempo for Black.

4. Bxf7†?!

An early, unjustified — but potentially troublesome — sacrificial attack. Premature or brilliant?

4. ... Kxf7

Declining the sacrifice with *4... Ke7* — losing a pawn and castling privileges, plus blocking the King-Bishop and Queen — is unthinkable.

5. Qf3† Nf6

To save the Knight.

6. dxe5

White threatens to win Black's pinned N/f6 and regain his sacrificed piece with advantage. How should Black respond?

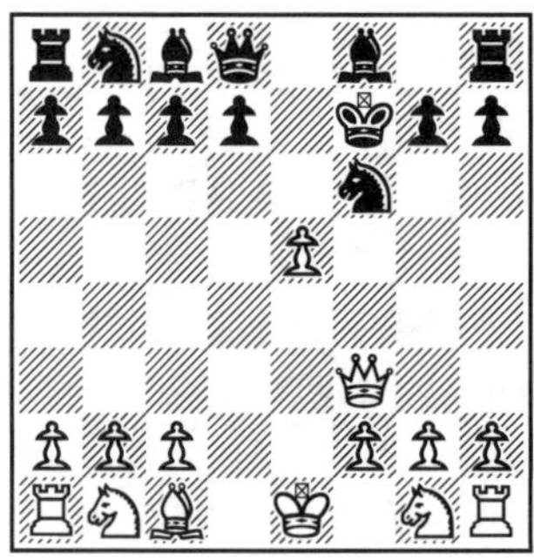

Diagram 186-Black to move

6. ... Qe8!

A precise, saving counterpin, pinning and attacking White's unprotected e5-pawn. *6... Qe7* would obstruct Black's King-Bishop.

7. Bf4 d6

Attacking White's bayonet e5-pawn before White can unpin it with *Ne2*. White's e5-pawn must be eliminated to save the N/f6.

8. Ne2

Unpins the e5-pawn and threatens *9. exf6*.

8. ... dxe5

9. Bg5 Nbd7

10. 0–0 Be7

A slight inaccuracy. Black should play *10... Qe6* first to prevent *11. Qb3†*, a move potentially awkward for Black.

11. Nbc3

White misses his chance to play *11. Qb3†*.

11. ... Rf8!

Black will "castle by hand."

12. Bxf6 Nxf6

13. Ne4

White presses his "attack."

13. ... Kg8

Insures King safety. Now *14. Qb3†* is simply and effectively answered by *14... Kh8*. The black King has found safe shelter.

14. Nxf6†

Throwing good pieces after bad. A Bishop behind, White should not make unforced or unprofitable exchanges.

14. ... Bxf6

14... Rxf6 is fine too, followed by *...Bd6* with free and easy development for Black, a piece ahead.

15. Qb3†

Far too late.

15. ... Qe6

A Bishop ahead, Black would welcome a Queen trade.

16. c4 b6

Prepares to activate the B/c8.

17. Rad1 Bb7

The initial tactical flurry has subsided, and Black, by patient consolidation and development, has emerged a Bishop ahead with a solid position. White's sacrificial PREMATURE ATTACK has been refuted. White has no compensation for his lost piece.

18. Rfe1

Planning *19. Nf4* or *19. Nd4* attacking the black Queen.

18. ... Kh8

There will be no discovered checks (*c5†*) after the black Queen vacates e6.

19. Nf4 Qg4

Black threatens *20... exf4*, then *21... Qxg2#*.

20. g3?

Loses a second piece. *20. Nd5* was White's only chance.

20. ... exf4

Black is a Knight and Bishop ahead.

21. Rd3

White has vulnerable light squares around his King—a weak-square complex.

21. ... Qh3

Threat: *22... Qg2#*.

22. f3 fxg3

New threat: *23... Qxh2† 24. Kf1 Qf2#*.

23. Re2 c5!

To support *24... Bd4†*, increasing the pressure on the white King.

24. hxg3 Bd4†

The white King has no flight squares.

25. Rde3 Rxf3

White's R/e3 is pinned, and Black threatens *26... Rf1#*.

26. Qd1

Guards against *26... Rf1#*.

26. ... Raf8

Renews the threat of mate on f1. All of Black's pieces participate in the attack.

27. Re1

Protects the first rank.

27. ... Rxg3#

White's early sacrificial PREMATURE ATTACK was unjustified and unsound. Black patiently consolidated and completed his development, then launched a virulent and successful counterattack which won more material and led to mate.

3. Sacrifices

(Curry's Opening)

Sacrifices often play a vital role in attacks. Timely sacrifices can open lines, expose and restrict the enemy King, improve the scope and mobility of attacking pieces, remove key defenders, and gain control of important squares. In this lively game, White makes three(!) sacrifices and pummels the black King into submission.

Expert Class B

1. d4 Nf6

A flexible move that develops a Kingside piece, prevents *2. e4*, and leads to numerous defenses.

2. Nf3 g6

Black intends to fianchetto his King-Bishop at g7 — usually a sturdy defense to *1. d4*.

3. Bg5

Threatens *4. Bxf6* doubling Black's Kingside pawns.

3. ... Bg7

4. e3 0–0

King safety first.

5. Bd3

An aggressive post. If *5. Bc4, ...d5* and White loses a tempo.

5. ... d5

Black is playing a Gruenfeld Defense against White's Curry Opening.

6. Nbd2

Rather than *6. Nc3*, to allow *c3* and *Qc2* with Kingside pressure.

6. ... Nbd7

7. c3 Re8

Prepares a central pawn advance.

8. Qc2 e5

Threatens *9... e4* winning material.

9. dxe5 Nxe5

10. Nxe5 Rxe5

Threat: *11... Rxg5*.

11. Nf3

Protects the B/g5 and attacks the black R/e5.

11. ... Re8

12. 0–0–0

White plans a thematic Curry Opening Kingside attack.

12. ... c6

Releases the black Queen to the Queenside for counterattack.

13. h4

White's Kingside attack begins.

13. ... h6

Puts the question to the B/g5.

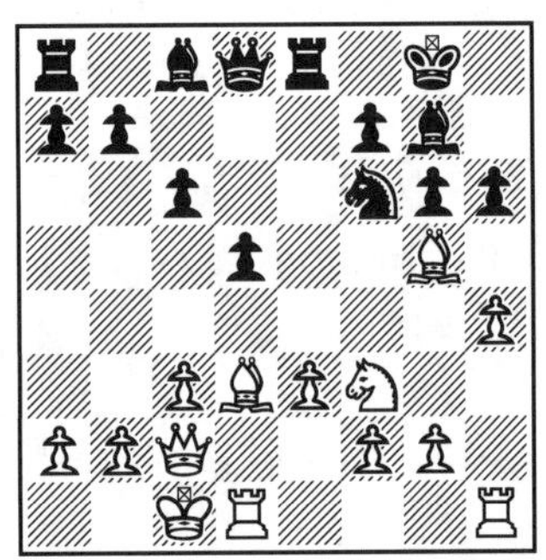

Diagram 187-White to move

14. Bxg6!?

Sacrifice #1 — to strip the black King of pawn protection (if *...fxg6, 15. Qxg6*).

14. ... hxg5

Wins a Bishop, but allows White to open the dangerous h-file.

15. hxg5!?

Sacrifice #2 — to open the h-file.

15. ... fxg6

Black gobbles all the offered material — White has sacrificed two Bishops.

16. Qxg6

Foregoing *gxf6* to penetrate with the Queen.

16. ... Ne4

Saves the Knight and threatens *17... Nxf2* winning a pawn and forking the white Rooks.

17. Rh7

Brutal threat: *18. Qxg7#.*

17. ... Qc7

Defends the B/g7.

18. Rdh1

New threat: *19. Rh8#!*

18. ... Kf8

The black King tries to escape.

19. Rh8†!

Sacrifice #3 — drives the black King into a mating net.

19. ... Bxh8

Declining the Rook sacrifice succumbs to mate in two: *19... Ke7 20. Rxe8† Kd7 21. Qe6#.*

20. Rxh8† Ke7

Forced.

21. Rxe8† Resigns

On *21... Kd7* (forced), *22. Qe6#.*

After a conventional opening, White played three strong SACRIFICES to denude and trap the black King, and Black was unable to withstand White's powerful sacrificial onslaught.

4. Weaknesses (Tartakower's Defense)

Tactics win chess games, and every successful tactic is based on one or more *weaknesses* in your opponent's position. Weaknesses can be tactical or positional, short- or long-term, temporary or permanent; but the secret of winning chess is to attack them. A positionally sound opening and early middlegame form the foundation for effective tactics.

Class C Expert

1. d4 d5
2. c4 e6

Declining the Queen's Gambit. Accepting the gambit with *2... dxc4* yields Black active piece play, but cedes the center to White after an early *e2-e4*.

3. Nc3 Nf6
4. Bg5 Be7
5. e3 0-0
6. Nf3 h6

Forces a decision by the white B/g5.

7. Bh4 b6

Black intends to fianchetto his Queen-Bishop.

8. Rc1

cxd5 first to hinder the impending fianchettoed black B/b7 is preferable.

8. ... Bb7
9. Bd3

9. ... dxc4

Opens the fianchettoed B/b7's diagonal with tempo by attacking White's B/d3.

10. Bxc4 Nbd7
11. 0–0 c5
12. Re1 Rc8

White's B/c4 is vulnerable after *...cxd4*.

13. Bd3 cxd4
14. Nxd4 Re8

Protects the B/e7 and unpins the N/f6 should the black Queen move.

15. e4 Nc5

White's N/d4 is *en prise*.

16. Bxf6 Bxf6
17. e5 Be7

A more flexible post than the tempting g5-square.

18. h3?

Trap—hoping for *18... Qxd4? 19. Bh7†!* winning the greedy black Queen.

18. ... Nxd3!
19. Qxd3

White's N/d4 is pinned — a WEAKNESS.

19. ... Bc5

Attacks the pinned Knight twice.

20. Red1 Qg5

Threatens *21... Qxg2#!*

21. f3

White's vulnerable f3-pawn (unprotected by the pinned g2-pawn—a WEAKNESS) is guarded by both the white Knight and Queen; but the Knight is pinned (another WEAKNESS!), and the Queen guards the weak, pinned Knight.

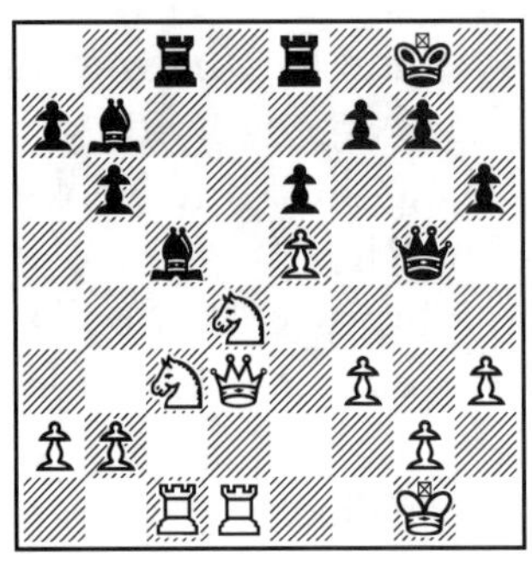

Diagram 188-Black to move

Black removes both White's f-pawn defenders with one stroke.

21. ... Bxd4†!
22. Qxd4 Bxf3

Black threats: *23... Qxg2#* and *23... Bxd1*.

23. Rd2

The white R/d2 is a vital guard preventing mate on g2; but this Rook is in line with the more valuable Queen (a WEAKNESS), and is thus susceptible to a skewer.

23. ... Red8!
24. Qf2

If *24. Qxd8†, ...Rxd8 25. Rxd8† Qxd8 26. gxf3 Qg5† 27. Kf2 Qxc1* and Black wins.

24. ... Rxd2
25. Qxf3

Holding the position for now. So far, White has lost only the Exchange and a pawn.

25. ... Rxg2†

Simplifies and wins a pawn.

26. Qxg2 Qxc1†

The white R/c1 was an unguarded piece — a WEAKNESS.

27. Kh2 Rd8

Threatens *28... Rd2!* winning the pinned white Queen — a WEAKNESS.

28. Ne4

Guards the sensitive d2 invasion square.

28. ... Qf4†

Decisive double attack on the white King and Knight.

29. Kg1

On *29. Ng3, ...Rd2!* wins; or if *29. Qg3, ...Qxe4* also wins easily.

29. ... Rd1†

30. Resigns

Mate is forced: *30. Qf1 Qxf1† 31. Kh2 Qg1#.*

Pressure from Black induced White to create a succession of small WEAKNESSES in his position, which Black adroitly exploited. Black's progressive middlegame tactics (pin, removing the guard, skewer, and double attack) were based directly on White's WEAKNESSES, forcing decisive positional and material concessions from White which led to checkmate.

5. Pawnstorm (King's Indian Defense)

A pawnstorm occurs when pawns are advanced toward the opposing King's position. The idea is to open lines with pawn exchanges so that attacking pieces can penetrate and checkmate. Pawnstorms usually occur when Kings are castled on opposite wings; otherwise, pawnstorming would denude and expose the attacking side's own King.

Expert Class B

1. d4 Nf6
2. c4 g6
3. Nc3 Bg7
4. e4

Seizes the center.

4. ... d6

Discourages *5. e5*, prevents a later *Ne5*, and releases the Queen-Bishop.

5. Be2 0–0

Black has adopted the popular and reliable King's Indian Defense.

6. Bg5 h6

This slight weakening of Black's Kingside will prove significant later. *6... c5* or *6... Nbd7* is the road to equality.

7. Be3

The attacked Bishop retreats to a flexible central post.

7. ... Nbd7

Prepares *...e5* or *...c5* to strike

at White's imposing center.

8. Qd2

Menacing 9. *Bxh6*.

8. ... Kh7

If 8... *h5* instead, 9. *Bh6* forces the exchange of Black's fianchettoed Bishop and weakens the black King's protection.

9. g4

A bayonet pawn thrust that threatens *10. g5* opening lines near the black King (the result of 6... *h6)*. White's PAWNSTORM has begun. (Note that if White takes time for 9. *0–0–0* first, Black can respond 9... *Nb6*; then *10. g4* would lose the pawn.)

9. ... Ne8

So if *10. g5*, ...*h5* closes Kingside lines.

10. h4

White pursues his energetic PAWNSTORMING attack, keeping his pawns flexible.

10. ... b6

Black attempts to develop some Queenside pieces for counterplay.

11. f4

The ultimate PAWNSTORM! White's unusual pawn formation is jocularly referred to as the "Curry 6-Pawns Attack."

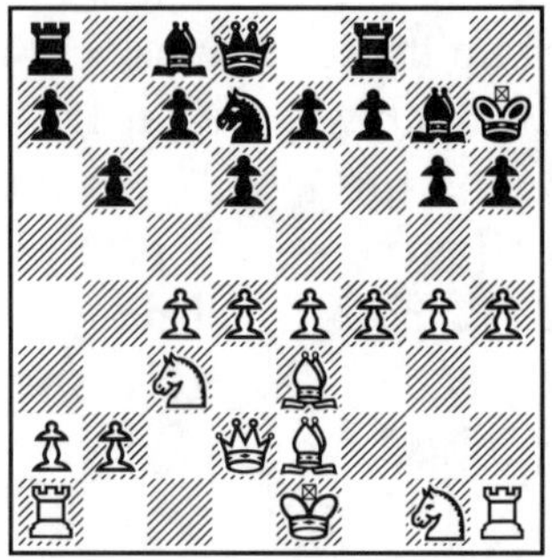

Diagram 189-Black to move

11. ... Bb7

Aims at the white R/h1.

12. Nf3

Develops a new piece and partially blocks the sensitive h1-a8 diagonal.

12. ... f6

For flexibility in meeting White's PAWNSTORM.

13. 0–0–0

King safety first, before attack. *0–0–0* also brings White's Queen-Rook into position for Kingside activity.

13. ... Rc8

Black aligns his Queen-Rook with the white King, intending ...*c5* with Queenside counterplay.

14. h5

White plans to open Kingside lines with pawn exchanges — the initial intent of a PAWNSTORM.

14. ... g5

Black tries to keep the position near his King closed. Attackers seek open lines; defenders usually require closed lines.

15. e5!

An excellent, fluid move to open lines toward the black King. White's PAWNSTORM is in full progress, and is becoming dangerous.

If instead *15. fxg5, ...fxg5* and White's Kingside PAWNSTORM is stalled.

15. ... Bxf3

Removes one potential attacker to diminish White's Kingside pressure. Well-timed exchanges often break up a promising attack.

16. Bxf3 fxe5

A further point of *15... Bxf3:* White's f4-pawn is pinned, and Black's e5-pawn is adequately guarded. Black also threatens *17... exf4* completely blocking White's PAWNSTORM. Has White lost a valuable pawn?

17. Be4†!

This sharp in-between move saves the imperiled white f-pawn and furthers White's PAWNSTORMING attack.

17. ... Kh8

18. fxg5 exd4

Recovers the pawn and attacks White's Bishop and Knight.

19. gxh6!

A strong counter-blow. If instead *19. Bxd4, ...e5!* closes lines and slows White's attack.

19. ... dxe3

Captures a piece and attacks the white Queen.

20. hxg7†!

Another superlative in-between stroke, which removes a key defender near the black King.

20. ... Nxg7

Brings a replacement defender to the critical vicinity of the black King.

21. Qxe3 Nf6

Rushes more resources to the vulnerable Kingside. Black hopes for *22... Nxe4* next to weaken White's attack.

22. Qh6+

Now that White's PAWNSTORM has opened lines with pawn exchanges, the attacking white pieces can penetrate the black King's position.

22. ... Kg8

Of course not *22... Nh7?? 23. Qxh7#.*

23. Bg6

Further penetration which traps the black King without a flight square. And Black's N/f6 cannot move because of *Qh7#.*

23. ... e5

Releases the black Queen for defense.

24. g5!

Wins a piece, as the attacked N/f6 is a vital guard shackled to defending h7 against mate.

White's attack is too strong; he now has a clear win.

24. ... Nge8

To maintain an essential guard on h7 after *25. gxf6*.

25. gxf6 Nxf6

White has several intriguing possibilities at his disposal, including *26. Nd5* (or *Ne4*) or *Rdf1* (or *Rhf1)* attacking the vital guard N/f6; but *26... Qd7* would prolong Black's resistance. White chooses the most convincing conclusion.

26. Rhg1!

The black King has no flight squares, and must submit to the upcoming discovered check. Black can forestall, but not prevent, checkmate.

26. ... Qe7

To defend against mate threats on Black's second rank. The black monarch expires after the desperate defense *26... Rf7 27. Bf5† Rg7 28. Qxg7#*.

27. Be8†

A precise discovered check that eliminates the black King's f7 flight square.

27. ... Resigns

Black can only futilely interpose pieces to delay checkmate.

Black weakened his Kingside pawn structure early, and White effectively exploited the black King's vulnerable position with an aggressive PAWNSTORM attack. Black's feeble Queenside counterattack died aborning.

6. Counterattack (Sicilian Defense)

Counterattack is often an effective defense, either on individual moves or as a general strategy. Counterattacks epitomize active play, but must equal or exceed the opponent's original threat; else material, or even the game, may be lost. Successful counterattacks usually require sharp tactics and accurate timing.

Class A Expert

1. e4

An excellent opening move which usually leads to more fluid and volatile positions than *1. d4*.

1. ... c5

The asymmetric Sicilian Defense, Black's most aggressive and ambitious counter to *1. e4*.

2. Nf3 d6

Prepares a later *...Nf6* without *e4-e5* evicting the black Knight, and releases Black's Queen-Bishop.

3. d4 cxd4

Black exchanges a wing pawn for a center pawn, to: 1) to establish a central Black pawn majority; 2) destroy White's temporary *ideal pawn center*; and 3) create a half-open c-file for Black's major pieces later.

4. Nxd4 Nf6

Develops a Kingside piece (furthers *...0-0)* and prevents the

Maroczy Bind (*5. c4)* by attacking the white e4-pawn.

5. Nc3 g6

The main alternative is 5... *a6*, leading to the Najdorf Variation.

6. Be3 Bg7

Entering the Dragon Variation of the Sicilian Defense, named for Black's serpentine pawn formation and fianchettoed King-Bishop.

7. f3

This move initiates the popular and very strong Yugoslav Attack — White intends *0-0-0* followed by a Kingside *pawnstorm*.

The move *7. f3* serves three useful functions: 1) prevents ...*Ng4* from attacking the white B/e3; 2) defends the e4-pawn, freeing the N/c3 from guard duty; and 3) serves as a support for a *g2-g4* thrust later.

7. ... 0-0

Whisks the black King to safety.

8. Qd2

Threat: 9. *Bh6* to eliminate Black's "Dragon" Bishop — a main offensive/defensive weapon — and weaken Black's castled position.

8. ... Nc6

Well-timed defense by COUNTERATTACK. Now if 9. *Bh6?*, ...*Bxh6!* nets Black a piece, since the white Queen is overworked (on *10. Qxh6*, ...*Nxd4)*.

9. Bc4 Bd7

10. 0-0-0

Prelude to a Kingside pawnstorm.

10. ... Qa5

Black initiates a Queenside COUNTERATTACK by aggressively positioning his Queen near the white King.

11. h4

White's Kingside pawnstorm begins.

11. ... Rfc8

Black increases the Queenside pressure (COUNTERATTACK) with a veiled threat against White's unguarded B/c4. This move also allows Black to retain his fianchettoed Bishop with ...*Bh8* if White plays *Bh6*.

12. Bb3

Prudently retreating the Bishop. If White immediately pursues his pawnstorm with *12. g4?*, Black wins the endangered B/c4 (*12... Nxd4 13. Qxd4 Nxg4! 14. Qd3 Nxe3 15. Qxe3 Rxc4)* and emerges a Bishop ahead. White can play "desperado" with *15. Bxf7† Kxf7 16. Qxe3*, but the white Bishop is still lost.

12. ... Ne5

Uncovers the R/c8 on the important c-file for COUNTERATTACK, and will eliminate one of White's strong Bishops on the next move.

13. Kb1

Unaligns the King with the black R/c8.

13. ... Nc4

Forces the exchange of one white Bishop by simultaneously attacking the white Queen and B/e3.

14. Bxc4

White relinquishes the less valuable Bishop. On *14. Qd3, ...Nxe3* and Black's fianchettoed Bishop reigns sovereign on the dark-square domain.

14. ... Rxc4

Black can now double (or triple) major pieces on the half-open c-file.

15. Nb3

Chases the black Queen and reinforces White's castled position.

15. ... Qc7

Maintains Black's COUNTERATTACK on the half-open c-file. *15... Qa6* was an alternative, followed by *...Rac8* with Queenside pressure.

16. Bd4!

A strong, multipurpose move by White to: 1) guard against a thematic Black Exchange sacrifice (*...Rxc3*) later; 2) prepare *Bxg7*, eliminating Black's strong fianchettoed Bishop, if the black N/f6 moves; and 3) threaten to win a pawn and disorganize Black with *17. Bxf6 Bxf6 18. Nd5! Qc6 19. Nxf6† exf6 20. Qxd6*.

Black must be careful.

16. ... Be6

Defends against a Knight invasion (*Nd5*) and aims another COUNTERATTACKING piece at the white King's position.

17. g4

White continues his Kingside pawnstorm, threatening *h5* and *hxg6* opening the h-file for attack.

17. ... a5

Black COUNTERATTACKS on the Queenside.

18. h5

Consistent Kingside attack, but the prophylactic *18. a4* first is more accurate (to prevent *...a4* from evicting the N/b3).

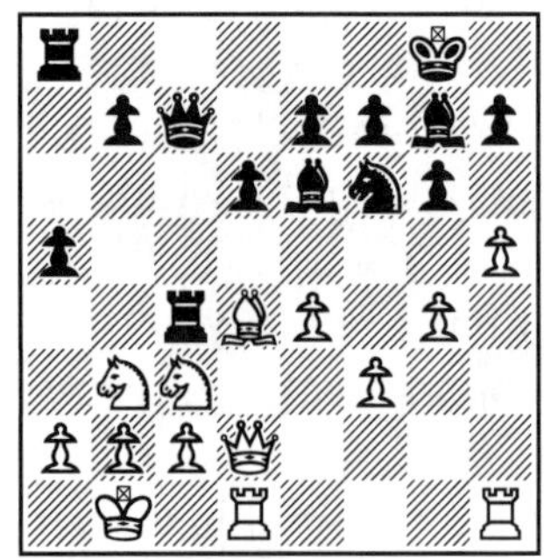

Diagram 190-Black to move

18. ... a4

Consistent Queenside COUNTERATTACK.

19. Nc1 Nxe4!

Black alertly snares a valuable center pawn and opens the "Dragon" Bishop's diagonal with the immediate peril of *20... Nxd2*.

20. Nxe4 Rxd4

Black has won a pawn.

21. Qh2 Rxd1

Black's best choice. This disarming move reduces White's pressure on the h-file and clears the aggressive "Dragon" Bishop's diagonal toward the white King.

22. Rxd1 a3

A well-timed pawn thrust to open lines near the white King. The tempting *22… Qb6* (threatening *23… Qxb2#)* is met by *23. Nd3*.

23. hxg6

23. b3? would be countered by the riposte *23… f5 24. Ng5* (or *Nd2) Qc3!* and Black mates on the next move.

23. … axb2!

A carefully calculated move in a taut position, since White has the in-between *Qxh7†* before saving his Knight.

24. Qxh7† Kf8

The terminus of White's aggression. White has no checkmate, and Black threatens *25… bxc1=Q†* winning a Knight. White must exercise caution in moving the threatened Knight (on *25. Nd3??* or *25. Ne2??, …Bxa2#!)*.

25. Nb3

Saves the Knight and prevents immediate mate by blocking the diagonal of the B/e6.

25. … Rxa2!!

A strong surprise *sacrifice* that shatters White's defense — the threat is *26… Bxb3 27. cxb3 Ra1#!*

26. Kxa2 Qa5†

White's N/b3 is pinned, and the aggressive white Queen is a helpless, distant spectator.

27. Kb1 Qa1†!

A second remarkable but logical sacrifice — the culmination of Black's persistent Queenside COUNTERATTACK — that forces mate.

28. Nxa1

A final forced move.

28. … bxa1=R#

The "Dragon" Bishop prevails!

Black met White's aggressive Kingside pawnstorm attack with a virulent and sustained sacrificial Queenside COUNTERATTACK, and won convincingly. Consistent COUNTERATTACK and carefully timed sharp tactics were the essential keys to Black's victory.

7. Positional Play (English Opening)

Positional play involves controlling important squares and lines for maximum power and flexibility, as a prelude to effective tactics. Superior positional play establishes the positions and creates the conditions for successful tactics and attacks.

Expert Class B

1. c4

The English Opening — a reversed Sicilian Defense with an extra move — is usually positional, with tactical possibilities. The initial aim is to gain control of the d5-square.

1. ... c5

Sound alternatives are *1... e5*, *1... e6*, *1... Nf6*, and *1... g6*, *1... f5* (Dutch Defense) is also playable.

2. Nc3

Controls the d5-square, planning a N/d5 outpost later.

2. ... Nc6
3. Nf3 e5
4. d3 Nge7

Permits *...f7-f5* later, if desired.

5. g3

White intends to fianchetto his King-Bishop at g2 to exert pressure along the h1-a8 diagonal, especially on the d5-square.

5. ... Nf5

Black controls the d4-square.

6. Bg2 Be7
7. 0–0 d6
8. Nd5!

The white Knight occupies a key central outpost.

8. ... 0–0
9. a3

White plans Queenside expansion with *b2-b4*.

9. ... Be6

Challenges White's outpost N/d5.

10. Nd2!

Now the B/g2 guards the N/d5, preserving the important outpost.

10. ... f6

If *...Bxd5*, *11. Bxd5*.

11. Nb1

Awkward-looking preliminary move enables *Nbc3* to reinforce the N/d5 outpost.

11. ... Qd7
12. Nbc3

White's N/d5 outpost is secure.

12. ... Kh8

Planless and cramped, Black waits. White's positional superiority (more active pieces, mobile pawns) is already evident.

13. b4 cxb4
14. axb4 Rfc8

Black anticipates Queenside action.

15. b5 Nd8
16. Bd2 Nf7
17. Ra3

White plans to control the a-file with major pieces.

17. ... Nd4

Black vainly tries to establish a central Knight outpost.

18. e3

Evicts the N/d4 promptly.

18. ... Bxd5

Eliminates one white outpost Knight and vacates the e6 retreat square for the N/d4.

19. Nxd5

Maintains a central Knight outpost; *19. cxd5?* would isolate the b5-pawn and block the B/g2.

19. ... Ne6

20. Bb4

For *Bxc5* if *...Nc5*.

20. ... Bd8

Escapes the Knight's attack and controls dark squares on the Queenside.

21. Qa1

White adds pressure to the a-file; the immediate threat is *Rxa7* winning a pawn. White's pieces are active, while the black pieces are passive.

21. ... b6

Allows the Q/d7 to guard the a7-pawn.

22. Nc3!

Discovers an attack (from the B/g2) on the R/a8 defending the a7-pawn.

22. ... Rab8

Saves the Rook, but loses the a-pawn.

23. Rxa7

First booty from White's superior POSITIONAL PLAY.

23. ... Bc7

Interposes the Rook's attack on the black Queen.

24. Qa6

Prepares *Ra1* tripling major pieces on the a-file; *Bc6* first restricts Black even more.

24. ... Nc5

Attacks the white Queen.

25. Bxc5 dxc5

...bxc5? would give White a passed b5-pawn.

26. Nd5

Reestablishes a central Knight outpost and attacks the pinned B/c7.

26. ... Qd6

Unpins the B/c7.

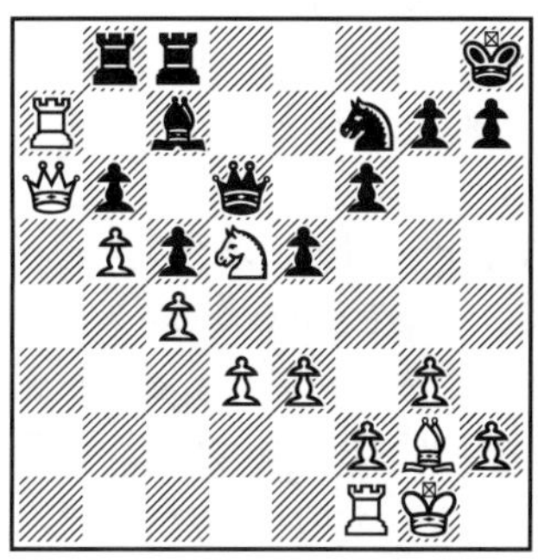

Diagram 191-White to move

27. Bh3!

This tactical stroke wins material — attacks the R/c8 defending the B/c7.

27. ... Rd8

Otherwise, *Bxc8* wins even greater material.

28. Rxc7

Wins the Bishop and attacks the unguarded N/f7. White is realizing the tactical payoff of his earlier superior POSITIONAL PLAY.

28. ... Ng5

Attacks the B/h3.

29. Bg2

The Bishop returns to a key diagonal.

29. ... h6

Provides a flight square (h7) for the black King.

30. Ra1

Controls the a-file; if *30... Ra8, 31. Ra7* or *31. Qxa8 Rxa8 32. Rxa8†* gains two Rooks for the Queen.

30. ... Ne6

The Knight heads for the Queenside, the scene of action, and attacks the R/c7.

31. Rc6

Attacks the black Queen and b6-pawn (thrice).

31. ... Qd7

The black pieces have very little maneuvering room.

32. Rxb6 Nc7

Harasses the white Queen.

33. Nxc7

Simplifies. With a 5-point (Bishop and two pawns) material advantage and a passed b-pawn, White seeks to eliminate pieces.

33. ... Qxc7

Threatens the R/b6 (and *...Rxd3*).

34. Rxb8 Qxb8

Maintains the *...Rxd3* threat.

35. Qa8!

White seeks to liquidate pieces and queen his b-pawn.

35. ... Qd6

Black avoids the Queen trade, and threatens *...Rxa8* and *...Qxd3*.

36. Qxd8†!

A temporary sacrifice which forces *...Qxd8* (or loss of the black Queen).

36. ... Qxd8

37. Ra8

Forces the exchange of the pinned black Queen for a Rook.

37. ... Resigns

After the forced Queen-for-Rook trade, the white b-pawn will queen.

With superior POSITIONAL PLAY, White established early control of an important central square (d5) and line (a-file) to dominate play. White's ensuing multiple central Knight outposts and tripled major pieces on the a-file supported effective tactics, enabled decisive penetration, and forced winning liquidation.

Summary

The important lessons in the preceding Study Games represent a sound and balanced foundation for improving your chess. Reinforce your knowledge of these lessons by reviewing the introductions to all the Study Games, then apply these winning principles in your games.

Chapter 14

SOLITAIRE CHESS

To learn to play chess, you must play *chess. In chess, as in life, ultimately you teach yourself.*

After studying the preceding chapters, you should now:

- Understand and apply sound chess principles
- Recognize, develop, and execute varied checkmate patterns
- Recognize, create, and avoid tactical and positional weaknesses
- Analyze and evaluate positions correctly
- Calculate variations accurately
- Apply tactics (including combinations and sacrifices)
- Develop sound strategy and plans
- Play effective defense
- Understand how to select the best move in any position

You need to practice applying these important skills. An excellent method to improve your chess is to simulate competition by carefully playing over well-played games, covering the moves and finding the best moves for the winner. This proven and effective "Solitaire Chess" training method will challenge and expand your knowledge and skills.

For your instruction, this chapter presents five interactive, self-grading Solitaire Games — typical amateur games — representing a variety of openings and defenses. The emphasis is on aggressive play, and the grading reflects the importance and difficulty of each move. The first two Solitaire Games are annotated from the winner's side, while the last three are unannotated — a more realistic situation. If you are unfamiliar with the opening or defense in any Solitaire Game, refer to the opening moves given in Chapter 3 ("Opening").

To gain maximum benefit from these instructive Solitaire Games:

- Set up the pieces from the *winner's* side and *play slowly*, as you would in a serious chess game.
- Clearly decide on your choice of move (preferably, record it) before uncovering the game move.
- On a "miss," try to determine why the move played in the game was better than your choice.
- Record your strength in each Solitaire Game, and note your progress.
- After each game, review the moves of the loser and try to determine what the losing moves were.

These helpful Solitaire Games will provide you with considerable entertainment and abundant instruction — enjoy and learn from them.

Solitaire Game 1

English Opening

Before the first move, cover the moves and find the best moves for *White*. Notes follow each White move for your instruction, and points are indicated in parenthesis for your self-evaluation. Compare your final score with the accompanying table to determine your strength in this game.

(COVER UP)

1. c4 (4)

Attacks the central square d5 — a potential outpost for White's Queen-Knight later. If *1... d5, 2. cxd5 Qxd5 3. Nc3* develops a white piece with tempo by attacking the black Queen.

1. ... e5

2. Nc3 (4)

Develops a piece, attacks two center squares (d5 and e4), and eyes *Nd5* at an opportune future moment.

2. ... Nf6

3. d3 (5)

Releases White's B/c1 and prevents *3... e4*. *3. Nf3* (5 points) is also good: if *3. Nf3, 3... e4 4. Ng5 Qe7 5. Qc2* wins the errant black e-pawn.

3. ... Bb4

4. Nf3 (5)

Develops a piece, attacks the

black e5-pawn, exerts control on d4, and prepares *0–0*. *4. Bd2* (4 points) is defensive (unpins the N/c3).

4. ... d6

5. g3 (5)

To fianchetto the white King-Bishop at g2, since this Bishop has a limited future on the clogged f1-a6 diagonal; also furthers *0–0* after the imminent fianchetto. *5. Bg5* (4 points) and *5. Bd2* (3 points) are also playable.

5. ... Bg4

6. Bg2 (5)

Defends the N/f3 and prevents doubled Kingside pawns (if *6... Bxf3, 7. Bxf3*); also prepares *0–0*.

6. ... Nc6

7. 0–0 (5)

Safeguards the King and unpins the N/c3; *7. Bg5* (4 points) and *7. Bd2* (2 points) are also playable.

7. ... 0–0

8. Bg5 (6)

Develops the last minor piece with a threat (*9. Nd5*, then *Nxf6†*, doubling Black's Kingside pawns and exposing the black King).

8. ... Bxf3

9. Bxf3 (6)

Regains the piece favorably. *9. exf3?* would double White's pawns, block the fianchettoed B/g2, and leave White's d3-pawn backward and weak.

9. ... Nd4

10. Bxb7 (7)

Wins a pawn with tempo (attacks the black R/a8), and prevents *10... Nxf3†* from doubling White's Kingside pawns and making the white d-pawn backward.

10. ... Rb8

11. Be4! (7)

Repositions the Bishop to an aggressive outpost. *11. Bg2* (3 points) is unnecessarily passive.

11. ... Re8

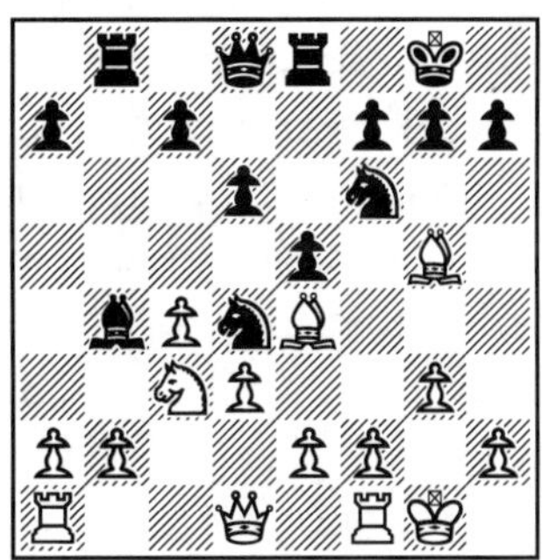

Diagram 192-White

12. Nd5! (8)

Seizes an important outpost and threatens *13. Nxf6† gxf6 14. Bh6* to expose and restrict the black King. *Note:* Continuing *13. Nxb4? Rxb4* would dissipate White's initiative.

12. ... Bc5

13. b3 (6)

Saves the threatened b-pawn. White's attack is strong — but why give your opponent anything, especially a free pawn and an enemy Rook on your second rank?

13. ... c6

14. Nxf6†! (8)

The threatened white Knight captures a black Kingside defender, doubles Black's Kingside pawns, and exposes the black King.

14. ... gxf6

15. Bh6 (7)

Saves the threatened Bishop and restricts the black King.

15. ... Qd7

16. e3! (7)

Releases the white Queen for a Kingside attack, and forces the black N/d4 to retreat (*...Ne6* or *...Nf5)* and interfere with the black Queen's control of g4, the white Queen's checking square (any other move loses the black Knight).

16. ... Ne6

17. Qg4† (7)

The lethal lady enters the attack.

17. ... Kh8

18. Qf5! (9)

Threatens *19. Qxh7 checkmate!*

18. ... Nf8

19. Qxf6† (8)

Forces mate next move. (*19. Bxf8* (8 points) *Rxf8 20. Qxh7* also mates.)

19. ... Kg8

20. Qg7# (6)

After the white Knight's disruptive capture on f6, White's Queen and two Bishops penetrated Black's Kingside position and forced an early checkmate.

Your Score:	*Rating:*
106-125	Outstanding
86-105	Excellent
51-85	Average
26-50	Fair
0-25	Novice

Solitaire Game 2

Sicilian (Dragon) Defense

After White's third move, cover the moves and find the best moves for *Black*. Notes follow each Black move for your instruction, and points are again indicated for your self-evaluation. Compare your final score with the accompanying table to determine your strength in this game.

1. e4 c5
2. Nf3 d6
3. d4

(COVER UP)

3. ... cxd4 (4)

Black exchanges a wing pawn for a center pawn to eliminate White's *ideal pawn center*, establish a 2:1 central pawn majority, and create a half-open c-file for Black's major pieces later.

4. Nxd4 Nf6 (4)

Develops a piece and attacks the white e4-pawn to prevent *5. c4*, the Maroczy Bind, which would stifle the positionally freeing *...d5* later.

5. Nc3 g6 (4)

Prepares to fianchetto the black Bishop at g7. The alternative 5... *a6* is the Najdorf Variation.

6. Be3 Bg7 (4)

Completes the fianchetto immediately (usually the best idea) to develop the Bishop and prepare ...*0–0*. If 6... *Ng4?* to attack the B/e3, *7. Bb5†!* wins material for White (e.g., *7... Bd7 8. Qxg4*).

7. f3 0–0 (4)

Safeguards the black King and activates the King-Rook.

8. Qd2 Nc6 (5)

Develops a piece, exerts control on the center, and prevents 9. *Bh6* to exchange Black's fianchettoed Bishop (if 9. *Bh6?*, ...*Bxh6!* and Black wins a piece — either the white B/h6 or N/d4 — since the white Queen is overworked).

9. Bc4 Bd7 (4)

Develops the last minor piece to the only available good square, and vacates c8 for a Rook.

10. 0–0–0 Qa5 (5)

Faced with a likely Kingside *pawnstorm* attack by White, Black initiates an early Queenside *counterattack* (5 points also for ...*Rc8*).

11. h4 Rfc8 (5)

Increases the Queenside pressure toward the white King, and threatens *12... Nxd4!* winning a piece — *12... Nxd4! 13. Qxd4* (if *13. Bxd4*, *...Rxc4) Ng4! 14. Qd3 Nxe3 15. Qxe3 Rxc4* — the unguarded white B/c4 is vulnerable.

12. Bb3 Ne5 (5)

Uncovers the important c-file for the black R/c8, and prepares ...*Nc4* attacking the white Queen and forcing the exchange of a white Bishop.

13. g4 Nc4 (5)

Attacks the white Queen and forces the exchange of a white Bishop for the Knight, removing a valuable defender/attacker near the white King.

14. Bxc4 Rxc4 (3)

Recovers material and prepares to double Rooks on the half-open c-file leading to the white King.

15. h5 Rac8 (5)

Black develops his last piece with increased pressure on the white King's position.

16. Nb3 Qc7 (5)

Triples major pieces on the sensitive c-file. *16... Qa6* is less forceful, and *16... Qe5* becomes complicated after *17. f4*.

17. hxg6 fxg6 (5)

Keeps the h-file closed to protect the black King while developing a possible flight square (f7).

18. Kb1 Be6 (5)

Adds pressure toward the white King, plus avoids the trap *19. e5 dxe5 20. g5!* and White wins a piece.

19. Nb5 Qd7 (6)

Saves the threatened Queen,

and prepares to bolster the Queenside attack with ...*b5* without an extra tempo (...*a6* will not be required, since the black Queen guards b5). If White injudiciously grabs a pawn with *20. Nxa7*, the a-file will be opened for attack.

20. N5d4 Bf7 (6)

Preserves the attacking light-squared Bishop (if Black allows *21. Nxe6 Qxe6 22. Nd4* with tempo on the black Queen, ...*b5* is delayed). In attacks against Kings castled on opposite wings, every tempo is important, since the side whose attack arrives first usually wins.

21. c3 b5 (6)

Intending ...*b4* to pry open an attacking line.

22. Qh2 b4 (6)

To open a file for attack against the white King. If White captures *23. cxb4*, then *23... Qa4 24. a3 e5!* and White loses a Knight.

23. Ne2 Qa4 (7)

Approaches the vicinity of the white King and avoids *24. e5 Nd5* (the black d6-pawn is pinned) *25. Qxh7+* and White wins a pawn.

24. Bd4 e5 (6)

Stops White's threat of *25. Bxf6 Bxf6 26. Qxh7†*, and deprives the B/d4 from guarding c3 and hindering Black's counterattack.

25. Be3 R4c6 (7)

Guards the threatened black d6-pawn, opens an attacking line for the B/f7 (threatens the immediate *26... Bxb3 27. axb3 Qxb3* winning a pawn and decimating White's defenses), and prepares to swing the Rook to a6 to attack twice the sensitive a2-square near the white King.

26. Nbc1 Ra6 (7)

Triple attack on a2. If White tries *27. b3, ...Bxb3! 28. axb3 Qa1† 29. Kc2 Rxc3† 30. Kd2 (30. Nxc3?? Qxc3† 31. Kb1 Ra1#!) Qb2† 31. Ke1 Rxe3* gives Black both material and positional advantages.

27. Rd2 Bxa2† (7)

Wins a pawn and exposes the white King. Now if *28. Ka1??, ...Bb3† 29. Kb1 Qa1#*.

28. Nxa2 Qxa2† (7)

The only logical follow-up — regains material and forces the white King onto the c-file in line with the black Rook.

29. Kc2 bxc3 (7)

Opens more lines to attack the white King and threatens *30... cxd2* winning a Rook.

30. Nxc3

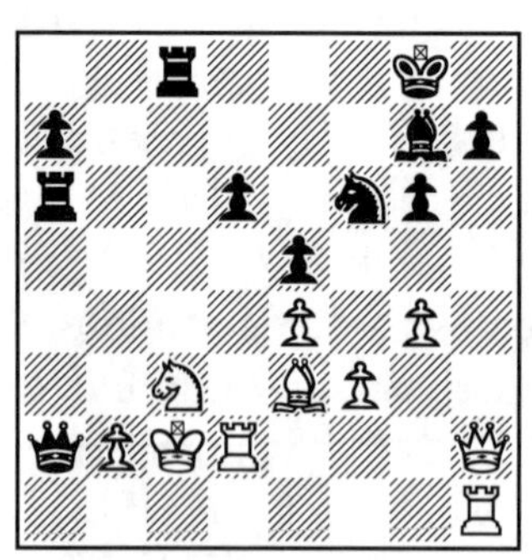

Diagram 193-Black

30. ... Rxc3†! (9)

This strong Exchange sacrifice exposes the white King and drives it into a mating net. *31. bxc3* is illegal (White's b-pawn is pinned); and if White refuses the sacrifice with *31. Kd1, ...Rxe3* and Black has won a Knight and Bishop.

31. Kxc3 Rc6† (8)

Restricts the white King (if *32. Kd3, ...Qc4#*).

32. Kb4

32. Bc5, sacrificing the Bishop for a flight square (e3), would hold out longer.

32. ... Qc4† (9)

Forces mate next move.

33. Ka3 Ra6# (6)

Black's vigorous Queenside counterattack prevailed over White's threatening Kingside pawnstorm in a well-played struggle featuring opposite-wing castling.

Your Score:	*Rating:*
151-175	Outstanding
121-150	Excellent
71-120	Average
36-70	Fair
0-35	Novice

Solitaire Game 3

King's Gambit

After Black's first move, cover the remaining moves and find the best moves for *White*. Points are indicated after each White move for your self-evaluation. Compare your final score with the table to determine your strength in this game.

1.	e4	e5

(COVER UP)

2.	f4 (5)	exf4
3.	Nf3 (6)	d6
4.	Bc4 (6)	Bg4
5.	d4 (6)	Nf6
6.	Nc3 (6)	Nc6
7.	Bxf4 (7)	h6
8.	0-0 (6)	Be7
9.	Qd2 (7)	Bxf3
10.	Rxf3 (7)	0-0

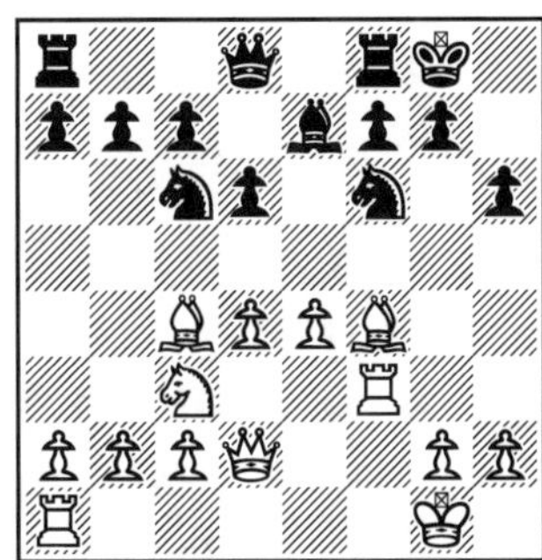

Diagram 194-White to move

11.	Bxh6! (8)	gxh6
12.	Qxh6 (7)	Qd7
13.	Rg3† (7)	Ng4
14.	Qg6†! (9)	Kh8
15.	Rh3† (7)	Nh6
16.	Rxh6# (6)	

Your Score:	*Rating:*
86-100	Outstanding
71-85	Excellent
41-70	Average
21-40	Fair
0-20	Novice

Solitaire Game 4

Gruenfeld Defense

After White's second move, cover the remaining moves and find the best moves for *Black*. Points are indicated after each Black move for your self-evaluation. Compare your final score with the table to determine your strength in this game.

1.	d4	Nf6
2.	Nf3	

(COVER UP)

2.	...	g6 (4)
3.	Bg5	Bg7 (4)
4.	Nc3	d5 (4)
5.	e3	0–0 (4)
6.	Be2	Nbd7 (4)
7.	Qd3	e6 (4)
8.	0–0–0	c5 (5)
9.	Ne5	Qa5 (6)
10.	Kb1	cxd4 (6)
11.	Qxd4	

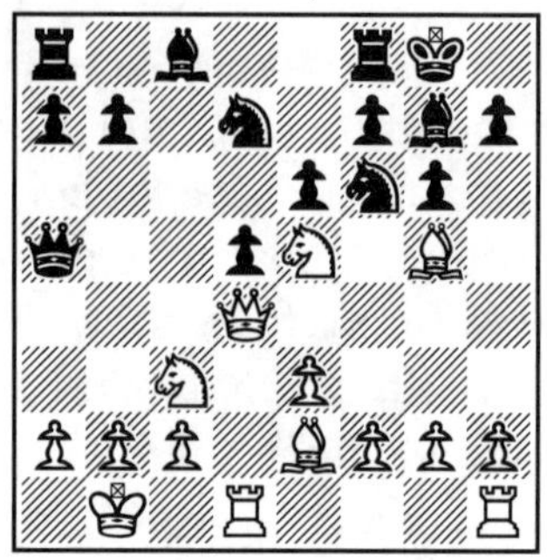

Diagram 195-Black to move

11.	...	Nxe5! (7)
12.	Qxe5	Ne4! (8)
13.	Qf4	Nxc3†! (8)
14.	bxc3	Qxc3 (7)
15.	Kc1	Qa3†! (7)
16.	Kd2	Bc3† (7)
17.	Kd3	Bb2†! (9)
18.	Kd2	Qc3# (6)

Your Score:	*Rating:*
86-100	Outstanding
71-85	Excellent
41-70	Average
21-40	Fair
0-20	Novice

Solitaire Game 5

Queen's Gambit

After Black's first move, cover the remaining moves and find the best moves for *White*. Points are indicated after each White move for your self-evaluation. Compare your final score with the table to determine your strength in this game.

1.	d4	d5

(COVER UP)

2.	c4 (4)	e6
3.	Nc3 (4)	Nf6
4.	Bg5 (4)	Be7
5.	e3 (4)	Nbd7
6.	Nf3 (4)	0–0
7.	Rc1 (4)	c6
8.	Bd3 (4)	dxc4
9.	Bxc4 (3)	Nb6
10.	Bd3 (4)	Nbd5
11.	0–0 (4)	Bd7
12.	Ne5 (5)	Qb6
13.	Nxd5! (7)	cxd5
14.	Bxf6 (6)	Bxf6
15.	Nxd7 (6)	Qxb2
16.	Qh5! (8)	h6
17.	Nxf6†! (8)	gxf6
18.	Qxh6 (7)	f5
19.	f4! (8)	Qd2

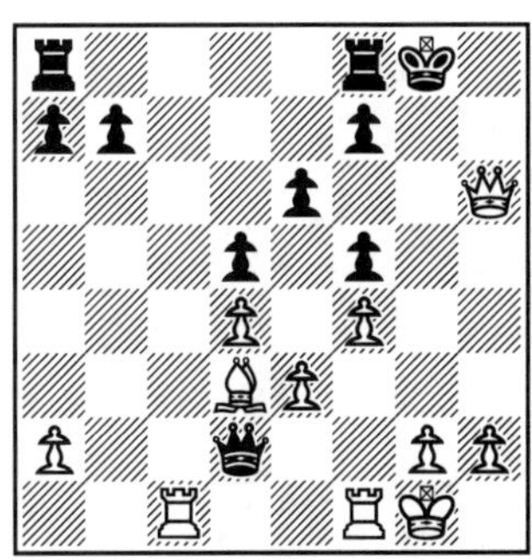

Diagram 196-White to move

20.	Rf3!! (10)	Qxc1†
21.	Bf1 (7)	f6
22.	Qg6† (8)	Kh8
23.	Rh3# (6)	

Your Score:	*Rating:*
106-125	Outstanding
86-105	Excellent
51-85	Average
26-50	Fair
0-25	Novice

Summary

The experience gained in playing through the preceding Solitaire Games should provide you with a better understanding of active, attacking chess. Strong chessplayers are aggressive, flexible, and patient, and the Solitaire Games emphasized these important qualities. Develop and maintain an active, aggressive playing style, and you will win many chess games!

Note: You can continue to practice this instructive "Solitaire Game" approach with chess games published in books, magazines, and newspapers. Simply cover and try to guess the winner's moves.

Chapter 15

CONTINUING YOUR IMPROVEMENT

Learning is essential to improve in chess.

The goal in chess is to be positionally sound and tactically accurate. We learn to play better chess through STUDY and PLAY. To improve, you will need to study chess and play many serious games.

Study

Knowledge is power in chess, and with proper instruction a chessplayer can learn more in just a few hours than he would discover for himself in many years of untutored, trial-and-error playing. Chessplayers, like champion athletes, should concentrate more on improving their *weaknesses* than their strengths. Strengthening weak areas brings faster and greater improvement. Identify and improve your weaknesses by recording your games for later analysis and study (chess scorebooks are available for a nominal fee from Chessco, 125 Kirkwood Blvd., Davenport, Iowa 52803; or, you can use a stenographer's notebook to record your games). Study selected chess books and magazine articles also, and analyze those games in addition to your own.

A chessplayer seriously desiring to improve should devote some time each week to studying. Setting aside a regular time for study is best. For maximum benefit, an intermediate chessplayer should allocate his study time approximately as follows: opening – 30%; middlegame – 50%; endgame – 20%.

Develop a study plan and list specific topics you intend to study, then follow your plan. Maintain a notebook of your chess goals, ideas, and progress. Include the lessons you learn from each loss and your plans for further study. If you are a rated chessplayer, set a challenging annual rating improvement goal, and work to accomplish it.The following books are recommended for your study and reference:

Intermediate Books (algebraic notation)

Openings: *Chess Openings*, M. Basman
Openings: *Gambits*, G. Burgess
Openings: *How to Play the Opening in Chess*, R. Keene & D. Levy
Strategy and Tactics: *The Genesis of Power Chess*, L. Ault
Strategy and Tactics: *How to Become a Candidate Master*, A. Dunne
Strategy and Tactics: *How to Reassess Your Chess*, J. Silman
Strategy and Tactics: *The Game of Chess*, S. Tarrasch
Games: *Thinkers' Chess*, S. Gerzadowicz
Endgame: *Exploring the Endgame*, P. Griffiths

Advanced Books (algebraic notation)

Chess Tactics for Advanced Players, Y. Averbakh
Opening Preparation, M. Dvoretsky and A. Yusupov
The Middlegame Books 1 and 2, M. Euwe and H. Kramer
Batsford Chess Openings 2, G. Kasparov & R. Keene
Strategic Chess, E. Mednis
My System 21st Century Ed., A. Nimzovich
The Chess Terrorist's Handbook, L. Shamkovich
Endgame Strategy, M. Shereshevsky
Batsford Chess Endings, J. Speelman, J. Tisdall & B. Wade
Thress Steps to Chess Mastery, A. Suetin

These instructive books represent a modest and wise investment in your chess game.

Start with the intermediate books and progress to the advanced ones. Magazines can supplement these excellent books.

Play

Continue playing serious games with opponents of various strengths, especially stronger players. White wins more often than Black (approximately 55 percent to Black's 45 percent, including draws), so play White at every opportunity to start with an advantage. Play *slowly* — the legacy of speed in chess is a multitude of discouraging mistakes and a series of lost games. Play at your own pace — do not hurry to accommodate a faster player or dawdle to match a slower opponent.

Join a local chess club or group to develop a variety of opponents. Play chess regularly, enter local club tournaments, and play matches (four to six games) with worthy opponents. Concentrate on playing *stronger* opponents — you will learn more from them.

Record all your serious games in your scorebook, and review them — preferably with a stronger player — to pinpoint your strengths and weaknesses. When first reviewing your games, *reverse* the board for a more objective perspective. *Learn a lesson from each loss*, record the lessons in a diary, refer to this diary often, and determine to avoid similar mistakes in future games. Reviewing all of your games is helpful, but reviewing your losses is most instructive — review all your losses.

Join the United States Chess Federation (USCF, 186 Route 9W, New Windsor, NY 12553) and read *Chess Life*, the official USCF monthly magazine. Play in the weekend USCF chess tournaments (listed in *Chess Life)* in your area. Tournament chess is the crucible in which your chess game will be tested under fire and improved. Entry fees in local and regional tournaments are usually modest, competition is often in sections according to strength, and class prizes are offered. Tournament chess offers you a challenging opportunity to assess your game and achieve a national USCF rating, and you will meet and compete with many interesting fellow chessplayers. Not all USCF tournament players are strong, so do not be afraid to compete in USCF tournaments — all chessplayers are welcome. You may win a prize!

For more leisurely competition, play postal chess. In addition to the U.S. Chess Federation, Correspondence Chess League of America (CCLA, P.O. Box 3481, Barrington, Illinois, 60011-3481) offers postal tournaments in open and class formats. Postal competition is usually double round robin in four-player sections (you play two games — one as White, one as Black — with three opponents simultaneously, for a total of six games) or in seven-player sections (you play one game with each of six opponents simultaneously). You can elect to play in an open (no restriction on strength) or class (similar strength) section. Other postal organizations offer similar competition. For a list of national postal organizations, write to the USCF.

Postal chess moves are normally sent on postcards, and you have an average of three days to respond to each move. Annual postal organization dues and postage costs are modest, and you will compete and correspond with chessplayers from all over the United States. You can also play *international* postal chess — you will enjoy the chess, collect many colorful postcards and stamps, and foster international goodwill.

Postal chess offers you: 1) an opportunity to experiment with various openings and defenses using reference books as desired; 2) more time to carefully analyze positions and consider your plans and moves; and 3) satisfying chess experiences at nominal cost. Many Grandmasters played postal chess early in their careers to strengthen their chess games. Some strong players will play a postal game with you and analyze your moves for a modest fee (see the "Classifieds" section of *Chess Life* magazine).

For best results, play both over-the-board (OTB) and postal chess regularly. Regular serious play at a local chess club will strengthen your game, and postal chess will help you develop keener analytical abilities. Also, frequently play your chess computer (if necessary, buy one — they are a bargain). Play your computer at progressively higher levels, and record your computer games in a separate scorebook. Playing your computer is an ideal method to practice new openings and defenses. For maximum benefit, simulate tournament conditions when playing your computer — play slowly, record your moves, and ***do not take moves back.*** Live with the consequences of your mistakes. Play your best to develop effective chess habits. Good chess habits pay off!

If possible, find a chess tutor — preferably a significantly stronger player who can analyze your games, point out your mistakes, and guide you toward better chess thinking. A good tutor can be invaluable. If no tutor is available, concentrate on studying *annotated* games of Masters and Grandmasters which explain the ideas and moves of both sides. Such synthetic "tutoring" can prove very beneficial.

Your chess improvement will likely be somewhat uneven. The typical pattern is rapid progress followed by a temporary plateau, further progress to a new plateau, then more progress and plateaus until you achieve chess mastery or reach your potential. Be patient — focus on the *trend* in your chess improvement, and ignore temporary plateaus and even minor setbacks.

Some important advice which will help you improve more rapidly is:

1. Never depend on unforced cooperation from your opponent; always develop your plans assuming best play on his part. Be grateful for, and capitalize on, opponents' mistakes, but do not rely on errors. The "move-and-hope-he-doesn't-see-it" school of chess is an elementary school. Strong players force or induce weak moves by their opponents.

2. Discipline yourself to take the time necessary to analyze and evaluate each position. Regular chess play is a game of accuracy, not speed, and sound chess requires time.

3. After analyzing a position, form a plan — modest or ambitious — and define the *specific tasks* required to accomplish your plan. Then evaluate responsive moves, and select the best one.

4. Some defense is required in every chess game. Defend as necessary, but defend *actively*, and do not allow your position to become cramped or passive.

5. Be careful of the sequence of your moves in tactical positions. The move order sometimes determines whether you win or lose material or emerge even.

6. Maintain constant vigilance, even when winning. Many unpleasant surprises await the overconfident or careless player.

7. Since a chessplayer tends to play in serious games the way he plays in casual games, develop good chess habits by always playing your best, even against your computer or weaker opponents in skittles games.

8. Play stronger players often — you will learn much from them, and they can critique your moves and help you improve.

9. Make playing your *best*, rather than winning, your goal in every chess game. Play your best, and wins will come.

10. When you lose a chess game, learn exactly *why* you lost — and focus on avoiding the same or similar mistakes in future games.

Develop an energetic, aggressive, and imaginative playing style, and try to avoid sterile wood-pushing which relies on technique alone. A balanced, energetic style will bring you the most victories and satisfaction.

Summary

Focused study and purposeful play are the keys to chess success. To improve your chess, continue to *study* and *play* — there is no substitute or magic shortcut to proficiency in chess. Developing a strong chess game requires time and effort, but offers immense satisfaction. Chess is a game of rich ideas and effective techniques. Learn as many of these as you can, and *apply* these winning principles and maneuvers in your games. An individual's progress in chess is typically somewhat uneven; but if you persevere, your trend will be upward. Put occasional losses and minor setbacks behind you, and continue your progress. Excelsior!

Appendix A

CURRY OPENING GAMES

1. Orthodox Defense
2. Queen's Indian Defense
3. King's Indian Defense
4. Gruenfeld Defense
5. Irregular Defense
6. Black Castles ...0–0–0
7. White Castles 0–0
8. Curry Opening Loses

1. Orthodox Defense

1.	d4	d5
2.	Nf3	Nf6
3.	Bg5	e6
4.	e3	Be7
5.	Nbd2	Nbd7
6.	Bd3	c5
7.	c3	0–0
8.	Qc2	c4
9.	Be2	h6
10.	h4	b6
11.	0–0–0	Bb7
12.	Bxf6	Nxf6
13.	Ne5	a5
14.	g4	b5
15.	g5	Nd7
16.	Ndf3	b4
17.	Nxd7	Qxd7
18.	gxh6	g6
19.	Rdg1	Rfb8
20.	Rxg6†	Kh8
21.	Rg7	f5
22.	Ne5	Qe8
23.	Qa4	Resigns

2. Queen's Indian Defense

1.	d4	Nf6
2.	Nf3	b6
3.	Bg5	e6
4.	e3	Bb7
5.	Nbd2	Be7
6.	Bd3	d6
7.	c3	0–0
8.	Qc2	Nbd7
9.	0–0–0	a5
10.	h4	c5
11.	h5	h6
12.	Bxf6	Nxf6
13.	Rdg1	cxd4
14.	exd4	Qc7
15.	g4	Nd5
16.	g5	Nf4
17.	gxh6	Nxd3†
18.	Qxd3	Bf6
19.	hxg7	Bxg7
20.	Ng5	Rfc8
21.	Qh7†	Kf8
22.	h6	Bf6
23.	Nxe6†	fxe6
24.	Rg8#	

3. King's Indian Defense

1.	d4	Nf6
2.	Nf3	g6
3.	Bg5	Bg7
4.	e3	d6
5.	Bd3	0–0
6.	Nbd2	h6
7.	Bxf6	Bxf6
8.	c3	Nd7
9.	Qc2	Kh7
10.	h4	h5
11.	Ng5†	Bxg5
12.	hxg5	Kg7
13.	g4	hxg4
14.	0–0–0	Rg8
15.	Rh6	Kf8
16.	Rdh1	Ke8
17.	Bxg6	Nf8
18.	Rh8	Rxg6
19.	Rxf8†	Kxf8
20.	Rh8†	Rg8
21.	Qh7	Resigns

4. Gruenfeld Defense

1.	d4	Nf6
2.	Nf3	g6
3.	Bg5	Bg7
4.	e3	d5
5.	Bd3	Nbd7
6.	Nbd2	0–0
7.	c3	e6
8.	Qc2	b6
9.	0–0–0	Bb7
10.	h4	c5
11.	h5	Rc8
12.	hxg6	fxg6
13.	Ne5	cxd4
14.	exd4	a6
15.	Ndf3	b5
16.	Nxd7	Qxd7
17.	Ne5	Qc7
18.	Bh6	Ne4
19.	f3	Nd6
20.	Bxg7	Kxg7
21.	Bxg6	Kf6
22.	Rxh7	Qa5
23.	Ng4†	Kg5
24.	Rh5†	Kf4
25.	Qd2†	Kg3
26.	Rh3#	

5. Irregular Defense

1.	d4	d5
2.	Nf3	Bg4
3.	Ne5	Bh5
4.	c3	Nf6
5.	Bg5	e6
6.	Nbd2	Nbd7
7.	Ndf3	Bd6
8.	Qc2	0–0
9.	g4	Bxe5
10.	Nxe5	Bg6
11.	Nxg6	hxg6
12.	h4	c5
13.	e3	cxd4
14.	exd4	Rc8
15.	h5	Qb6
16.	hxg6	fxg6
17.	0–0–0	Nxg4
18.	Bh3	Nxf2
19.	Rde1	Nxh1
20.	Bxe6†	Rf7
21.	Qxg6	Rcf8
22.	Rxh1	Nf6
23.	Bxf6	Resigns

6. Black Castles ...0–0–0

1.	d4	d5
2.	Nf3	Nf6
3.	Bg5	e6
4.	e3	Be7
5.	Nbd2	Nc6
6.	c3	b6
7.	Bd3	Bb7
8.	Qc2	Qd7
9.	0–0–0	0–0–0
10.	Ne5	Nxe5
11.	dxe5	Ne4
12.	Nxe4	dxe4
13.	Bxe4	Qe8
14.	Bxb7†	Kxb7
15.	Qe4†	c6
16.	Bxe7	Qxe7
17.	Rd4	Kc7
18.	Rhd1	Rxd4
19.	Rxd4	c5
20.	Rd6	Qe8

21.	Qc4	Qe7
22.	b4	Kb8
23.	bxc5	bxc5
24.	Qb5†	Ka8
25.	Rd7	Rb8
26.	Qc6†	Resigns

7. White Castles 0–0

1.	d4	Nf6
2.	Nf3	b5
3.	Bg5	Bb7
4.	Nbd2	e6
5.	e3	b4
6.	Bd3	Be7
7.	c3	Na6
8.	Qc2	h6
9.	Bf4	c5
10.	c4	d5
11.	Ne5	0–0
12.	0–0	Rc8
13.	b3	Nh5
14.	Bg3	Nxg3
15.	fxg3	Bf6
16.	Ndf3	Bxe5
17.	Nxe5	dxc4
18.	Bxc4	cxd4
19.	Rad1	Qg5
20.	exd4	Nc7
21.	Qe2	Nd5
22.	Rd3	Rc7
23.	Qd2	a5
24.	Qxg5	hxg5
25.	Rd2	f6
26.	Nd3	Re8
27.	Nc5	Ba8
28.	Re1	Rce7
29.	Rde2	Kf7
30.	Bb5	Rb8
31.	Bd7	Nc3
32.	Bxe6†	Ke8
33.	Bd7†	Resigns

8. Curry Opening Loses

If Black initiates an early Queenside pawnstorm, White should consider 0–0, as the following debacle illustrates.

1.	d4	d5
2.	Nf3	Nf6
3.	Bg5	e6
4.	e3	Be7
5.	Nbd2	Nbd7
6.	Bd3	0–0
7.	c3	c5
8.	Qc2	c4
9.	Be2	b5
10.	0–0–0	Qa5
11.	Kb1	b4
12.	h4	Rb8
13.	Ka1	bxc3
14.	bxc3	Ba3
15.	Rb1	Ba6
16.	Bxf6	Nxf6
17.	Rxb8	Rxb8
18.	Rb1	Bb5
19.	Ne5	Rb6
20.	Ndf3	Ba4
21.	Qd2	Ne4
22.	Qe1	Rxb1†
23.	Kxb1	Qb5†
24.	Ka1	Qb2#

Appendix B

CONDENSED CHESS COURSE

In chess, logical thinking is more valuable than inspiration.
— Purdy

Strong chess is played according to sound principles. Specific (and general) knowledge is required. Following is a comprehensive and concise collection of practical, Master-proven chess ideas, maxims, and tips — virtually a complete chess course — to help you strengthen your chess and win more games.

Highlight and periodically review the guidelines you find most beneficial, then *apply* these winning ideas, maneuvers, and techniques in your games.

In General

Offense

• UNDERSTANDING, not memory, is the essential key to chess success — the chessplayer who understands *why* will consistently defeat opponents who know only *how*. Play by sound general principles adapted to the specific requirements (offensive opportunities and defensive necessities) in each position.

• Play SLOWLY. Haste and carelessness are greater enemies than your opponent. *Accuracy*, not speed, is essential in chess. Be patient — the reward for speed is a legacy of lost games.

• Respect all opponents, but fear none.

• *Expect to win*, whenever the opportunity arises — opening, middlegame, or endgame. Win by attack or by attrition. Remember, checkmate is the goal!

• To find the best moves, and avoid becoming intimidated or overconfident, play the *position* on the board — not the opponent.

• Patience is the byword in the opening and early middlegame, especially as Black. Best results are achieved by first building a solid, strong, active position — safe King, active pieces, strong center, and sound pawn formations — then seeking tactical and attacking opportunities.

• Try to gain a material or positional advantage early, and increase it. Improve your position with every move, and accumulate small advantages — they win.

• Be aggressive! Attack opponents' weaknesses! Play forcing moves (checks and captures, and threats to check and capture).

• *Attacks are only justified by existing or potential weaknesses.* Avoid useless checks and premature attacks that waste time and scatter pieces.

• Play with a series of sound, flexible plans. Plan early and continuously. Base plans on strengths and weaknesses in the position, and modify as necessary or desirable (plans are made for a few moves only, not for the entire game).

• Correct ANALYSIS is the foundation of strong chess. Accurate and complete analysis of each position — for both sides — enables a player to develop sound plans and effective moves. When analyzing a position, search for the *central features* — especially identify and examine *weaknesses* — and base your plans on these features. Look at King safety, material status, possible tactics, piece placement and mobility, pawn structure, control of significant squares, and time (tempi).

• In tactical situations, always analyze each candidate move to a *quiet* position — one in which all checks and captures have been exhausted or neutralized (your "horizon").

• Disguise your plans — play least committal moves first, especially when preparing an attack.

• Do not be myopic and become too involved in your own plans. Play *both* sides of the board. Analyze your opponent's strengths, weaknesses, and possibilities as well as your own.

• Stay calm, relaxed, and focused during each game (tension and panic rout logical thought).

• When even or ahead, play hard. When behind, play harder!

• Use time wisely. Think and plan on your opponent's time during the game. Avoid time trouble. When in time trouble, try to think and play calmly.

• Do not relax and become overconfident and careless when ahead. Apply the "killer instinct" throughout the game.

• Focus on playing your best, rather than only on winning. Play your best, and the wins will come.

• Have a sound and *specific purpose* every time you touch a chessman — try to improve your position with every move.

• Every piece and pawn in a chess game should do *useful* work.

• When you find a good move, always look for a *better* one!

• Play according to the OFFENSIVE OPPORTUNITIES and DEFENSIVE NECESSITIES in each position.

• Seek the *initiative* (ability to create threats).

• The most consistently effective strategy is to win with minimum risk — avoid risky variations and speculative lines of play, unless behind. When ahead, play for the *certain* win, even if slower.

• Play *aggressively*, but soundly. Avoid risky, trappy, and unsound moves — unless desperately behind.

• When ahead in material or position, reduce your opponent's chances for counterplay by *minimizing* his tactical opportunities.

• Seek chess "bargains" — try to gain more than you relinquish on every move.

• Avoid playing moves which help your opponent.

• *Hinder* your opponent when possible.

• In every chess position, first ANALYZE accurately, then PLAN soundly, and finally EXECUTE effectively (A-P-E).

• Examine and respect the small tactical and positional details in each position — they often contain the keys to victory.

• Keep the normal values of the pieces in mind (Queen–9, Rook–5, Bishop–3+, Knight–3, pawn–1), and remember that these values vary according to the position, mobility, and potential of the pieces. Whether attacking or defending, count the *number* and consider the *values* of both attackers and defenders on a target piece, pawn, or square before exchanging or occupying, to insure against losing material.

• The *sequence* of moves is often important — in a series of exchanges, capture with the lowest-value attacker or defender first, unless an alternative capture is clearly more advantageous.

• Chess is not Solitaire — sound chess begins with respect for your opponent's ideas, moves, threats, and ability.

• To win a chess game, you must first not *lose* it — avoid mistakes, such as leaving pieces *en prise* (unguarded) or exposing your King. Before each of your moves, ask yourself: "Does this move IMPROVE MY POSITION?" and "Is this move SAFE?" Avoiding mistakes is the beginning of improvement in chess. THINK before you move!

• Determine the *purpose* of each move by your opponent — ask yourself: "What is the THREAT?" and "What has CHANGED in the position?" Concentrate on offense and attacking, but recognize and answer all threats.

• The two most common (and often fatal) mistakes in chess are *moving too fast* and *overlooking your opponent's threats* — "sit on your hands" until ready to move.

• Search for multipurpose moves, and recognize possible multiple purposes of opponents' moves.

• Superior force usually wins, so stay even or ahead in material throughout the game (except for gambits, combinations, or sacrifices to force checkmate or a winning endgame).

• TACTICS decide all chess games. Successful tactical play involves recognizing, creating, and attacking *weaknesses* to win material and to checkmate. Always be alert for tactical opportunities and threats.

Examine every possible check and capture — for both sides(!) — on each move.

- Look for frequent TACTICS:
  - — Superior force
  - — Pins
  - — Skewers
  - — Knight forks
  - — Double attacks
  - — Discovered attacks
- Look for less frequent TACTICS:
  - — Overworked defenders
  - — Vital guards
  - — Removing defenders
  - — Deflecting defenders
  - — Sacrifices
  - — In-between moves
  - — Vulnerable back rank
  - — Interference
  - — No retreat
  - — Trapping pieces
  - — Desperado
  - — *Zugzwang*
  - — Queening combinations
  - — Underpromotion

• Play COMBINATIONS — sequences of forcing tactical moves, often involving a temporary sacrifice, which lead to a tactical or positional advantage.

• Anticipate your opponent's *best* replies to your moves (ask yourself, "What move would *I* play against this move of mine?"); then other moves by your opponent should pose no problem. While not *relying* on an opponent's errors, do take advantage of any mistakes that occur.

• POSITIONAL play, the control of important squares and lines, involves active piece placement and a sound pawn structure, as well as creating weaknesses in your opponent's position.

• Sound *positional play* provides the necessary foundation for effective tactics — incorrect or inferior positional play is seldom redeemed by tactical salvation. Positional superiority precedes and supports effective tactics.

• Do not sacrifice material without a clear reason and sufficient compensation (e.g., open lines for attack, expose the enemy King, remove key defenders, simplify to a winning endgame, etc.).

• Accept opponents' sacrifices, unless clearly dangerous.

• Remember the three special moves in chess: castling, pawn promotion, and capturing *en passant*.

Defense

• King safety is always *paramount* — avoid exposing your King to attack. Protect your King at all times.

• Keep pieces and pawns defended. Unguarded pieces and pawns are targets.

• Avoid tactical and positional weaknesses, and remedy any weaknesses promptly. Especially avoid Knight forks, double attacks, and discovered attacks. Avoid being pinned or skewered, and break pins early.

• Defend only as required, and avoid cramped and passive positions.

• Defend *actively*, rather than passively. When attacked, consider *counterattack* first.

• Be certain that your defenders are not pinned, overworked, unstable, or too valuable.

• Defend against short-term threats with moves that promote your *long-term goals*.

• Proper *timing* is often the key to effective defense — defending too soon dissipates the initiative, defending too late is ineffective.

• Always consider the six possible ways to parry a threat:
— Counterattack
— Capture the attacker

— Pin the attacker
— Interpose
— Guard
— Move away

• Defend as *economically* and *permanently* as possible, and remember that a pawn is the cheapest defender.

• Close lines — and keep lines closed — when defending your King.

• When in check, always consider all three escape methods — capture the attacker, interpose, or move the King — do not automatically move your King.

• Exchange pieces when cramped (for freedom) or under attack (for safety).

• Exchange passive pieces for your opponent's active pieces, unless behind in material.

• Avoid unnecessary exchanges when behind in material.

• Avoid placing your King or Queen on the same files as opposing Rooks, or on the same diagonals as opposing Bishops, even with intervening pieces (because of discovered attacks).

• Avoid a back-rank mate — provide your castled King a safe flight square.

• Play difficult positions with determination, and seek counterplay.

• Faced with loss of material, lose the least possible ("desperado").

Specifics

Opening

• Remember: a chess game begins on the *first* move!

• In the opening (first 10 to 15 moves of a chess game), work to: 1) control the center; 2) develop all pieces to effective squares; and 3) safeguard your King. Every move in the opening should contribute to one or more of these three opening objectives; if it does not, it is probably weak or an outright mistake.

• The purposes of pawn moves in the opening are to control the center, release pieces, defend your piece-and-pawn formation, and restrain opposing pawns and pieces.

• Open by advancing a *center* pawn *two squares* on the first move.

• Try to establish an Ideal Pawn Center (both center pawns safely abreast on the fourth rank), and support your pawns with pieces.

• Make only two or three pawn moves in the opening, and maintain at least one central pawn to avoid being overrun in the center.

• Play to gain control of the center — attack central squares (d4, d5, e4, e5) with pawns and pieces.

• Develop pieces rapidly and safely toward the center, and develop with a threat when possible, to limit your opponent's options. Defend by developing a *piece* when possible.

• Develop each piece to its most *effective* square — strong, safe squares on which your pieces have scope, mobility, and aggressive or defensive prospects.

• Aim your pieces at the center, the opposing King, and at weak points in your opponent's position.

• Develop *all* pieces in the opening.

• To facilitiate castling, develop pieces first on the side where you intend to castle.

• Develop minor pieces (Knights and Bishops) first; usually, develop the Knight before the Bishop on each side, since the best squares for Knights are usually known earlier.

• Do not block your Bishops' diagonals, especially with pawns.

• Neutralize (restrict, oppose, or exchange) opponents' fianchettoed Bishops, especially when aimed at your King.

• Develop Rooks to *open* files (or files likely to become open), especially central files.

• Develop the Queen, but not too early, and usually close to home to avoid harassment by opposing minor pieces and pawns.

• Move each piece only *once* in the opening — do not waste time (tempi) moving the same piece multiple times, leaving other pieces undeveloped.

• Avoid time-wasting pawn-grabbing of wing pawns — especially with the Queen — at the expense of development and position (center pawns are generally worth capturing).

• *Castle early*, usually on the Kingside.

• Do not disrupt your King's pawn shelter by moving the pawns in front of your castled King without a clear, sound reason.

• Prevent your opponent from castling, if possible.

• Avoid prolonged symmetry in the opening — imbalances in the position are necessary to create winning chances.

• Do not lose material (without adequate compensation) in the opening.

• Occasionally, play GAMBITS — sacrifices of material (usually a pawn or two) in the opening to gain a lead in development, control the center, seize the initiative, and open lines for attack — for fun, and to sharpen your tactics.

• If you accept a gambit, expect to play some defense — and be prepared to return the extra material to improve your position.

• *Pin* your opponent's pieces, and maintain effective pins until the exchange is favorable.

• *Attack* pinned pieces, especially with pawns.

• Avoid being pinned; if pinned, break pins *early*.

Middlegame

• Middlegame goals are to: 1) checkmate the enemy King, 2) win material, and 3) establish a winning endgame.

• In the middlegame, active, coordinated pieces, open lines, and aggressive play are the keys to success.

• The most important middlegame principle is to establish and maintain a SAFE and ACTIVE position (passive positions contain the germs of defeat).

• CENTRALIZE and COORDINATE your pieces early in the middlegame — pieces are effective only when they are *active*, and cooperate.

• Move Knights to *outposts*, and support them with pawns and pieces.

• Seize and control open files and diagonals with pieces.

• Double long-range pieces on important files and diagonals.

• Double Rooks on the seventh rank when possible.

• Be certain that all advanced pieces have safe retreat squares.

• Gain control of *important squares* — central squares and the squares around both Kings.

• Gain space with pawn advances, and seek improved development during exchanges.

• Refrain from aimless moves, captures, or exchanges — move pawns and pieces only to gain an advantage or avoid a disadvantage.

• Avoid the exchange of attacking pieces, except to eliminate important defenders.

• Avoid exchanging Bishops for Knights without compensation — Bishops are usually slightly stronger than Knights, except in closed positions.

• VISUALIZE your chess goals in every position. Imagine your pieces and pawns safely in IDEAL position, then determine the moves necessary to reach that position.

• An attack on a wing is usually best met by a counterattack in the center; close the center before embarking on a wing attack.

• When Kings are castled on *opposite* wings, pawnstorms to open lines toward both Kings are the usual method of attack.

• Successful attacks are based on *weaknesses* in the opponent's position — identify and target *specific weaknesses* to attack.

- The usual sequence to attack a King is: open lines, penetrate with pieces, restrict the opposing King, eliminate key defenders, then deliver winning checks.

- Open lines (with pawn exchanges and sacrifices or, if necessary, piece sacrifices) when attacking; close lines when defending.

- Try to expose and restrict the opponent's King — move your pieces into its vicinity, then penetrate with your pieces to weak squares around the enemy King.

- Attack with several pieces, rather than only one or two.

- When attacking, play forcing moves (checks, captures, and threats to check and capture) to limit — and increase the predictability of — your opponent's replies.

- When meeting a threat with an *in-between* move, make certain that your threat equals or exceeds your opponent's.

- Play to MAXIMIZE your advantage — win all you *safely* can.

- Be prepared to exchange one advantage for another more favorable (e.g., exchange a Bishop for a Knight to double an opponent's pawns in front of his castled King).

- If no tactics or attacking opportunities are available, try to IMPROVE YOUR POSITION — especially by mobilizing your inactive, or least active, pieces.

- Pawn structure is the skeleton of a chess game; strategy is more clearly defined when the pawn structure is rigid, since options are more limited and pawn targets are fixed.

- Attack pawn chains at their *base*, if possible.

- Establish and maintain strong pawn formations — avoid weak (isolated, doubled, backward) pawns.

- Make exchanges which give your opponent weak pawns.

- An open or half-open file is the usual compensation for doubled pawns; occupy and control such files with Rooks and the Queen.

- Usually, capture with pawns *toward* the center.

• Simplify (trade pieces) when ahead to make the win easier and more certain. Complicate the position when behind.

Endgame

• Endgame goals are to: 1) checkmate the enemy King, 2) promote pawns, and 3) create passed pawns.

• In the endgame, sound, mobile pawn structures and an active, aggressive King lead to victory.

• PLANNING is especially important in the endgame, since King position is usually critical and pawn moves are irreversible.

• The minimum mating material against a *lone* King is a King and Rook.

• To win an endgame with only *pieces* remaining, you must normally be at least *minimum* mating material *ahead*.

• *Activatee* your King (usually centralize) early in the endgame — for both offense and defense — and maintain an *aggressive* King position throughout the endgame.

• Learn and apply endgame fundamentals: "queening square," opposition, triangulation, and *zugzwang*.

• Seize and maintain the *opposition* in K + P endgames — the opposition determines whether the game is a win or a draw.

• Avoid moving your King outside the "queening square" of opposing passed pawns.

• Keep your Rooks active in the endgame.

• Place Rooks *behind* passed pawns.

• Bishops of opposite colors are drawish in the endgame, since they can be sacrificed to prevent a solo opposing pawn from queening.

• Place pawns on *opposite*-colored squares than your Bishop so as to increase the Bishop's mobility.

• Protect *weak* pawns by maintaining them on *opposite*-colored squares than your opponent's Bishop.

• Every pawn is a potential Queen, and every new Queen was once a passed pawn — do not lose pawns carelessly.

• Develop queening threats on both sides of the board — the enemy King is not elastic!

• CREATE and ADVANCE passed pawns at every *safe* opportunity, and promote passed pawns to new Queens as quickly as possible.

• To promote pawns, advance *unopposed* pawns first — especially those farthest from the defending King.

• An offside (away from the Kings) pawn majority can produce a winning passed pawn — either a new Queen or an effective decoy.

• Capture or blockade opposing passed pawns early, before they threaten to queen.

• If an opposing passed pawn reaches the sixth rank, strong measures should be taken immediately!

• If you are only *one* pawn ahead in the endgame, exchange *pieces*, not pawns — save your valuable pawns for promotion to Queens.

• When *behind* in the endgame, exchange *pawns*, not pieces — eliminate your opponent's potential new Queens.

• Kings *lead* pawns to queening in a K + P(s) endgame.

• In a K + P endgame, a King on the *sixth* rank ahead of a safe pawn on the same file (except a Rook file) is a certain win.

• Remember, a King and a Rook-pawn (even with a Bishop of opposite color than the pawn's promotion square) is a draw if the defending King can reach the promotion square.

• Be alert for endgame *tactics*, especially sacrifices.

• With only one pawn against your opponent's none in an endgame with minor pieces remaining, protect against your opponent's sacrificing a minor piece for your solo pawn and forcing a draw by insufficient mating material.

• Avoid stalemating your opponent — leave him moves when his King is not in check.

• Remember the option of *underpromoting* a pawn, to avoid stalemate (Rook or Bishop) or give a winning check (Knight).

• Remember and apply the five types of draws: insufficient mating material, stalemate, threefold repetition, 50-move rule, and by agreement.

• Do not resign prematurely — play for a draw when behind. Aside from hopelessly drawn positions, offer a draw only when behind or in time trouble. Accept draws only after careful reflection.

• You cannot win a chess game by resigning — resign only when the position is absolutely hopeless.

Bad Chess Habits

Bad chess habits cause many discouraging losses. Following is a list of 50 common bad chess habits:

1. Playing too fast and being impatient (sound chess requires time)
2. Neglecting to castle
3. Failing to develop all pieces early
4. Moving the same pieces multiple times in the opening
5. Underestimating the importance of controlling the center
6. Expecting to win in the opening, and playing premature attacks
7. Unwise pawn-grabbing at the expense of development and position
8. Giving useless checks and making idle threats
9. Relying on opponents' errors or inferior moves
10. Making hasty or careless moves ("I'll just see what happens")
11. Making unsound trappy moves ("Hope he doesn't see it")
12. Attacking with only one or two pieces
13. Exchanging pieces or pawns without a specific, sound purpose
14. Creating weaknesses in your position (exposed King, unguarded, pinned, forkable pieces and pawns, weak pawns, holes in pawn structure)
15. Overlooking opponents' threats (not asking after *each* of your opponent's moves, "What is the *threat?*")
16. Missing tactical opportunities (not asking after *each* of your opponent's moves, "What has *changed* in the position?")

17. Losing material carelessly (neglecting to ask before each of your moves, "Is this move *safe?*")
18. Believing a significant early material deficit can always be overcome
19. Not keeping accurate account of material at all times
20. Being mentally lazy (not looking far enough ahead, not anticipating opponents' best defenses to your threats)
21. Having no systematic method of searching for a move
22. Failing to analyze each position accurately and completely
23. Not analyzing the consequences of all possible checks and captures — for both sides — on each move
24. Not planning (playing only move-to-move)
25. Inflexibly persisting with inappropriate or faulty plans
26. Becoming so involved in your own plans and threats that you ignore or underestimate your opponents' plans and threats
27. Not playing adequate defense (not breaking pins early, not keeping all pieces and pawns defended, walking into Knight forks, aligning your King or Queen with enemy pieces, not considering all possible defenses to threats)
28. Ignoring or discounting positional possibilities (open files and diagonals, outposts, Rooks on seventh rank, strong or weak pawns) for *both* sides
29. Ignoring or underestimating the value of pawns and the importance of pawn play (passed pawns, pawn majorities, pawn exchanges and sacrifices, weak pawns, holes in pawn structure)
30. Being too passive (blocking pieces with pawns, always retreating rather than advancing or counterattacking when threatened)
31. Being unwilling to trade Queens
32. Always accepting sacrifices
33. Never playing sacrifices
34. Not creating, protecting, and advancing passed pawns quickly in the endgame
35. Not activating your King early and using your King aggressively in the endgame
36. Playing the opponent, rather than the position on the board
37. Becoming intimidated and playing too cautiously or passively against stronger opponents; becoming overconfident and

playing carelessly against weaker opponents
38. Concentrating on staying ahead of your opponent on the clock more than on the board
39. Not relaxing by taking frequent mental breaks during a game
40. Always playing to win, even when only a draw is realistic
41. Resigning prematurely
42. Agreeing prematurely to draws
43. Becoming overconfident and careless in winning positions
44. Carelessly allowing losing opponents to achieve stalemate
45. Not recording and reviewing your own games
46. Not studying chess regularly
47. Not trying new ideas, even in casual games
48. Listening to too many chess advice-givers (confusing)
49. Playing only weaker opponents
50. Becoming emotionally upset after losses instead of learning a pertinent lesson to improve your future play

To improve your chess immediately, select five applicable bad habits from the foregoing list and begin to remedy them promptly.

Your Continued Development

- To improve your chess game, combine STUDY and PLAY: study and play, study and play, study and play ...

- Divide your study time: Opening–30%; Middlegame–50%; Endgame–20%.

- As you improve, you will learn the value of — and develop skill in exploiting — first pieces, then pawns, and finally squares.

- Always play "Touch-Move" — never take back a move; it is against the rules of chess and detrimental to your improvement.

- Avoid having a favorite piece.

- Learn chess notation, then record and review your games.

- Play stronger players frequently, and learn from them — playing stronger players strengthens your chess.

- Play White when possible — White wins more often than Black.

• Learn and play standard openings and defenses which *suit your style*, whether tactical or positional.

• Play both King- and Queen-pawn openings, and play gambits occasionally.

• Specialize in only a few openings and defenses.

• In serious games, play openings and defenses you know well; practice other openings and defenses in casual ("skittles") games or against a computer.

• Remain calm and alert throughout a chess game — take occasional mental breaks to ease the tension.

• Emphasize playing your best, rather than considering winning all-important.

• Enjoy your WINS and learn from your LOSSES! Learn at least one lesson from each loss — defeats are great teachers.

• Chess is the game of kings and the king of games, but, for perspective, remember — chess is only a game.

Summary

Chess knowledge is chess power! The preceding helpful guidelines represent the accumulated practical wisdom of countless chess Masters over the centuries. Learning and applying the foregoing guidelines will strengthen your chess game. Apply them consistently and appropriately — but not automatically, for exceptions exist — and you will win more games.

GLOSSARY

advanced pawn — a pawn moved beyond the fourth (White) or fifth (Black) rank

annotations — critical comments on chess moves

attack — a move or series of moves designed to checkmate or win material

back-rank mate — checkmate of a confined King on the first or eighth rank

backward pawn — a pawn whose supporting pawns on adjacent files have advanced beyond the pawn; thus, the pawn cannot be defended by other pawns

"bad" Bishop — a Bishop restricted by pawns of its own color

balanced position — a position in which the material and positional advantages and disadvantages of both sides are approximately equal

base pawn — the rear pawn in a pawn chain

battery — two or more pieces of the same color acting along a rank, file, or diagonal

blunder — a serious mistake which violates one or more basic chess principles and allows checkmate, loses significant material, or seriously deteriorates a position

capture — transfer of a chessman to another square, displacing an enemy chessman

castling — a combined move of a King and Rook to safeguard the King and activate the Rook (the King is first moved two squares toward the Rook, then the Rook is placed on the adjacent square on the opposite side of the King). Castling is illegal if: 1) the King would move into, out of, or through check; 2) intervening pieces exist; 3) the King or Rook on the castling side has previously moved

center — the four central squares (d4, d5, e4, e5) on the chessboard

center control — exercising power over the important central squares by occupation or attack

check — an immediate attack (threat to capture on the next move) against a King

checkmate — a game-ending attack (check) on a King which is impossible to escape (by capturing the attacker, interposing, or moving the King)

chessmen — Kings, Queens, Rooks, Bishops, Knights, and pawns

clearance — vacating a piece from a square so that a more effective piece can utilize the square

closed file — a file occupied by pawns of both colors

closed position — a position in which few, if any, pawn exchanges have occurred, much of the pawn structure is blocked, and few open lines exist

combination — a series of forcing moves, often involving a temporary sacrifice, which leads to a tactical or positional advantage, or minimizes a disadvantage, if successful

connected pawn — a pawn protected by one or more pawns

connected passed pawn — a passed pawn protected by one or more pawns

counterattack — responding to an attack by waging an equal or greater attack on the opponent

defense — parrying opponents' threats (e.g., counterattack, capture, pin, deflect or interpose against attacking piece, guard threatened chessman or square, move away, block lines)

desperado — an inevitably lost chessman used to gain as much material or cause as much damage as possible

development — moving minor pieces and Queen off the back rank, and Rooks to open, half-open, or central files

diagonal — a row of same-colored squares running obliquely, or slant-wise, across the chessboard

discovered attack — an attack by a piece uncovered when a chessman aligned between the piece and its target moves off the same rank, file, or diagonal

double attack — simultaneous attack against two chessmen or significant squares by another chessman

double check — simultaneous check by two pieces (must result from a discovered attack)

doubled pawns — two pawns of the same color on the same file

draw — a tie in which neither side wins or loses (types of draws: insufficient mating force, stalemate, threefold repetition, 50-move rule, and by agreement)

endgame — final phase of a chess game when material is reduced and the main objective is to promote one or more pawns to enable checkmate

en passant *(e.p.)* — an optional capture by a pawn on its fifth rank immediately after an opposing pawn has advanced *two* squares on an adjacent file. The enemy pawn is captured as though it had moved only *one* square. The *en passant* capture option exists for one move only.

en prise (ahn-**preez**) — an attacked and unprotected piece or pawn

Exchange — winning a Rook for a Bishop or Knight (minor Exchange), or a Queen for a Rook (major Exchange)

fianchetto — flank development of a Bishop on a wing

FIDE — Federation Internationale des Echecs, world chess governing body

fifty-move rule — a draw can be claimed if no captures or pawn moves are made within 50 moves (extended for certain rare endgame positions)

file — a column of eight vertical squares on the chessboard

forcing move — a check, capture, or threat to check or capture

gambit — sacrifice of material (usually a pawn or two) in the opening to gain a lead in development, open lines, control the center, gain the initiative, and develop an early attack

half-open file — a file occupied by a pawn(s) of one color (also known as a semi-open file)

hanging pawns — a pawn island consisting of two connected pawns abreast on half-open files

hole — a square in front of an isolated, doubled, or backward pawn on which an enemy piece can be placed and not be profitably captured or easily evicted (outpost)

hypermodern chess — initially controlling the center from a distance with pieces (often fianchettoed Bishops), then counterattacking the center with flank or central pawn thrusts at an opportune time

ideal center — safely supported central pawns on e4 and d4 (e5 and d5, for Black)

in-between move — a counter-threatening move interposed before answering a threat (also known as *zwischenzug)*

initiative — the ability to create threats, usually the result of superior development and position

insufficient mating force — a drawn position in which neither side has existing or potential material to checkmate

interference — breaking the line of communication between an enemy piece and the chessman or square it protects

isolated pawn — a pawn without a pawn(s) of the same color on adjacent files

"j'adoube" (jah-**doob)** — a universal (French) warning given before adjusting chessmen to avoid the "touch-move" requirement (in English: "I adjust")

kibitz — to offer unwelcome gratuitous advice to chessplayers during a game

Kingside — the four files (e, f, g, h) on the Kings' original side of the chessboard

Knight fork — simultaneous attack by a Knight on two or more chessmen

line clearance — removing chessmen from a significant rank, file, or diagonal

major pieces — Queens and Rooks

material — all chessmen except the King

mating force — material sufficient to force checkmate (against a lone King, a King and Rook constitute minimum mating force)

middlegame — the phase of a chess game between the opening and the endgame, characterized by strategy, positional play, tactics, attacks, and defense

minor pieces — Bishops and Knights

mobility — freedom of action for pieces

move — the transfer of a chessman to a vacant square

notation — a system of recording chess moves and positions (Algebraic and English Descriptive are the most popular notation systems)

offside pawn majority — extra pawn(s) on wing opposite enemy King

open file — a file not occupied by pawns

of either color (pieces may be on the file)

open line — any rank, file, or diagonal free of pawns

open position — a position in which several pawn exchanges have occurred, and files and diagonals have become open

opening — the first 10 to 15 moves of a chess game, characterized by development of pieces and struggle for control of the center

opposition — occurs when Kings are aligned on a rank, file, or diagonal an odd number of squares apart (a vital endgame maneuver to penetrate with a King and escort a pawn to promotion)

outpost — a significant square in or near enemy territory on which a piece can be placed and not be profitably exchanged or easily evicted

oversight — a minor mistake which loses slight material or position

overworked defender — one chessman simultaneously defending two or more attacked chessmen or significant squares

passed pawn — a pawn facing no hostile pawns on the same or adjacent files between the pawn and its promotion square on the last rank

pawn chain — a series of connected pawns on a diagonal

pawn-grabbing — unwisely capturing pawns, especially wing pawns, at the expense of development and position

pawn island — a cluster of connected pawns on adjacent files

pawn majority — extra pawn(s) in any sector (center, Kingside or Queenside)

pawn promotion — promoting a pawn to a Queen, Rook, Bishop, or Knight immediately upon the pawn's reaching the last rank

pawn wedge — an advanced pawn protected by one or two pawns

perpetual check — an endless series of checks, eventually leading to a draw by threefold repetition

phalanx — pawns abreast on the same rank with supporting pawns on adjacent files

pieces — Queens, Rooks (major pieces) and Bishops, Knights (minor pieces)

pin — an attack along the same line against a chessman aligned with a more valuable chessman on a rank, file, or diagonal

position — configuration of chessmen on the chessboard

positional play — placing pieces or pawns in optimum position for offense and defense by controlling important squares and lines

premature attack — an unjustified or insufficiently prepared attack

promotion square — the square on which a pawn promotes to a new piece (Queen, Rook, Bishop, or Knight)

protected passed pawn — a passed pawn defended by one or two pawns

queening — promoting a pawn to a Queen

queening combinations — tactical moves to promote a pawn to a Queen

queening square — the square geometric space on a chessboard within which a King can catch and capture an enemy passed pawn before or immediately after the pawn promotes

Queenside — the four files (a, b, c, d) on the Queens' original side of the chessboard

quiet position — a position in which neither checks nor captures are imminent

rank — a row of eight horizontal squares on the chessboard

rating — a numerical index of a chessplayer's strength

resign — concede defeat

reversed opening — playing a Black defense as White, with an extra move in hand

sacrifice — yielding material for a tactical or positional advantage

sector — an area of the chessboard (center, Kingside, or Queenside)

semi-open file — a file occupied by a pawn or pawns of one color (also known as a half-open file)

simplifying — trading pieces to reduce material, minimize counterplay, and reach a winning endgame

skewer — an attack along the same line against a chessman aligned with a less valuable chessman on a rank, file, or diagonal

skittles — casual chess games

stalemate — a draw, in which a King is not in check and the side has no legal move by any chessman, including the King

standing Queen — a newly promoted Queen which cannot be captured

strategy — plan for exerting maximum offensive and defensive force in a chess game

subcenter — the twelve squares adjacent to the center on the chessboard (e3, d3, c3, c4, c5, c6, d6, e6, f6, f5, f4, f3)

tactic — immediate threat to checkmate or win material

tempo — one move for either side (*tempi* is plural)

tension — possible checks, captures, and threats

threat — possibility of forcing checkmate, winning material, or achieving a positional advantage

threefold repetition — a draw can be claimed if the same position occurs three times, with the same side to move (the repetitions need not be consecutive)

"touch-move" rule — requirement that a touched chessman must be moved, and a touched enemy chessman must be captured, if legal (unless "*j'adoube*" first)

transition — the interval between the opening and middlegame, or middlegame and endgame

trappy move — a move which loses material or position if the threat is properly countered

triangulation — an endgame King maneuver to lose a move (take *two* moves to reach an adjacent square), and thereby establish *zugzwang* for the opponent

tripled pawns — three pawns of the same color on the same file

unbalanced position — a position in which the advantages and disadvantages of both sides are unevenly distributed

underpromotion — promoting a pawn to a Rook, Bishop, or Knight instead of to a Queen (to avoid stalemate or give a winning check)

USCF — United States Chess Federation, governing organization of chess in the United States

variation — possible sequence of moves

vital guard — an essential protector of an important chessman or square

vulnerable back rank — an inadequately defended King confined to its first rank and subject to checkmate on that rank

weak square — an inadequately protected significant square

weakness — tactical or positional defect in a position

zugzwang — having to move, and any move loses material or the game

zwischenzug — a counter-threatening move interposed before defending against a threat (also known as an "in-between" move)

EPILOGUE

Strong chessplayers have superior chess knowledge and skills: they know more, evaluate positions more correctly, develop sounder plans, analyze variations more accurately, defend more tenaciously, and play better moves.

You are now a strong chessplayer. You have significantly increased your knowledge and skill in all phases of chess — opening, middlegame, and endgame — and you have experienced the satisfying benefits of your improvement by winning more chess games. You now know the principles and techniques necessary to win at chess!

Continue your chess progress by broadening your knowledge of openings, and by studying games of Masters and Grandmasters to gain new winning middlegame ideas. Be certain to stay tactically sharp — do tactical problems and exercises at every opportunity. Continue to develop your skill at positional play and pawn play, and seek to improve your defensive capabilities. Study advanced endgame manuals to extend your endgame expertise. Continue to play and learn from stronger players.

You can now play chess with skill and confidence. I wish you continued progress in chess and every success in your future games!

— RHC

RON CURRY

Expert Ronald Curry has successfully competed in national and international chess tournaments, and has taught chess classes and given private lessons for over twenty years. He has also coached scholastic and college chess teams.

Curry was honored with the prestigious Meritorious Service Award by the United State Chess Federation for his teaching.

An honors graduate of Cornell, and a member of Mensa, Curry is a retired business consultant who enjoys his hobbies of chess, golf, tennis, collecting pipes, and music.

A Small List of Accomplishments

Inventor of the Curry Opening (1971, see *Chess Life* article 9/86);
USCF Certified Senior Tournament Director;
Author of numerous chess games collections (published locally);
Instructor, Delaware scholastic Gifted Student Program;
Delware Amateur Champion (1973);
2nd place, ICCF Master Class Tournament (1983);
Semi-Finalist, CCLA Grand National Tournament (1990);
Coach, University of Delaware chess team (1993—);
Newark, Delaware Chess Club Champion (1973-1974-1975);
Games published in *Chess Life* and *The Chess Correspondent*
... and much more.

WHAT OTHERS ARE SAYING

Anyone can hype themselves, what's really fun is to get endorsements from others, especially those who paid *you* for their lessons.

What follows on the next few pages are some excerpts by those who worked from Curry's original manuscript.

At last. An instructive book the average chessplayer can understand... Without qualification, your most helpful new book has improved my chess game more than any other chess book I have ever read (and I have read many) over the past fifty years I have been addicted to chess. I really believe if such an instructive manual as yours had been available in 1940 when I 'pushed my first pawn,' I would be a Master today... I have also had remarkable success altely with your 'Curry Opening.' I have found any defense other than the King's Indian or Gruenfeld is doomed from the start. And I have enjoyed several impressive wins against both the King's Indian and Gruenfeld Systems...

Edward (Ned) F. Smith, Jr. (1991, 1995)

...As a former technical writer for a large company I can definitely say that this book is not a half-hearted or amateurish attempt, but is a serious, important contribution to the chess literature, aimed at increasing the beginning and lower rated players' understanding of the game... I am a senior citizen who for the past five years has been attending Ron Curry's excellent chess lectures at the Fraim Senior Center in Wilmington, Delaware. Ron's lessons and his book have helped me increase my rating from 1350 to 1685 on the club ladder, and I have recently had two draws out of two games against masters in simultaneous exhibitions...

Bill Marsh (1991)

I am a retired chemist who joined Mr. Curry's chess class a couple of years ago as a beginning chess player with no preconceived ideas of proper chess play or poor chess habits to worry about... *Win at Chess*... has been one of the key factors in my improvement in chess. Although Curry aims his book at the intermediate player, I believe the serious beginning player will benefit a great deal from studying his book...

Henry Krysiak (1991)

...(Your book) includes many helpful suggestions for improvement, e.g., four questions to ask before every move, and to look for the BEST move (a personal weakness)...

Jim Murphy (1991)

...I find your book *Win at Chess!* to be excellent...It is packed full of specific suggestions for improving one's game in so many aspects. Your instructions are simple, direct, and effective...

Wallace Adams (1992)

...The president of our club, Sid Smith, bought one of the copies, as you know. He *raves* about it. Says he spends some time almost every day with it. From my games with him, I find his game has definitely become stronger...For me it is the best general book on chess that I have encountered.

Paul R. Arms (1992)

...In general, I find that I pay more attention to details that I had not even watched before. It has made me a more careful player...Your ideas have made me less of a defensive players. And I particularly like the "Curry Opening," it has made my white opening a lot stronger right away!!

Sidney B. Smith (1992)

What others are saying

...In essence (Win at Chess) teaches common sense, and understanding of the necessary knowledge required, to play chess at its best...The why, when, and how to make a move, or series of moves, based on sound reasoning, is explained in detail where needed. It is a *complete* home or class room *study course*...It is the best teaching manual of any, so far as I believe.

Frank A. Riley (1992)

...Most importantly, this book emphasizes fundamental principles rather than focusing on managing moves. The principles are laid out in a logical progression with numerous examples and exercises to test one's progress...

Sharon B. Jacobs (1992)

...You are without doubt the best teacher I have ever had. Only a dedicated teacher who loves his subject can give a lesson to his class each week that is fresh, exciting and instructive...the text, too, is fresh, exciting and instructive...

Joseph F. Glackin (1992)

...This book indicates that you have spent years studying a library of chess books and have done a superior job sorting out the knowledge that one must have to become a good chess player...

Ed Stokes (1992)

I've gone through your excellent book *Win at Chess* several times, each time I'm amazed at how much information you have put in your book.I would certainly recommend it for any player from beginner to expert...

Jerry Uniacke (1993)

•

Now you, reader, have in your hands a work which has been updated, sifted, reorganized, and applied to a method of winning chess for the Intermediate Player. Ron and I offer our best wishes for your success. Let us know what you have gleaned from this book.

Bob Long
Publisher

* COLOPHON *

Typeset in Adobe's Goudy Oldstyle with Thinkers' Press C.R. Horowitz, 12/14
Copy entry, rewrites, diagrams: Pat Scoville
Cover: Rob Long & Bob Long with help from Electric Image
Layout: Pat Scoville & Bob Long
Proofreading: Bob Long, Paul Sholl, and Ron Curry

Thinkers' Press is known worldwide for its quality chess literature. We provide quick delivery and postpaid shipping of all of our products. You can be assured of top-notch materials; what we sell through this catalog is guaranteed or your money back. Please order by catalog number.

THE OPENING

Alekhine's Defense Four Pawns Attack: *GM Larry Christiansen, Manuel Joseph, Bob Raingruber, flexi*

Ultimately, this attack is probably the one Black fears most. Designed like our King's Gambit book, it arms White with a very powerful weapon for his 1. e4 arsenal. Published in 1989. OP57882. **$12.95**

Bronstein-Ljubojevic: Four Pawns Attack: *Tom Tucker & Bob Long, flexi*

A 20-page supplement to the above book on a highly-tactical line not contained in the ADFPA book. Controversial and exciting. OP57889. **$4.00**

Benoni Defence Taimanov Variation 8 Bb5 (A67): *Maurizio Tirabassi, flexi*

While Black seems to keep coming up with ways of diverting White's latest innovations, in this line he has been running into a brick wall. Black's congestion and development problems last throughout the game. Published in 1993. OP77529. **$12.50.**

Bird Variation in the Ruy Lopez *Rotariu and Cimmino, flexi*

128 pages. ICCF GM Rotariu explores the correspondence weapon 1. e4 e5 2. Nf3 Nc6 3. Bb5 Nd4 by giving hundreds of annotated and unannotated games such as Rohde-Christiansen 1985 (won by Black). 17 main lines plus complete games indices. © 1992. **$14.00**

Blackmar-Diemer gambit keybook: *Rev. Tim Sawyer, flexi*

Master Sawyer's compilation of 743 (mostly) annotated games, arranged in 7 chapters (Avoided, Declined, Bogoljubow, Euwe, Ziegler, Gunderam, and Teichmann), presents a great number of scintillating games where Black is often crushed under the weight of a mighty piece onslaught by White.

While this opening is exciting, controversial, and dangerous, it will also add many points to your rating. Chapter one is loaded with ways of beating Black when "he" avoids your opening. The whole book is chock full of brilliant tactical counterstrokes. OP57887. **$21.95**

Caro-Kann Defence Advance Variation (B12): *Tirabassi, flexi*

More than the Seirawan ECO book. 3... c5, 3... Bf5, 3... Na6 are covered. Includes the hot 3... Bf5 4. Nc3 e6 5. g4 line. Many games and analyses. 128 pages. OP77558. **$14.00**

Caro-Kann Defence Knight Variation 4... ♘f6 (B15-B16): *S. Curtacci, flexi*

Popular with Seirawan and many others. Our Italian IM offers this system as a secret weapon because the lines are not as numerous nor complex as many others are. Figurine algebraic notation with 100s of decisive annotated and unannotated games. Indices, 96 pages. *ECO* style. OP72982. **$12.50**

Cambridge Springs Variation in the Queen's Gambit (D52-QO15.2): *S1E, flexi*

Ten major chapters including the Anti-Cambridge Springs. This rough and tumble chess variation begins: 1. d4 d5 2. c4 e6 3. Nc3 Nf6 4. Bg5 Nbd7 5. e3 c6 6. Nf3 Qa5. 282 games and analysis. © 1994. OP92788. **$12.50**

Dutch Defence Leningrad Variation 7... Nc6 (A89): *Luccioni, flexi*

If you are playing to win a critical game, many of the best players turn to the Dutch Defense. The Leningrad is such a solid line that you must know a lot of variations. OP87982. **$14.00**

English Opening (A21): *Maurizio Tirabassi, flexi*

96 pages. Covers the "new" 1. c4 e5 2. Nc3 Bb4!? 200 games plus extensive analysis as well as original analysis of this hot system to combat the English. © 1994. OP77557. **$12.50**

English Opening Lukin's Variation (A21): *S1E, flexi*

This very enterprising line goes: 1. c4 e5 2. Nc3 d6 3. Nf3 f5 4. d4 e4. A combination Old Indian/Dutch/English. White has had no end of grief looking for a good 5th move. © 1994. OP95525. **$16.50.** If you want the book + ChessBase disk (PC) combo then it's SW95527 for **$28.95.**

French Defence Tarrasch Variation C03: *Luccioni, flexi*

1. e4 e6 2. d4 d5 3. Nd2. 216 pages covering 24 "main" lines. Extremely comprehensive. © 1995, OP97527. **$17.00.**

French Defence Winawer Variation C15-C19: *Myers, flexi*

46 complete games + extensive bibliography covering 27 chapters. An amazing book and excellent introduction for beginner and advanced player. © 1994, OP87987. **$17.50.**

The Göring Gambit: *Cimmino, flexi*

128 pages on C44. 210 games plus lots of analysis on one of the most difficult and yet fascinating gambits in the history of chess (1. e4 e5 2. Nf3 Nc6 3. d4 ed 4. c3). © 1993. OP77552. **$14.00**

Grünfeld Indian Exchange Variation 7 Nf3 c5 8 Be3 (D85): *S1E, flexi*

More English instruction than the usual S1E book. With the introduction of 7... c5 White's advantage in the past has become "unclear." 247 games or fragments. © 1994. OP95299. **$16.50.** Or get the book + ChessBase disk (PC) combo. It's SW95522. **$29.95**

Italian Game C53-C54: *S1E, flexi*

288 complete or partial games are referenced. To many this is known as the Giuoco Piano. Lots of old and new games are given. Includes the Möller and d3 lines. Of the "main lines" are older games! There are number of 1993 references. Also includes the Evans Gambit. © 1994, OP95528. **$16.50.** Or get the book + ChessBase disk (PC) combo. It's SW95529. **$28.95**

The King's Gambit As White 3: *Bob Raingruber and Lou Maser, flexi*

Rewrites to the Berlin and Fischer systems plus new additions to various declined methods in this "heavily expanded" edition. More problems and almost three times as many games as before. OP58295. **$22.95**

Keres Defence: *G. Falchetta, flexi*

A system in vogue in order to solve the problem of the QB: 1. d4 d5 2. c4 Bf5. White's objectives are on the Q-side but Black can also get active play there as well as a solid game. Figurine algebraic notation, hundreds of annotated games, clearly diagrammed, and many decisive contests. Indices, 128 pages. © 1992. OP72988. **$14.00**

Semi-Slav Defence Botvinnik Variation (D44): *Konikowski and Thesing, flexi*

244 pages. Botvinnik's variations in any opening are usually important and this one is particularly true. 1. d4 d5 2. c4 c6 3. Nf3 Nf6 4. Nc3 e6 5. Bg5 dc4. © 1993. OP77572. **$15.50**

Ruy Lopez (Vol. 1) Exchange Variation: *Falchetta, flexi*

Lots of analysis in 175 pages as well as 132 well-annotated games. More to come. OP87985. **$15.50**

Sicilian Defence Najdorf Variation 7... ♕c7 (B96): *S. Curtacci, flexi*

91 pages. A hot line of interest with thousands of copies sold in Germany alone. Other moves have been 7... Be7, 7... Qb6, and 7... b5. Current practitioners are Kasparov, Chandler, Tukmakov, Gelfand and many others. Black's play has resulted in great tactical and positional tension.

The author suggests you fasten your seat belt. If, however, you have a faint heart, this book is not for you, he says! New winning chances for Black. OP72985. **$12.50**

Sicilian Defence Najdorf Variation (B98-B99): *Curtacci, flexi*

292 pages. 21 lines, a huge and easy to read index of variations. Over 300 complete games plus lots of analyses on 1. e4 c5 2. Nf3 d6 3. d4 cd4 4. Nd4 Nf6 5. Nc3 a6 6. Bg5 e6 7. f4 Be7. White presses and Black tries to complicate. © 1993. OP77559. **$18.50**

The LDL Sicilian: *Alex Dunne, flexi*

An eight-chapter dissertation of the Lasker-Dunne-Line. Featuring a "new" winning method against the Sicilian Defense using a fianchetto system.

This suggestion by the great Lasker is 30 pages in length and designed to fit inside a standard business envelope. OP58298. **$5.00**

Schaak: *collected by Jaap van der Kooij (Dutch), flexi*

These regularly updated pamphlets each contain an average of 100 correspondence games (mostly master level) on a particular opening. Presented in easy-to-read Dutch algebraic and unannotated.

The collection is too large to list here (over 210 items), but you may contact Thinkers' Press for a complete listing by name of opening, *ECO* number, and move order.

Prices are **$4.00** each; **$3.50** each for 8-24 copies; **$3.00** each for 25-99 copies; **$2.00** each for 100-150 copies. The complete set of 212 number is **$315.00.**

TREATISES

The Genesis of Power Chess: *Leslie Ault, flexi*

Dr. Ault's contention is that a thorough grounding in strategy and tactics is necessary for strong, consistent, and effective play. Examples from master play and Ault's own master praxis will convince you of his approach. The emphasis often revolves around getting a winning endgame or great pawn play—typical master achievement. One of our most important works. 352 pages, 700+ diagrams. © 1993. TR72872. **$25.95**

Practical Chess Analysis: *Mark Buckley, 3rd printing, flexi*

A brilliant exposé of how masters analyze. The methods and aims are illustrated through many fine examples. If you really want to follow a long thread of analysis, in your head, the author shows you how it can be done, really! Systematize the way you think so can carry these logical chains of reasoning, in your mind, to their conclusion including long chunks of analysis.

Buckley is a Senior Master from California. To be reprinted in 1995 for the 3rd time! TR58527. **$22.00.**

Win At Chess: *Ron Curry, flexi*

This expert has been teaching improvement to amateurs and average players for years with his own special brand of philosophy, techniques, and openings. The success and comments of his students offer proof of the worthiness of his methods. This is to be our entrant in the intermediate level instructional chess market. 272 pages. Summer 1995. TR77992. **$20.00.**

How to Become a Candidate Master: *Alex Dunne, 3rd printing, flexi*

Most of us non-masters want to make the "expert" rating, and this book contains 50 annotated games whose sole purpose is to get you to win more often and tone up that killer instinct.

A wide variety of opening, middlegame, and endgame play is displayed to get you used to winning in *any* phase of the game. There is also a "think and grow rich" tone presented throughout by the author. TR58288. **$18.95**

Answer Guide to How to Become a Candidate Master: *Alex Dunne, 2nd printing, flexi*

This book came about due to the tremendous popularity of the preceding book. Besides the brief biographical background of the author, there are answers to the questions posed in the book, ratings of the combatants, and corrections to the first edition of HTBACM. Published in 1986. TR57885 **$4.95**

Thinkers' Chess: *Gerzadowicz, flexi*

The best tips from 26 different game sources. The author annotates all skill levels from 1400-2400—compiled from the most interesting games supplied by readers of *The Chess Gazette.* Deep instructional ideas and just plain fun with words, the players, and chess. © 1995. TR87277. **$17.95**

Strategical Themes: *Unger, flexi*

Four principle applications, little known or used by the average player, are illustrated with (60) games and discussion (analysis): the pawn roller, centralization, the bad bishop, and the double fianchetto. One master told me this is the best exposition of the bad bishop he has seen. TR59828. **$13.95**

Chess Master . . . At Any Age: *Rolf Wetzell, flexi*

Rolf Wetzell was 50 years old when he attained a master's rating after years of fruitless pursuit at the 1800 level.

Using all kinds of psychological insights, analysis, discussions with friends, etc., he finally made it. He shows you how and what he found necessary to do when one isn't blessed with instant natural talent. The charts, aphorisms, philosophies, dietary and other considerations abound. This is a HOW TO book that really worked. Includes 16 dissected games using his methods. One of our hottest books in years. 300 pages. TR77997. **$23.95**

GAME COLLECTIONS

CJS Purdy's Fine Art of Chess Annotation and Other Thoughts: *compiled* *by Ralph J. Tykodi, flexi*

100 superbly annotated games by the man Fischer referred to as one of the best annotators of chess games.

For years Purdy, an Australian, edited *Chess World* magazine and a large majority of his readership was in the USA. In 1953 he won the world's First Correspondence Championship.

Included with the master-grandmaster level games are many aphorisms/maxims from his writings to help you improve your chess ("Purdyisms") and avoid those nerve-wracking blunders. See near back for additional details. GC58279. **$16.95**

New York 1991: *S1E, flexi*

100 selected games from this powerful event. GC95289. **$11.00.** As an introduction to the superb S1Editrice line from Italy, we will offer this book to you at **$4.00** with the purchase of ANY other S1E book from this catalog.

BIOGRAPHICAL

The Journal of a Chess Master: *Stephan Gerzadowicz, flexi*

An amazing collection of annotated games mostly from correspondence events played against many of the best players around and annotated in a belles-lettres style that William Shakespeare would have loved.

Several times finalist in national correspondence events, "Gerz" elucidates on the Pirc/King's Indian/Modern systems, and others, from years of experience on either side of the board! Rave notices and reviews (so much so that a second volume is in preparation). BI58292. **$19.95**

Henrique Mecking Latin Chess Genius: *Stephen Gordon, flexi*

One of the brashest, brightest players, of the 70s and the first player of great significance from South America.

Master Gordon annotates 24 of Mecking's best games and provides another 320 in the most complete collection ever of this Brazilian fireball. Also includes his recent return to chess.172 pages. BI72989. **$17.95**

Persona Non Grata: *GM Viktor Korchnoi & Lenny Cavallaro, flexi*

Korchnoi's defection from the USSR and his battle for the World Chess Championship, at Baguio City in the Philippines, is the theme. It contains many items missing from his Anti-Chess" such as photos, seven annotated games (3 by Kortchnoi, the other 4 by Alburt and Shamkovich), an afterword, letters, and other appended items (ten in all). Kortchnoi's notes are a motherlode of information on such topics as the passed pawns. Published in 1981 during his match with Karpov. BI58522. **$8.95.** We also have a very small supply of hardcovers

(BI58525) at **$22.50** each.

Grandmaster Fearless: *edited by Long, flexi*

This pamphlet came on the heels (1982) of "Persona Non Grata" and will be included FREE with any order for that book. His results in the USSR championships include title wins 4 times! Bronstein's article praises his play. 13 games (6 with notes). Also, Kortchnoi's scores against all world champions he has played (Karpov was the only player with a better percentage at that time). BI58287. **$3.00**

Viktors Pupols, American Master: *Larry Parr, flexi*

A book about a player who is just as interesting in person as he is in the book. His knowledge of chess, illustrative positions, and chess humor makes Pupols a fascinating and humorous study. All types of openings, opponents and a 100 tournament first-places!

Tired of boring chess or boring chess masters?, grab this book and reminisce about driving to far away tournaments, dealing with obnoxious people, and discovering new chess theory. Pupols' Latvian Gambit flattened Fischer numerous times when Bobby was just a youngster. Foreword by Seirawan. BI59852. **$6.50**

Confessions of a Chess Grandmaster: *GM Andrew Soltis, 2nd. ed, flexi*

Do only born geniuses have a chance to become a GM? This and lots of other questions are discussed in this autobiography.

Soltis' gift as a writer and chess player is in evidence here. Virtually all new, original information, whether it is about Fischer, Zuckerman, or the Russian GMs.

Soltis discusses his penchant for "bizarre" systems in "normal" openings and gives lots of details, especially in his Sicilian lines. He also discusses why he decides to drop certain variations just as they become popular. BI58282. An expanded edition will be printed in 1996. Our biggest book.

ENDGAME

What Every GM Knows About the Endgame...: *GM Andrew Soltis, flexi*

This will be the best endgame book ever written for instructional purposes. One column has a diagram and analysis, the "adjacent" column has a discussion of "techniques" with GM Noah Tall and his student Pat. These techniques include the mismatch, zugzwang, Lucena, Philidor, elbowing, triangulation, the opposition and much more. Most of the examples are from current Grandmaster play! Mistakes and improvements by the world's best with instructional value less hundreds of hours of memorizing! Available Fall 1995. EG87279.

REFERENCE

The Complete Guide to Correspondence Chess: *Alex Dunne, flexi*

Everything about correspondence chess is here: players, rules, organizations, history, games, advice, rosters of winners, computers and cheating.

Dunne has been the "Check Is In The Mail" columnist for *Chess Life* for the past ten years. Nothing else like this in print. Now with every purchase get a 16-page supplemental update of addresses, prizes, events and lots of other information. RE58285. **$16.95.**

Russian for Chessplayers: *Hanon W. Russell, flexi*

A revised and expanded edition of his earlier book—this is completely re-typeset. The vocabulary is twice the previous size and now a pronunciation guide to the names of Soviet players has been included. How to handle nouns, verbs, and translate on the fly using HWR basics. RE58529. **$12.95.**

Lasker & His Contemporaries

In 1978 we began publishing translations, theories, photos, new articles, and some incredible game annotations cover Lasker and the other giants of chess from the Golden Age. An oasis in a Sahara of chess literature. All are 8.5" x 11" format and, unfortunately, several are in short supply.

Issue One: Capablanca—Lasker negotiations, Lasker's Profundity, the Earliest Recorded Lasker Game, Annotated Games, and the Ten Best Controversy. 36 pp. Some rust on staples. EN59855. **$15.00**

Issue Two: The Great Steinitz Hoax, Karl Schlechter, 1903 Lasker—Chigorin, Lasker the Mathematician, and the 1910 Lectures in South America. 40 pp. EN59857. **$15.00**

Issue Three: Lasker vs. the Devil, New York 1893, Frank Marshall, Chess and Strategy, Lasker's Forgotten Games, and "old" Lasker in the USSR. 48 pp.

EN598958 **$15.00**

Issue Four: Doomsday Encounter, Khrulev on Lasker, Marshall and Lasker, Cambridge Springs, 1894 Match, Lasker's Visit to Spain, Chess Nerves, and the Annotated Lasker. 56 pp. EN59859 **$15.00**

The Lasker Poster: A beautiful, full size, two-color rendering of the artwork designed by Bob O'Hare for *Lasker & His Contemporaries.* Orange-brown and black. Few left. Price includes shipping. **$15.95.**

CHESS HAMMERS

Originally published as "Chess Analysis Reports." Use these just like a jackhammer to your opponent's game.

This is winning chess, ideas that you won't find in the regular opening books. And, if you look close enough, you will find lines that probably refute current thinking—no kidding!

There are 38 of these and you can get them all at special prices, see at the end. These typeset idea-starters run from 3 to 5 pages. Contributions by Masters Tom Tucker, Allan Savage, Tim Sawyer, and your editor, Bob Long.

1. Colle System: A New Idea for White. 1 d4 d5 2 Nf3 Nf6 3 e3 c5 **4 ???**

2. Richter-Veresov: A New Idea for White. 1 d4 d5 2 Nc3 Nf6 3 Bg5 Nbd7 4 Nf3 g6 **5 ???**

3. Nimzo-Indian Defense: A Gambit System for Black. 1 d4 Nf6 2 c4 e6 3 Nc3 Bb4 4 Qc2 0-0 5 a3 Bc3 6 Qc3 **???**

4. Old Catalan: A New Idea for Black. 1 d4 d5 2 Nf3 Nf6 3 g3 **???**

5. Catalan: A Surprise Weapon for Black. 1 d4 Nf6 2 c4 e6 3 g3 **???**

6. Colle System: A New Idea for Black. 1 d4 d5 2 Nf3 Nf6 3 e3 c5 4 c3 **???**

7. French Advance: An Interesting Idea for White. 1 e4 e6 2 d4 d5 3 e5 c5 4 c3 Nc6 5 Nf3 Qb6 6 Be2 cd 7 cd Nh6 8 Nc3 Nf5 **9 ????** Includes 6 games.

8. Symmetrical English: A Gambit for White. 1 c4 c5 **2 ???**

9. French Defense Burn Variation: A Gambit Idea for White. 1 e4 e6 2 d4 d5 3 Nc3 Nf6 4 Bg5 de **5 ???**

10. Sicilian Defense Moscow Variation: An Unusual Resource for Black. 1 e4 c5 2 Nf3 d6 3 Bb5 Nc6 4 d4 cd 5 Qd4 **Qa5** 6 Nc3 Qb5 7 Nb5 **???**

11. Ruy Lopez Classical Defense: A Gambit Idea for White. 1 e4 e5 2 Nf3 Nc6 3 Bb5 Bc5 **4 ???**

12. Caro-Kann, Panov-Botvinnik Attack: A Blow to the Gunderam Attack. 1 e4 c6 2 d4 d5 3 ed cd 4 c4 Nf6 5 c5 e5 6 Nc3 ed 7 Qd4 **???**

13. Réti System: An Unusual Idea for White. 1 Nf3 d5 2 c4 d4 **3 ???**

14. Caro-Kann Advance Variation: A New Resource for Black. 1 e4 c6 2 d4 d5 3 e5 **???**

15. Center-Counter Defense, "Modern"

Variation: A New Resource for Black. 1 e4 d5 2 ed Nf6 3 c4 **???**

16. French Tarrasch, Guimard Variation: An Underestimated Resource for Black. 1 e4 e6 2 d4 d5 3 Nd2 Nc6 4 Ngf3 Nf6 5 e5 Nd7 6 Nb3 Be7 7 Bb5 **???**

17. The English Defense: Black Fights Back! 1 d4 e6 2 c4 b6 3 a3 **???**

18. Réti vs. Dutch: An Old Gambit Springs to Life. 1 Nf3 f5 2 e4 fe **3 ???**

19. QGA: A "Beginner's Move" for Black. 1 d4 d5 2 c4 dc 3 Nf3 Nf6 4 e3 **???**

20. Center-Counter with Colors Reversed: A Surprise for White. 1 e4 e5 2 d4 ed 3 Qd4 Nc6 **4 ???**

21. The Old Indian Defense: Pseudo-Saemisch System for White. 1 d4 Nf6 2 c4 d6 3 Nc3 e5 4 d5 Nbd7 **5 ???**

22. Trompowski's Attack: Black's Critical Answer. 1 d4 Nf6 2 Bg5 Ne4 3 Bf4 c5 4 f3 Qa5 5 c3 Nf6 6 d5 **???**

23. The Larsen-Nimzovich 1 b3: White's Punishment. 1 b3 e5 2 Bb2 Nc6 3 c4 **???**

24. The Bishop's Opening: An Unusual Defense for Black. 1 e4 e5 2 Bc4 **???**

25. Caro-Kann Defense: A New Idea for Black. 1 e4 c6 2 d4 d5 3 Nd2 de 4 Ne4 **???**

26. QGD: Anti-Alatortsev. 1 d4 d5 2 c4 e6 3 Nc3 Be7 4 cd de **5 ???**

27. English Opening, Mikenas System: Improvements in the 8... h6 Line for Black. 1 c4 Nf6 2 Nc3 e6 3 e4 d5 4 e5 d4 5 ef dc 6 bc Qf6 7 d4 c5 8 Nf3 **???**

28. French Defense, Alekhine-Chatard Variation: The Recommended Defense Crumbles. 1 e4 e6 2 d4 d5 3 Nc3 Nf6 4 Bg5 Be7 5 e5 Nfd7 6 h4 a6 **7 ???**

29. Refuting the King Pawn Nimzovich Defense. 1 e4 Nc6 2 d4 d5 3 Nc3 de 4 d5 Ne5 5 Bf4 Ng6 6 Bg3 f5 **7 ???**

30. The Center Counter Wing Gambit: The End of Tunbridge Wells 1912. 1 e4 d5 2 ed Qd5 3 Nc3 Qa5 **4 ???**

31. Lisitsin Gambit 1 Nf3 f5 2 e4 fe 3 Ng5 **???**

32. Krejcik Gambit 1 d4 f5 **2 ???**

33. Alekhine's Defense 1 e4 Nf6 **2 ???**

34. Budapest Defense, Quiet Line 1 d4 Nf6 2 c4 e5 3 de Ng4 4 Nf3 Bc5 5 e3 Nc6 6 Be2 Ngxe5 7 Nxe5 Nxe5 8 Nc3 0-0 9 0-0 Re8 **10 ???**

35. Schlechter Gambit, Another ECO Unmentionable 1 f4 e5 2 fe **???**

36. Scholar's Mate Attack, What They Didn't Teach You in School 1 e4 e5 **2 ???**

37. Hillbilly Attack, Caro-Kann Comes to Dogpatch 1 e4 c6 **2 ???**

38. King's Gambit, ECO Fails Again! 1 e4 e5 2 f4 ef 3 Nf3 **???**

Each "Chess Hammer" is **$3.00.** Buy all 38 for just **$57.00.** More titles are expected.

CHESS PREVIEWS

Want to see some fresh, innovative, eye-opening, jam-packed information about chess openings? You know, stuff that will drive your opponents nuts?

The original idea was to provide a free gift for each monthly purchase of a certain amount to all of our good and regular customers. They were 14-16 pages in length and put together by Master Tom Tucker. There were semi-annuals that added new material from the previous 5 issues. In fact, the semi-annual is a good composite and would give you a good picture of what it is all about. Try a few of these, you will be pleasantly surprised at how GOOD this material is!

1. The French Defense: Tarrasch 3... a6. 1 e4 e6 2 d4 d5 3 Nd2.

2. The King's Indian Defense: Smyslov's Variation 5 Bg5. 1 d4 Nf6 2 c4 g6 3 Nc3 Bg7 4 Nf3 d6.

3. The English Opening: Neo-Keres 3... c6. 1 c4 e5 2 g3 Nf6 3 Bg2.

4. The Closed Two Knghts' Defense 4 d3. 1 e4 e5 2 Nf3 Nc6 3 Bc4 Nf6.

5. Torre Attack 3... h6 Variation. 1 d4 Nf6 2 Nf3 e6 3 Bg5.

6. Semi-Annual Update. Previous 5 openings updated + 10 games.

7. Modern Benoni 7 Bf4 Variation. 1 d4 Nf6 2 c4 c5 3 d5 e6 4 Nc3 ed 5 cd d6 6 Nf3 g6.

8. Slav Defense Exchange Variation 6... Bf5. Killer stuff.

9. Pirc Defense Classical System 5 Be2. 1 e4 d6 2 d4 Nf6 3 Nc3 g6 4 Nf3 Bg7.

10. Dutch Defense Modern Stonewall 6... Bd6. 1 d4 f5 2 c4 Nf6 3 g3 e6 4 Bg2 d5 5 Nf3 c6 6 0-0.

11. LDL Sicilian. The Emergence of a Main Line. 1 e4 c5 2 g3 Nc6 3 Bg2 g6 4 Qf3.

12. Semi-Annual Update. An update of issues 7-11. 11 complete games.

Priced at **$4.00** each. Buy a complete set of all 12 for just **$36.00.** Get an accompanying binder, postpaid, for just **$3.95.** Chess Hammers and Previews are available only through Thinkers' Press.

I really believe in Thinkers' Press literature and not just because I am the publisher!

At one point in my publishing career I owned over 2,000 different chess titles + thousands of magazines. I kept noticing one thing over and over—most of the books looked bad whether there was anything good in them or not.

Do you recall how discouraging it was to pick up a book (to learn something), only to be put off because it was poorly organized, or there was no index when there should be, or the type was hard to read, or the material was a mishmash rehash of stuff you've seen before?

Well, now that there is desktop publishing, you are in for the treat of the same old stuff only on a broader scale—everyone's doing it!

My years of experience in typography and publishing doesn't make me a genius, just someone who cares about the final product and who tries to make each succeeding effort better than the one previous.

The price of our books is based on our costs and effort—not whether we think it will be a best seller.

We love all the comments we get about our books. We love it so much that it drives us on towards our next project—and we have lots of them coming up—for example, **Chess Centurions** by Alex Pyshkin on the Soviet and Russian championships from 1891-1991. A colossal work.

GM Soltis' book on the endgame, **What Every GM Knows About the Endgame...** will be the best book on the endgame ever published—I've seen them all! You'll actually learn how to play the endgame—for real!

We expect to publish a 10-volume CJS Purdy set—the likes of which you have never seen. Don't overlook our first volume.

Thanks to everyone who purchases Thinkers' Press products.

Bob Long

PS: Our business as a publisher and retailer has allowed the creation of two programs to help stave off the rampant economic insecurity which seems to constantly plague all of us: a) setting up a Thinkers' Press chess reseller network; b) setting up an interactive distribution group to market products not related to chess.

If you are more than a little curious, drop me a line and I will send some materials on these programs. As usual, there is no obligation.

S1Editrice

Three annual yearbooks for correspondence chess players. Similar to the *Chess Informants,* these same size books have 350-400 games per issue and are annotated by the best postal chess masters around. Thinkers' Press has become the exclusive North American distributor for all S1E books. Their line of opening books are featured in earlier pages of this catalog and denoted by their figurine algebraic notation, though usually there is an introduction in English.

Chess Correspondence Yearbooks:

OP72852	CCYB#2	$24.95
OP72855	CCYB#3	$24.95
OP72857	CCYB#4	$24.95
OP78227	CCYB#5	$24.95
OP72858	CCYB#6	$24.95
OP72859	*CCYB#7	$21.95
OP77528	*CCYB#8	$22.95
OP79757	*CCYB#9	$23.95
OP87897	CCYB#10	$22.00
OP89779	CCYB#11	$22.00
OP92958	CCYB#12	$22.00

* Includes *Chess Theory* booklet.

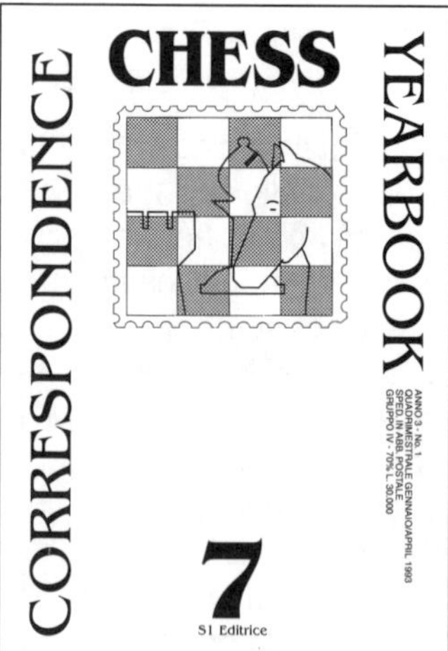